FOUR SPIRITUALITIES

FOUR SPIRITUALITIES

EXPRESSIONS OF SELF, EXPRESSIONS OF SPIRIT

A PSYCHOLOGY OF CONTEMPORARY SPIRITUAL CHOICE

Peter Tufts Richardson

DAVIES-BLACK PUBLISHING
Palo Alto, California

Published by Davies-Black Publishing, an imprint of Consulting Psychologists Press, Inc., 3803 East Bayshore Road, Palo Alto, California 94303; 1-800-624-1765

Special discounts on bulk quantities of Davies-Black books are available to corporations, professional associations, and other organizations. For details, contact the Director of Book Sales at Davies-Black Publishing, 3803 East Bayshore Road, Palo Alto, California 94303; 415-691-9123; Fax 415-988-0673.

MBTI and *Myers-Briggs Type Indicator* are registered trademarks of Consulting Psychologists Press, Inc.

Cover and interior photography by Peter Tufts Richardson
Cover photograph: Detail, Church of the Restoration, Unitarian Universalist, Philadelphia

00 99 98 97 96   10 9 8 7 6 5 4 3 2 1
Printed in the United States of America

Library of Congress Cataloging-in-Publication Data
Richardson, Peter T.
    Four spiritualities : expressions of self, expressions of spirit : a psychology of contemporary spiritual choice / Peter T. Richardson.
        p.   cm.
    Includes bibliographical references and index.
    Paperback ISBN 0-89106-083-9
    Hardback ISBN 0-89106-085-5
    1. Spiritual life.   2. Personality—Religious aspects.   3. Typology (Psychology)—Religious aspects.   I. Title.
    BL624.R52   1996
    248.4—dc20
                                        95-44375
                                        CIP

FIRST EDITION
First printing, 1996

To Eleanor,
soul mate and
life companion

CONTENTS

LIST OF PHOTOGRAPHS

PREFACE

I BOUGHT MY FIRST COPY of the Koran on the way home from eighth grade in the spring of 1954 for 50 cents from a creaky circular rack in the Rexall drugstore. Within a year I had a basic library of world religious heritage, all for 35 and 50 cents each: Confucius, Lao-tzu, the Buddha, the Bhagavad Gita, and a life of Martin Luther. I had seen a wonderful movie about Luther called *Here I Stand*, and I rushed out to buy the book. In that fateful year, I found both my vision and my vocation: a vision of a harmony of human religions, where there was freedom for mutual stimulation, dialogue, and appreciation, and a vocation to prepare myself to bring that vision into the hearts and minds of all in the circles around me.

I have been collecting scriptures, commentaries, and studies of our world spiritual inheritance ever since. But I did not have a sorting tool to differentiate what I needed in order to grow spiritually myself. I traveled many fascinating roads more appropriate for the spiritual journeys of people very different from myself.

In the summer of 1957 I was visiting my great aunt and uncle in Maine when another teenager down the street invited me to his youth fellowship meeting. They invited me back to lead the meeting the following week, and I created the topic "The Four Ways." The words I used then were "meditation," "intellect," "devotion or love," and "works." My efforts were shot down, and I put my notes away in a box that I exhumed only after the present manuscript was finished! My talk was typed on my uncle's ancient Remington and marginal notes jotted with my high school fountain pen. You can imagine the rush of feelings when I recognized the beginnings of this project, long forgotten, exactly thirty-eight years ago. What if I had been confirmed and supported in these observations instead of ridiculed? I have always known, somewhere deep within, that this book needed to be written.

I invite you to share these discoveries with me and to refine them to fit your own spiritual aspirations. Dig out the seeds of your own inspiration, perhaps long kept hidden in your deeper self for fear of being caught out on a limb without support. Your own truth is too important, too precious, to be kept hidden even from yourself. I hope somewhere in these pages your eyes will widen in recognition that yes, indeed, your own spiritual reality is more like one of the four forms of spirituality than the others, and that the parameters of that recognition will appear warm and friendly, beckoning for your spiritual journey.

This book cannot lead you through your journey. Only you can truly engage your spirituality. This book will confirm you in your awareness that there are very different ways of entering into the spiritual life, and it will suggest the four great avenues explored by countless sages and teachers who have journeyed before us. It will confirm for you that many share your orientation, and may embolden you to set out on a path that is appropriate for you regardless of what others may say.

In these intervening decades I have spun my wheels many times, encountering spiritual perspectives intriguing but eventually unsatisfying for my quest. But other alternatives engaged native elements deep within. As a minister of religion, I quickly discovered that I could not be all things to all people. We are very different from one another. But I could attempt to bring the gift of careful listening into my relationships. My ear is always trying to understand and appreciate the inner religious genius of each person.

Particularly in listening to interfaith couples, I discovered not only that religions were different, but that forms of spirituality also differed within each religion. To understand the religion of your partner is often a matter of searching for elements of that religion you are able to resonate with. And we experience a profound acceptance that it is good we are different, that we deepen in different ways. There are parallel spiritualities within and among religions.

Six years ago I brought these considerations to my study of psychological type theory developed by Carl Jung and Isabel Briggs Myers and made a powerful discovery. Four very different approaches to human spirituality can be illuminated by working with the *Myers-Briggs Type Indicator*® (MBTI®), the most popular personality inventory in use today. At last there is a way to bring together in a matching, sorting process a guide for discovering appropriate "native spiritualities" for very different individual personalities who inhabit our families, religious communities, and nations. These same Four Spiritualities are—in outline—exactly what I had differentiated long ago in my youth when I was reading paperback editions of world scriptures bought at the corner drugstore in Westwood, Massachusetts.

Each of the chapters for the Four Spiritualities has two mentors whose contributions are developed at more length. For the Journey of Unity they are the Buddha and Buckminster Fuller; for the Journey of Devotion, Mohammed and St. Francis; for the Journey of Works, Moses and Confucius; and for the Journey of Harmony, Rabindranath Tagore and Jesus. Each pair of mentors will be very different, one from the other, showing the great diversity as well as the remarkable patterns of similarity within each of the Four Spiritualities.

Then in chapter 8, Deepenings, we will discuss how from your native spirituality you can deepen your journey by relating to the other three around the mandala circle. You will benefit from the dynamics of polarity, and what I label deasil and widdershins "spinning of the wheel." In an important way, all spirituality is for you, but absorbed from your own unique base of spiritual integrity.

The final chapter, Destination, places your return into the context of your life. Spiritual growth occurs at various junctures in the life cycle and therefore will affect the contexts in which you live and work, including the temple or religious community in which you are engaged and which you will influence. Your spiritual journey has great import for those who surround you and share the planet with you!

I invite you with this offering of *Four Spiritualities* to begin your own sorting process that will engage the deepest levels of your yearning for spiritual progress.

ACKNOWLEDGMENTS

I am grateful to all who have influenced this project at least indirectly over the years, from parental and teaching influences in my youth, the many acquaintances through thirty years in the ministry, and the support of my wife, Eleanor.

Several people read early versions of the manuscript and gave exceedingly valuable critiques of content and form: Reverend Rolfe Gerhardt, Adrian Dawson, Susan Foster, Bob Pratt, and Reverend Doris Hunter. The responses of Nancy Millner and Reverend Spencer Lavan were most encouraging along the way. Together with the editors at Davies-Black Publishing, Lee Langhammer Law, Melinda Adams Merino, and John Walker, the work became far more readable.

My congregation in Andover has been very supportive not only in showing interest as the writing progressed but by attending workshops in which many of the ideas in *Four Spiritualities* could be refined and better interpreted. In addition, my previous congregation in Maine sponsored a five-month sabbatical in Egypt and Europe, which opened up appreciation and experiences in a deep diversity of spiritual environments. This continued with a trip to India to attend meetings of the International Association for Religious Freedom. Special thanks to my aunt, Dorothy Pearson, for sponsorship in both these pilgrimages.

A parishioner in Maine gave me a book on the MBTI and, alas, it was several years before I actually read it. A special thanks to Al Adams for piquing that first curiosity and to colleague Reverend Glenn Turner for accelerating that interest. MBTI teachers Jean Kummerow, Judy Provost, Bob McAlpine, and Nancy Zimmer have had a lasting influence.

With the positive response and support this project has received all along, the writing and honing process has been a pleasure and I look forward to the journey *Four Spiritualities* will make in its own right!

INTRODUCTION

BETTER IS YOUR OWN DHAMMA, HOWEVER WEAK,

THAN THE DHAMMA OF ANOTHER, HOWEVER NOBLE.

LOOK AFTER YOUR SELF, AND BE FIRM IN YOUR GOAL.

Dhammapada

THE SPIRITUALITY NATIVE TO YOUR personality yearns for growth and expression. Out of your individuality flows a spirituality. And for all of humanity, the individual's spiritual journey will flow uniquely in one of four classic variations: the Journey of Unity, the Journey of Devotion, the Journey of Works, or the Journey of Harmony. My research shows a remarkable pattern around the world, whereby each individual's story—never known before in all time—emerges into its fullness in the context of one of these Four Spiritualities. They are found in the various permutations of religion in the many branches of human culture.

Our longing for a greater spiritual presence in our lives today is offset by a confusion and chaos of conflicting claims from gurus, psychics, religious orthodoxies, fundamentalisms of many persuasions, entrepreneurs, new age spiritual guides, Eastern religions, and mainline denominations. Which approach is right for you? Millions have been wooed by alternatives that worked well for others but have dropped out deeply disillusioned because they had not found appropriate pathways for their own needs. *Four Spiritualities* will be of great assistance for your personal sorting process.

The key for me in sorting through the myriad spiritual traditions and the claims of each, was the discovery of a natural division of spiritualities in accord with Jungian typology and the *Myers-Briggs Type Indicator* (MBTI). Widely used in educational, religious, counseling, organizational, and business consulting, the MBTI personality inventory helps people identify one of sixteen personality types closest to their own preferences. From a very early age, our unique individuality begins to emerge in recognizable patterns, identifying our broad approaches to life more with one than the other fifteen personality types. The MBTI can be a powerful means for self-understanding and a starting place for the spiritual journey. Even though the MBTI is a psychological tool grounded in rigorous scientific research, it is readily accessible to and useful for nonspecialists.

Psychological type theory provides a basis for appreciating and incorporating into personal practice the rich diversity of religious orientations, beliefs, ethical and wisdom traditions, and spiritual practices. Just as there is a recognizable differentiation of human personality types, so, too, is there a differentiation within the spiritual cultures of Western, Middle Eastern, Asian Indian, Far Eastern, and the nature-centered traditions. I see the Four Spiritualities as a Rosetta stone for our spiritual life, gaining us entrance from our own experience into every branch of religious culture.

I have conducted a number of workshops using the MBTI for personal and spiritual growth. Some participants seem quite content once they "have their letters"—the four letters used to distinguish one's type from the other fifteen. However, to stop at this point can give one a somewhat reductive and static awareness of the strengths and weaknesses of one's personality—not enough to appreciate the truly dynamic nature of typology and its great potential as a key to unlocking avenues of spiritual growth. *Four Spiritualities* seeks to clarify the foundations of personality according to Jung and the MBTI and to show the Four Spiritualities that open up from these foundations.

This book makes no attempt to persuade you to join one or another organized religion or spiritual practice. It does provide valuable tools for your own process of matching your personality characteristics with examples of the Four Spiritualities found in the various religious traditions. The choice of an appropriate milieu for your journey must be yours.

Each of us participates in the building of the world. In our age, the noosphere (to borrow the term of Teilhard de Chardin), or the cultural milieu surrounding the human community of earth, is beginning to come together in a unity not seen since the Paleolithic age.[1] In the words of René Maheu, director-general of UNESCO: "The immanence of the universal in every cultural and scientific experience is what gives its essential character to the spiritual solidarity of mankind."[2] Central for the contribution each of us makes is the honoring of all Four Spiritualities, not holding our own journey up as more important than the others.

As the millennium approaches, one fact is clear: We live in an emerging interfaith culture for one humanity on one planet. The fate of all and the fate of each are our shared fate. The idea that religions can exist in splendid isolation without positive reference to one another is obsolete and even dangerous.

In an interfaith world, we need a common language for mutual understanding and appreciation. Whether we are in the image of God, or the gods and goddesses that wear human faces, the common denominator of recognition is our human nature. Revelations, pantheisms, humanisms—all must be apprehended and undertaken by the human sensibilities we share. Each of the world's religions has its strengths for one or several of the Four Spiritualities and its weaknesses for the others. It is important to employ many sources and not have too narrow a framework for spiritual growth.

The MBTI has thus far been found to be reliable and valid across cultural boundaries. Rooted in human nature itself, it identifies personality types without prejudice of accident of birth. You will find the Buddha, Moses, Confucius, Lao-tzu, Jesus, Mohammed, Patanjali, Socrates, Tagore, and many others—names familiar and unfamiliar—walking side by side in these pages. *Four Spiritualities* shows the parallels between personality types and how they practice human religion in widely divergent settings.

When Julius Caesar invaded Gaul, he encountered whole new pantheons of gods, goddesses, and their worship. But with remarkable facility, he translated the parallels of his Roman pantheon with those of the Gallic tribes.[3] Our approach will be not to draw equivalencies among the divinities but rather to work with the underlying types of human personality that create, experience, and benefit from the diversity of religious traditions. With large numbers of families in interfaith constellations today, this appreciative look at the Four Spiritualities found beneath the surface in the many religious traditions will be helpful as we seek to develop a practical, active tolerance.

Whether in youth, midlife, or elderhood, we live in a time of excitement about spirituality. At times, it seems as if we live in a veritable spirituality explosion. Without reliable tools for keeping our perspective, it is easy to be confused or misled. This book will present the Four Spiritualities developed over the millennia and that humans have wrestled with both as the shadows and the illuminations of life. It will outline the MBTI as a basic tool and structure for our investigations of the spiritual, and discuss various preparations essential for the spiritual life. Then it will present the Four Spiritualities, showing ways they deepen our spirituality, and finally comparing the strengths of the parallel journeys we are on and exploring the meaning of embarking on the most important journey of our lives. We identify spirituality as a journey, for we find inner motivations for embarking, energy that propels us deeper in our native spirituality, and then we return from this depth to integration and balance in the whole spiritual context of our living.

I.

BEGINNING

CHAPTER ONE

CONSIDERATIONS

HAVING GIFTS THAT DIFFER ACCORDING TO THE GRACE

GIVEN TO US, LET US USE THEM.

Romans 12:6

ANY PARENT OF A SECOND child will tell you, "This one is different." Almost from birth, our differences are observable. Relatives immediately begin making comparisons: "She has Uncle Jim's chin"; "His nose looks like Aunt Joan's—isn't that too bad?" But personality comes in early, too: "She's very active, outgoing, curious"; "He's quiet but seems intense."

In youth with the approach of adulthood, or at midlife when we may begin a process of personal assessment, in times of crisis at work or at home when we seek insight into ourselves and our relationships, or in our reflections as elders, we strive to understand ourselves more systematically. What is this personality that experiences, expresses, forms my uniqueness? How am I different from and similar to others? Some are very different, or somewhat different, and others quite similar to me in my approach to life. Am I missing out, being who I am? Or is my personality one important way among many of being? And, ultimately, is there a way of bringing who I am into spiritual growth, of touching meaning, engaging my purpose in life, tapping an inner awareness and power, finding connections with realities deeper or larger than self alone?

We seek some way of sorting through these considerations, something more dependable than the anecdotal observations of relatives, something we can manage ourselves that has an objective base so that we can be assured our feet are on the ground while the whole range of variables is considered. The MBTI personality inventory can serve as this foundation for the spiritual journey. Even if you have come upon the Four Spiritualities independently, as I did through a study of religious sources and traditions, you will find, as I have, that a knowledge of the MBTI helps to sharpen and deepen your journey and helps you to appreciate the journeys of others.

Swiss psychologist Carl G. Jung (1875–1961) and Isabel Briggs Myers (1897–1980) of the United States were both motivated to seek a way of explaining why people are so different from one another and why large numbers of people are very much like each other but different from all others. How can we sort our similarities and differences into reliable patterns that can improve our knowledge of self and others? Jung's break with Freud propelled him to find an explanation for why their close working relationship had deteriorated into their epic parting of the ways. Myers began her quest when she first introduced her fiancé into her family circle. He was so markedly different, even opposite, from her. His strengths were her weaknesses and vice versa. Why? Eventually working with Educational Testing Services, she studied large populations of students—from junior and senior high schools through graduate programs for doctors and lawyers—using early versions of the instrument. From this, she developed the MBTI. She found that people differ in general, eminently describable ways. Jung found eight basic human types, refined by Myers into the sixteen personality types of the MBTI instrument.

First, all of us are *extraverted* or *introverted* in the various situations of our lives, but each of us leads with one or the other preference. Second, we all employ our *sensing* and *intuitive* faculties continually in the course of experiencing our situations, but each of us leads with one more of the time. Third, we all come to conclusions about the situations of our lives and decide what actions to take using our *thinking* and our *feeling* powers, but each of us prefers to lead with one more than the other. And fourth, we orient toward our experience and opportunities inherent in the many situations around us, sometimes in a *judging* way, that is, toward closure, focusing on tasks at hand, and at other times in a *perceiving* way, toward openness, considering many options. But each of us prefers one approach more often than not.

When we reflect on our preferences in each of these four areas, we can begin to unlock a powerful self-awareness. We will see more clearly the parameters of our own uniqueness and the manner in which others diverge from us in one, two, three, or all four of these basic patterns of personality. We are all cousins in our humanity, but like cousins, we can differ greatly from one another, despite our family resemblances.

The MBTI instrument was devised to use these four sets of preference alternatives in a scientific way to let us compare and contrast sixteen primary personality constellations or *types*.[1] I would urge the serious aspirant to find someone who can administer the MBTI inventory, perhaps a counselor, clergy person, or personnel director. Basic to the use of the instrument is the principle that only you can know what your true preferences are, thus the term *Indicator*. Therefore, while you are waiting for your MBTI results, an important second opinion is your own. The following discussion of the four pairs of preferences will assist you in forming your own assessment to have in hand when you review your formal MBTI results.

☙ THE FOUR MBTI PREFERENCE PAIRS

Recognizing which of the two alternatives in each of these four sets of characteristics fits you may be likened to your handedness. You will use both hands as situations warrant, but one hand, either the left or the right, will be your hand of preference the greater part of the time. You come to call yourself either left-handed or right-handed. It is difficult to imagine having two right hands or two left hands. You can operate far better when one leads and the other is available as needed.

After studying the detailed descriptions that follow of the four choices we need to make to ascertain the bold outline of our personality type, make your choice in each set—for Extraversion or Introversion, Intuition or Sensing, Thinking or Feeling, and Judging or Perceiving. You will find something familiar in all the definitions and discussions of each of the letters. But in each of the four sets, one will be the clear leader, whereas the other you use on a standby, as-needed basis. You are the expert regarding yourself, and upon reflection you will recognize your own preferences.

Life Attitudes: Extraversion (E) or Introversion (I)

People who prefer Extraversion focus on and are energized by events in the outer world. They are broadly focused, gregarious; they like action, talking, groups, and tend to have many friends.	People who prefer Introversion focus on and are energized by the inner world of ideas. They are deeply focused, deliberate, good listeners, and tend to have a few close friends.

It is likely that most spiritual literature has been written by Introverts. Introverts generally can readily center in reflection. Entering a shrine or temple and sitting quietly for an extended period of time would be a major act of spiritual discipline for an Extravert but would come quite naturally to an Introvert. Extraverts tend toward responding to stimuli and are more likely to find their native spirituality through action thus sparked. In the words of Isabel Briggs Myers:

The conduct of Extraverts is based on the outer situation. If they are Thinkers, they tend to criticize or analyze or organize it; Feeling types may champion it, protest against it, or try to mitigate it; Sensing types may enjoy it, use it, or good-naturedly put up with it; and Intuitives tend to try to change it. In any case, the Extravert starts with the outer situation.[2]

About 75 percent of the population are Extraverts, while 25 percent are Introverts, a large enough imbalance that enables Extraverts to set the norm for society.[3] Since spirituality is often seen as an alternative to our "normal" existence, it is clear why so many assume that spirituality is an alternative to an Extraverted activist norm that is responsive rather than reflective.

A well-honed approach to spirituality will look at whether your home base is Extraversion or Introversion and then work in two ways: (1) your spirituality in your own life attitude (E or I), and (2) alternative possibilities for your spirituality if your life is to come into greater balance with appropriate use of your nonpreferred attitude. It is important to begin in a comfort zone with a good sense of self. Extraverts tend to lose track of themselves when forced into situations of intense quiet, with a lack of external stimuli to respond to and a good deal of required inner reflection. Introverts tend to lose track of themselves when thrust into the turmoil of constant response to others and into situations where they do not have time to sort and relate what is happening to the continuities of their inner orientation. Introverts like to relate the new to what already has meaning for them in their inner life. Extraverts enjoy variety and the novelty of experience and feel that it is all part of the process of becoming that is life. Introverts want to prepare for where they are going with novel situations before they get there. Extraverts enjoy brainstorming out loud, not knowing where it will lead, whereas Introverts would prefer to reflect and reveal their considered opinion only at the end of the reflecting process. When you know your native approach to spirituality, then you can manage the doses of the opposite life attitude that enrich your spiritual journey. Do not allow others to persuade you that spirituality should be one way or the other. Enter the waters on your own terms, and gradually find the balance best for you.

Perceiving Functions: Sensing (S) or Intuition (N)

People who prefer Sensing base their perception on what is present here and now. They are realistic, practical, observing facts directly, step by step, with common sense.

People who prefer Intuition base their perception on the possibilities in situations, patterns, hunches, imagination, reading between the lines, with expectancy for the future.

Jung called both Sensing and Intuition the *irrational* functions because they involve our perceiving, how we take in information, preceding the *rational* decisions, or judgments, of Thinking and Feeling. Sensing and Intuition take in perceptions of actualities (S) and possibilities (N), the literal (S) and the imagined (N), what is (S) and what might be (N). A person preferring Sensing and a person preferring Intuition can be standing in exactly the same place, looking at exactly the same scene, at the same time, and perceive two different worlds.

According to Jung and psychologist James Newman, there are three levels in each perceiving process: (1) the perceiving itself, (2) personal memory, and (3) the collective unconscious.[4] Sensors perceive through physical experience, whereas Intuitives perceive through symbolic, abstract qualities. These are then refined in experiential (S) or symbolic (N) memory, which, when deep, tap into the instincts (S) or archetypes (N) in the collective unconscious. Terence Duniho identifies Sensing as "attached inputting," and Intuition as "detached inputting."[5] Sensing originates in direct experience, whereas Intuition originates in imagination. Sensing works by attaching itself directly to the experience; Intuition operates in a detached way in symbol, metaphor, and abstraction. Knowing through experience (S) is often relatively mute, for it is sufficient unto itself to be remembered. Knowing through surmise, the "mind's eye" (N), however, almost always demands language to make itself known, to be captured in memory.

And how do we know in the consciousness that a perception is or has been taking place? By the spotlight of Extraversion or Introversion. When we pay attention to our own experience, it remains accessible to us. When that attention is sustained, older memories are added, and if these memories are powerful, we gain access into instincts (S) and archetypes (N) that are brought up to illuminate our conscious experience. Moments of such attention are often considered spiritual, for they add depth of reality (S) or meaning (N).

The *Tao Te Ching* gives us numerous examples of Intuitive spirituality. For example, the Tao is described as follows:

> There was something formless yet complete,
> That existed before heaven and earth;
> Without sound, without substance,
> Dependent on nothing, unchanging,
> All pervading, unfailing.[6]

Jesus had only to invoke the Sensing function with one line: "He who has ears to hear, let him hear."[7] While the world of spiritual experience comes to us from Sensing, the reservoir of inspiration belongs to Intuition. Newman reports how sensation "entails the direct physical perception of nonverbal emotional cues such as body language, facial expression, and tone of voice."[8] It is as efficient at picking up cues from within as from the environment. We can see how much more profound are the realities of Sensing experiences than any description in words would portray. Poetry is more often directed by the mysteries, illusions, yearnings, and abstract transformations of Intuition.

About 75 percent of the population are Sensing types and 25 percent Intuitives. The norm in society is therefore a Sensing spirituality. Indeed, it is so overwhelmingly Sensing that Intuitives often must search to find religious communities in which their numbers are concentrated enough for encouragement and support.

Judging Functions: Thinking (T) or Feeling (F)

People who prefer Thinking base their decisions on objective, impersonal, analytical, purposive, principled logic. Discerning cause-and-effect relationships, they aim for clarity, fairness, firmness, and truth.	People who prefer Feeling base their decisions on subjective, people-centered values. They aim for harmony, mutual appreciation, trust, tact, persuasion, worthwhileness, and humane sympathy.

Jung called these the rational functions because we engage them in making our decisions. When the spotlight of consciousness shifts from input (S and N) to output (T and F), we use a different kind of cognitive process, incorporating perceptions in the forming of judgments. According to Newman, Thinking regulates the left side of the brain (NT), the "intellectual sphere of consciousness." Feeling regulates the right side of the brain (SF), "the emotional sphere of consciousness."[9] Duniho characterizes Thinking as "detached outputting" and Feeling as "attached outputting."[10] Thinking is detached in its objective expressions of truth, right, and order. Feeling is attached in its modulation of experience into arrangements of value, worth, and meaning. Thinking sorts for honesty and Feeling for harmony.

The spiritual quest needs both sorts of direction, a healthy skepticism and doubt that is firm-minded (T), and a passionate quest for meaning that appreciates human qualities with warmth (F). Feeling works within the complexities of experience, recognizing nuances and tones, always reworking judgments to encourage appreciation for what is good, aesthetically and ethically valuable, and conducive to supportive and trusting relationships. Thinking seeks to objectify religion, to bring to it order and system, theological or philosophical coherence, according to principles of justice. Our spiritual quest can be guided and shaped by systematizing, questioning, verifying (T) or by valuing, humanizing, binding us together appropriately (F). The goal of the spiritual life is enlightenment (T) or gratitude (F). For a balanced journey, we need to walk in one while honoring and accommodating the other.

Humanity seems to be split about fifty-fifty between Thinking and Feeling types, but 61 percent of men prefer the Thinking function and 68 percent of women prefer the Feeling function.[11] In men, Thinking is most commonly combined with Sensing (41%), while in women, Feeling is most commonly combined with Sensing (47%). According to Jungian analyst Loren Pedersen, "the current linguistic pop fad of 'he said/she said' " can more readily be understood as "differences in typology, supported by sex-role socialization."[12] The norms for men (ST) and for women (SF), reinforced and exaggerated by society, mean an uphill struggle for Feeling men and Thinking women. Often, it is the outsiders in the minority who find each other, forming communities to pursue the spiritual search in the reassurance of mutual recognition and support. It is essential to differentiate the social messages of what we "should" be, received since early childhood, from our own inner messages, permitted now to come into their own, of who we actually are. This independence from sexual stereotypes, and from misogyny and misandry, are requisites for the beginnings of spiritual progress.

Life Orientations: Judging (J) or Perceiving (P)

People who prefer Judging tend to live their lives in a planned, orderly way. They want things settled, organized, decisive; they like closure and enjoy finishing things.

People who prefer Perceiving tend to live their lives in a flexible, spontaneous way. Adaptable and tolerant, they keep options open, seeking to understand life rather than control it.

The final MBTI scale is divided fairly evenly, with approximately 50 percent of the population Judging types and 50 percent Perceiving types. Addressing clergy served by the Alban Institute, Roy Oswald and Otto Kroeger stress that the percentage of Judgers attracted to organized religion is far higher than that found in the general population.[13] This is easy to understand, as Judgers like closure and predictability. Perceivers prefer openness and variety, which are often stifled in formal institutions. Implications for the spiritual journey are clear: Judgers will tend toward well-defined, disciplined, and consistent pathways; Perceivers will look for something new to experience, do, or actualize beyond today's horizon. Thus, for better balance, Judgers will need to seek out variety to spice their journey, and Perceivers will learn to sustain their efforts through time.

Now take a moment to choose a letter from each of the preference pairs—E or I, S or N, T or F, J or P—to form the four letters of your own type. Keep in mind that we use all of the eight functions much of the time, but in each of the four sets there is one that, when combined with one each from the other three sets, forms a home base where you are most comfortable when you have your druthers and are truly yourself.

Even at this point, some will ask, "Yes, but can't I be all eight equally?" According to Jung, it is desirable to aim toward balance, but only so that we can utilize all eight appropriately as situations require. And it usually takes half a lifetime for us to grow to this level of type development. However, balance cannot mean stasis. To cite the handedness analogy again: If you were truly ambidextrous in the split-second moment of decision, which hand would you extend to save yourself? A moment's hesitation could mean disaster. You cannot be left- and right-handed simultaneously, or prefer them equally. Likewise, with Sensing and Intuition, for example, you cannot be perceiving the realities and the possibilities simultaneously. The spotlight of consciousness is in one direction or the other. You begin with one preference and, as Robert Frost tells us in "The Road Not Taken," "way leads on to way." Our perceiving now influences our perceiving a moment from now. The tendency is cumulative, reinforcing as it proceeds. If we begin with Sensing as our true preference, we may visit Intuition, but we will be primarily grounded in our Sensing. That will be our reality and will see us through. If we were to attempt to resist the leadership of our true preference to be both equally, we would risk being indecisive in both, inefficient in responding and adapting to the challenges life puts in our path.

☙ THE SIXTEEN PERSONALITY TYPES

When you combine the four letters of your personality type, the result is synergetic. You have far more than the characteristics of the four preferences side by side. Now you have a dynamic system, whereby the separate qualities are transformed in their relationship with the other three.

It is beyond the purpose of this book to discuss each of the sixteen types separately in any detail. For detailed descriptions of your type and how it compares with the other types, consult one of the excellent sources that explore them far more extensively than is possible here.[14] However, you need not be a specialist in psychological type to grasp how the dynamics of your personality can guide you toward forms of spirituality appropriate for your journey.

FIGURE 1 The Sixteen MBTI Personality Types

ISTJ	ISFJ	INFJ	INTJ
ISTP	ISFP	INFP	INTP
ESTP	ESFP	ENFP	ENTP
ESTJ	ESFJ	ENFJ	ENTJ

The well-known display of the sixteen MBTI types shown in figure 1 should be thought of as a tool for understanding how your type relates to other types, overlapping with all others in particular ways but standing as very different in other ways. First, locate the position of your type in the figure. The profound differences between personality types and how powerfully synergetic the four letters for the preferences taken together can be will be apparent when you read the description of the type opposite from your own in one of the sources cited in note 14. For example, an ENFP is very different from an ISTJ. ESFPs are strikingly opposite INTJs.

When the figure is divided into quadrants, the lower left accounts for approximately 52 percent of humanity, the upper left 24 percent, the lower right 20 percent, and the upper right 4 percent.[15]

In their experience from childhood onward, Introverted Intuitives are likely to be as strangers in the native spirituality of others. They have been living in a largely Extraverted and/or Sensing social environment. Thus, Introverted Intuitives need to discover that their own native spirituality is as legitimate and as deep as what they have been experiencing. For Extraverted Sensors, the opposite problem is likely to occur. They will find themselves in such familiar environs spiritually that they may miss noticing the implicit invitation to deeper experience that has been there all along. For one, the invitation to journey has been missing, and for the other, the spiritual milieu has been so routinized as to be invisible (like the concept of water for a fish). In addition, when spiritual growth reaches out for balance from one's native spirituality to its opposite, Introverted Intuitives may have to be accepting of a spirituality they had experienced as smothering, and Extraverted Sensors may have to do considerable searching to find their alternative pathway at all.

In this book, as we match personality with the Four Spiritualities, we will be looking primarily at the middle two letters—S or N, T or F—known as the *cognitive functions* because they have to do with mental processes, how the mind works. The life attitudes (E or I) and life orientations (J or P) are important for our spirituality in specific ways, offering certain nuances that enrich the spiritual journey, as we shall see in a later section of this chapter. But in the dynamics of type, they modify and orient the cognitive functions.

Thus, we will see, for example, that INFJs and ENFPs, sharing the same two middle letters, will be attracted to an Intuitive Feeling (NF) approach to spirituality as their home base. But INFJs will experience their spirituality from an Introverted Intuitive base, while ENFPs will experience their spirituality from an Extraverted Intuitive one. Even though Introverted and Extraverted Intuition work from different arenas of experience, cognitively they work in the same mental processes and, as this book explores, in the same spirituality as well.

The Four Spiritualities, coordinated with the four possible pairs of the cognitive functions, are found in the general population in these percentages: ST, 38 percent; SF, 38 percent; NF, 12 percent; NT, 12 percent.[16]

⟶ DEEPER DYNAMICS: THE FOUR COGNITIVE FUNCTIONS

Of the two middle letters in your type—S or N, T or F—one will be your *dominant* function, your home base of operations as a personality. The other will be your *auxiliary*, the second most important function. To decide which is your dominant, look to the fourth letter of your personality type, J or P. This will tell you how you extravert, with your perceiving function (S or N) or with your judging function (T or F). Then look at the first letter (E or I) of your personality type. If you prefer Extraversion, how you extravert will be your dominant function. If you prefer Introversion, then the other letter will be your dominant, and how you extravert will be your auxiliary function.

For Introverts, the dominant function is introverted; for Extraverts, the dominant is extraverted. The sixteen types thus have the following dominant and auxiliary functions, as shown in table 1. For example, for ESTJ, first we look at the J and determine that T is how this person extraverts, and since she is an Extravert, T is also the dominant function, with S as the auxiliary. In an opposite example, INFP, first we determine from the P that N is the

TABLE 1 The Sixteen MBTI Types and Their Dominant and Auxiliary Functions

MBTI Type Preference	Dominant Function		Auxiliary Function
INTJ	Introverted Intuition	with	Thinking extraverted
INTP	Introverted Thinking	with	Intuition extraverted
ENTP	Extraverted Intuition	with	Thinking introverted
ENTJ	Extraverted Thinking	with	Intuition introverted
ISFJ	Introverted Sensing	with	Feeling extraverted
ISFP	Introverted Feeling	with	Sensing extraverted
ESFP	Extraverted Sensing	with	Feeling introverted
ESFJ	Extraverted Feeling	with	Sensing introverted
ISTJ	Introverted Sensing	with	Thinking extraverted
ISTP	Introverted Thinking	with	Sensing extraverted
ESTP	Extraverted Sensing	with	Thinking introverted
ESTJ	Extraverted Thinking	with	Sensing introverted
INFJ	Introverted Intuition	with	Feeling extraverted
INFP	Introverted Feeling	with	Intuition extraverted
ENFP	Extraverted Intuition	with	Feeling introverted
ENFJ	Extraverted Feeling	with	Intuition introverted

way this person extraverts. However, since he prefers Introversion, the F is the introverted dominant function and N is the auxiliary.

We have a dominant function because, in the words of Isabel Briggs Myers, "a ship needs a captain."[17] When there is no clear dominant, a person is relatively undifferentiated and undeveloped. Opposites T–F and S–N, as we have seen, would interfere with each other, countermand each other, and the result would be an inefficient and ineffective personality. In addition, when our preferred functions are developed, one will be in the service of the other. A Perceiving auxiliary will serve a Judging dominant; a Judging auxiliary will serve a Perceiving dominant. The less preferred functions, called *tertiary* and *inferior*, have their own roles in the whole picture of personality, as we shall see.

Our dominant is important to our spirituality because it will lead us as we prepare for the journey, as we navigate the journey, and as we reengage with all elements of our lives on our return. But it will be chastened, refined, and balanced for a more thoroughgoing wholeness of person in its collaboration with the auxiliary and from the insights and stimulation of its polar opposite, called the *inferior function*, and from the opposite of the auxiliary, known as the *tertiary function*.

Our Two Most-Preferred Functions

The role the dominant plays for Introverts is very different from the one it plays for Extraverts. For Introverts, the question is, How does that relate to me? For Extraverts, the question is, How do I respond to that? For Introverts, the auxiliary takes care of the external world and the dominant works on the most central issues inside. It is hard for others to see the introverted dominant at work. However, in cases where the introverted dominant is a judging function (T or F), when something important is challenged or threatened, others can be surprised in a hurry as the relatively easygoing perceiving exterior is transformed by inner judging intransigence. For Extraverts, the auxiliary is the pathway to the inner life workings so that the Extravert does not become lost in his or her Extraverting, disconnected from reflective ideas within. Spiritual issues at this level of dominant and auxiliary working together as a team can therefore be quite different for Introverts and Extraverts. Introverts need to work on communication with others, cultivating relationships that are revelatory and mutual. Extraverts need to schedule quiet time in which they can regenerate the inner bases of their relationships.

Balancing. It is important to note that the dominant and auxiliary are neither both perceiving nor both judging. We need one of each for psychological balance. If the dominant is perceiving, there needs to be a way for a person to make decisions and to move along. If the dominant is judging, there needs to be a way for a person to be informed, to take in enough information for prudent decisions. Much of our preparation for the spiritual life involves this kind of balancing.

A Caution for Sensing Types. Because Sensing types are directly grounded in experienced reality, they perceive what is actually present to their senses in the here-and-now. They often will go directly from this experience into action, either in a Judging (planned and closure-oriented) mode or in a Perceiving (open-ended and opportunistic) mode. Thus, Sensing Judgers are known as "the realistic decision makers" and Sensing Perceivers are known as the "adaptable realists."[18] This has great advantages in emergencies, when quick action may save the day. But much of the rest of the time, it is important for spiritual balance that Sensing types remember to honor the judging function, Thinking or Feeling. Remember that the four functions are cognitive in nature; they create the knowledge base on which action depends.

We have the perceiving functions for input and the judging functions for output. To act first (which is a temptation for Extraverts anyway) without a built-in congruity with one's whole nature in the long run threatens the integrity of the self. The "being out there" needs the balance of the "being in here," a requisite for spiritual growth.

Cognitive Function Pairs. The Four Spiritualities are matched with the four possible combinations of the most preferred functions: N and T, S and F, S and T, N and F. I believe the spiritual journey can be illuminated by the type dynamics at work in this pairing. Thinking when it is attached to Intuition leads to a spirituality very different from when it is attached to Sensing. Likewise, Feeling when it is attached to Sensing leads to a spirituality very different from when it is attached to Intuition. The judging functions proceed very differently from the same perceiving base, giving us four ways of engaging in the spiritual quest that can be recognized in all the major branches of human culture.

Our Two Less-Preferred Functions

In order of development, our dominant comes to rule our conscious lives. Our auxiliary assists the dominant with the opposite attitude. If the dominant is introverted, the auxiliary is extraverted. Next, the tertiary, or third, function, opposite the auxiliary, usually in the same attitude as the dominant, comes on board, but in a minor role. The fourth, or inferior, function is last, because it is opposite our dominant (and has the opposite attitude as well). We prefer our dominant, and, hence, our inferior remains relatively primitive and undifferentiated, hidden in the unconscious.

Under stress or crisis, when our dominant is not coping well in our conscious life, often the inferior will kick in, bringing with it lots of chaotic and minimally processed perceptions or judgments. People will see us at our worst. As chapter 2 points out, much can be learned from the less-preferred functions, especially the inferior, for they operate less in the consciousness and more in the unconscious. They help us to integrate the self by accessing the rich depth and learning to be absorbed from the unconscious. The inferior function is our greatest source for learning about new sides of ourselves and alternative potentialities to complement those strengths we now possess. Avenues for spiritual growth are discovered in those moments when we are off balance, or "beside ourselves."[19] In these moments of discomfort and vulnerability, insights for personal and spiritual growth suggest themselves. Determine, therefore, which of the cognitive functions is your inferior function and how it tends to act out when you are under stress. Look at past experiences, and see whether they offer lessons, pointers to sources of spiritual awareness.

Honoring the Weak, Balancing the Strong. Balance is all-important in Jungian dynamics, not the balance of stasis but the balance in the creative relationship of the polar opposite elements of the personality: Sensing and Intuition, Thinking and Feeling, in readiness for situations to bring them forward. The push-pull of polarity deepens us. We learn from the interaction of the inferior with the dominant, the tertiary with the auxiliary. When arranged in the form of a mandala as shown in figure 2, all four cognitive functions in their juxtaposition around the circle give the personality a more centered and spiritually-poised orientation.[20]   The ship still has a captain, but the whole crew is working together. Again, locate your least and most preferred functions. Honor the presence of the weakest for it gives creative balance to the whole and dynamic energy for spiritual growth. For this reason, we will return to the circle motif in chapter 8 when we discuss the Four Spiritualities mandala.

☙ DEEPER DYNAMICS: LIFE ATTITUDES AND ORIENTATION

Spirituality is the heart of life coming into being when balance and composure reign among the cognitive functions. In addition, our spirituality is manifest in an authenticity of identity, a quality of connectedness to life and cosmos, an integrity and wholeness. In sublime reaches, it is "likeness to God"[21] or jen, human-heartedness.[22] We can attach to these nuances of spirituality the qualities of Extraversion and Introversion, Judging and Perceiving.

For Extraverts

When Extraverts sustain their Extraversion with their dominant function so relentlessly that they neglect their auxiliary function, the pathway to their inner conscious life, life becomes shallow and the authenticity of their spirituality is endangered. They need to take time to go inward, to reflect on what is important for them and what, though perhaps exciting or engaging, does not contribute to their personal mission or purpose in life.

For Introverts

When Introverts sustain their Introversion with their dominant function so intensely that they neglect their auxiliary, which is their primary way of relating to the world around them, they are in danger of losing their spiritual

FIGURE 2   The Polarity of Most and Least Preferred Functions

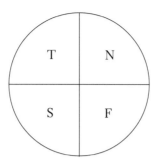

connection with the rest of life and nature. They need to develop strategies for overcoming their isolation and self-absorption so that they can participate in their full humanity and make a difference in the world of life around them.

For Judgers

When Judging types accentuate their decisiveness until it becomes straight and narrow—all work and no play—the spiritual aim of wholeness is endangered. They need to take the time to consider alternatives to the planned route and examine the options for bringing into being the many aspects of fulfillment possible in their human nature.

For Perceivers

Perceiving types often hold so many options open and explore such a variety of interests and adventures that the integrity of the center of their lives becomes hard to nurture or even ascertain. Those with this preference need to plan and experience closure at least in aspects of their lives that involve their very identity.

For the Judging and Perceiving orientations, these cautions can be doubled if people extravert with their dominant function—Extraverted Perceivers with either Sensing or Intuition, and Extraverted Judgers with either Thinking or Feeling. And as we have seen, many Sensors have an additional tendency to go from their sensing base of reality directly into action without the balanced deliberations of their judging function.

⟨⟩ A WORD OF REASSURANCE

You don't need to become an expert in the field of psychological type before you can engage the form(s) of spirituality appropriate for you. Glean what general knowledge you can from this opening chapter, particularly around the following seven items:

- Remember your four letters.
- Understand something of the nature of each letter.
- Notice that the four nonpreferred letters have continuing importance as well.
- Keep in mind that personality type is dynamic and not reductive and always in creative motion and development.
- Have confidence that human nature tends toward balance and health, not stasis but a creative growth.
- Be aware that the polarity of influences across the circle contributes to this health and wholeness.
- Focus on the four cognitive function pairs and the one pair that defines your home spirituality. Learn all you can about your own and appreciate the other three as well. Engage all in the course of your growth and understanding.

From this point, I recommend that you read chapters 2 and 3 in the same way to establish in bold outline a platform for your spiritual journey.

Once the platform is in place, I recommend that you read next the chapter that describes your spirituality:

NT	Journey of Unity	chapter 4
SF	Journey of Devotion	chapter 5
ST	Journey of Works	chapter 6
NF	Journey of Harmony	chapter 7

At this point, a reading of the other three chapters will suggest itself to you simply because you will want to learn about the other spiritualities for greater perspective in understanding your own. Differences between spiritualities sharpen direction for us in our own journeys. Chapter 8 will deepen this process, building on concepts introduced in earlier chapters.

In the final chapter, Destination, themes of concern are included when you reenter the larger context of your social life. The spiritual journey is intensely personal. Only you can engage it for yourself. Once it is under way, you need to begin to explore how the changes in you may have consequences with others and how the quality of your work can affect the well-being of the society around you. Every journey has a preparation and beginning, an intense and engaged progress, and a return into the context of your life once again.

CHAPTER TWO

EVALUATIONS

THE LITTLE SPACE WITHIN THE HEART IS AS GREAT AS
THIS VAST UNIVERSE. THE HEAVENS AND THE EARTH
ARE THERE, AND THE SUN, AND THE MOON, AND THE
STARS; FIRE AND LIGHTNING AND WINDS ARE THERE;
AND ALL THAT NOW IS AND ALL THAT IS NOT.

Chandogya Upanishad

EVERY SERIOUS TRAVELER MUST FREQUENTLY wonder, Where am I on the path so far? We need to evaluate our pilgrimage from its origins in our childhood to the present time. But progress is seldom linear and never neat. Carl G. Jung gives us a way of organizing our thoughts about how the self develops and helps us to recognize those moments when we are about to reach a milestone on our spiritual journey. This chapter will first outline Jung's general theory of the self. This will serve as a valuable reference for the overall goals of spiritual growth as we next look at two developmental theories of type. There are many different ways of measuring progress in the journey, but these two will mark an essential beginning.

ᥴ JUNG'S MODEL OF THE SELF

The question, Where am I on the path so far?, is more complex than it might appear to be. According to Jung's model of the self, there are several levels from which we may attempt to answer the question. Each represents a different stage of individuation and thus a different vantage point. And there is never a final perspective, only lifelong negotiations between adaptation and a more complete balance. We are cautioned that complacency is a sign of new dangers, new lessons about to be learned in awkward or painful transitions.

FIGURE 3 Jung's Model of the Self

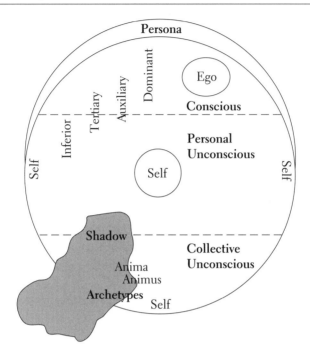

Jung's model of the self, illustrated in figure 3, includes three major levels he calls the *persona*; the *conscious realm,* centered in the ego; and the *unconscious realm,* consisting of both a personal and a collective unconscious.[1] The self, or psyche, is centered in the unconscious but embraces the conscious as well. The unconscious is far larger than the conscious, for the collective unconscious in one sense extends around the globe of nature and human nature.

The Persona

The *persona* is an appendage developed early in life containing all that society would like us to be. In it are sex roles, filial duties, outward virtues of citizenship and civilization, accoutrements of social standing and image, the work we are meant to do in the eyes of society. The persona can be regarded as a mask when it hardens beyond its adaptive usefulness and becomes impermeable, immune to influences from within as well as outside the self. As a mask, it continues to receive the rewards of society, and we are invited to move with it and identify it as our own self. However, there is the tug of real self, centered in the unconscious, and out of these countervailing forces the conscious ego between them gains in strength and assumes command. The persona will remain useful in its adaptive role, a thin membrane for the adaptive self, assuming a subordinate place in the whole picture.

Life Story

Each of us lives a story, a narrative of birth, childhood, youth, the adult chapters, and our elder years. Wherever we are in this emerging story, it is profoundly helpful to spiritual self-understanding not only to review the narrative but also to see how we have adapted along the way to influences upon us from the profoundly beneficent to the powerfully abusive. We have been blessed and wounded along the way. Our reactions to experiences have shaped us and created in us patterns of response to the situations of our lives. Some of these patterns operate out of what Jung calls the *personal unconscious*, unknown to us. A few may even be too painful to bring up to conscious memory. Testing the waters of the unconscious, finding themes beneath the running narrative of our story, and having new experiences that jog loose memories of experiences long ago—all enable us increasingly to dwell in the meanings and enrich the learnings thus far in our life stories.

Much material in the personal unconscious awaits healing moments. Jung believed we all have a tendency toward wholeness, that the self or psyche is self-regulating. Through the years of our story, unresolved issues land in the personal unconscious, combining with content from deeper regions of the unconscious and *shadow*. The shadow consists of those opposing aspects of self that are very difficult to acknowledge or own and that counter our conscious identity. We are likely to project this negativity onto others rather than to face and negotiate an integration of shadow and self. The route to balance here is in large measure through the inferior function, which provides our primary access to the unconscious (see figure 3). In recounting your life story, examine your difficult relationships, even enemies and evils, to see what insights they hold for this inner opposition with the self.

Good type development, bringing all four functions into positive creative interplay, overcoming fear, makes the balanced self emerge and makes spiritual deepening possible. Wholeness comes into being when the collective elements of persona and the unconscious move into closer interplay with the strengthened ego that is capable of managing the richness of polarities at work. The struggle of our life story, the spiritual journey, reveals the human longing to bring the self to wholeness, what Jung calls *individuation*.

Ego and the Emergence of Cognitive Functions

As long as we identify primarily with our persona, the unconscious will sabotage our efforts, for the ego is weak and the collective world rules. Key to the emergence of ego strength is the development of the four cognitive functions of typology—Sensing (S), Intuition (N), Thinking (T), and Feeling (F). The early emergence of the dominant gives the conscious ego its principal characteristic, its "captain," around which to organize our conscious life. So proficient do we become in meeting the world with reference to our dominant that its opposite, the inferior function, remains almost wholly immersed in the unconscious.

As the auxiliary function comes on line, the ego gains in strength; this is particularly essential when the dominant is introverted and the ego needs to assert a presence in the outside world. The reverse is the case when the dominant is extraverted, for the consciousness requires an inner life, a centered base. The opposite of the auxiliary, the tertiary, usually but not always has the opposite attitude as well, which it shares with the dominant.

Role of the Unconscious

But the ego is only part of the whole self. Always, whether the introverted function is dominant or auxiliary, there is a larger inner world just beyond reach that asserts itself when the ego experiences its weak moments and turns to utilizing the third and particularly the fourth, or inferior, function. This presents the spiritual opportunity to listen to dreams, to fantasies, to eruptions of chaotic reactivity from the unconscious, and to find ways to assimilate the lessons to be learned there for the conscious life. To push these revelations back down into the personal unconscious only delays their appearance again in a further, perhaps stronger, eruption another day, for the inferior function resides primarily in the unconscious and awaits another time of weakness or unusual openness to assert its important presence.[2]

The Jungian model shows our connection with the collective unconscious beyond the level of the personal unconscious. The personal unconscious contains all issues that we have deferred or even repressed from our attention or simply have not invested the time and energy to address when they first surfaced. Nothing is lost, but rather it assumes many guises, mixing with primordial archetypes, with symbol and metaphor, brought to it in the shadow. The power of today's good to be transformed into tomorrow's evil works in these levels of the unconscious.

What Jung calls the *animus* and *anima* in us reside in the unconscious as well—the male qualities in the female, the female qualities in the male—always crying for reinforcement and maturing so that individuals become more balanced and relationships between the sexes may deepen. Anima, of course, is the Latin word for soul even as psyche is in Greek. Jung sees the conscious individual as being part of a larger self (see figure 3) and like the shadow, in certain respects, the self is continuous with the collective being of life.

Jung identifies what he calls the *transcendent function*: when polarities in the psyche or self have remained conjoined for many years and a life experience jogs them loose. Old material is often combined with collective archetypes, perceived as metaphors (N), or experienced directly as deep and original revelations (S), and rises to the surface to be received into the consciousness. We may find ourselves at the threshold of union with a reality far larger than ourselves, the soul or psyche engaging with the transpersonal world soul, or God. It is at such points that we will recognize opportunities for our spiritual development.

All of these considerations relate to the question, Where am I on the path so far?, and to the centrality of the four cognitive functions in the mediation of spiritual growth in consciousness. The process is never finished. Cradle to grave, we can live always with expectancy for new discoveries, new progress, new wisdom.

ᑕᔆ DEVELOPMENTAL HYPOTHESES

As we evaluate the emergence of our true type from earliest childhood to the present time, we would all like to be able to recognize the bold outline of that emergence: first the dominant preference in the Extraverted or Introverted attitude, then the auxiliary preference in the opposite attitude, and, likewise in due course, the tertiary and inferior functions. And we should be able to identify the ascendancy of the life orientations—Judging and Perceiving—as these functions lined up in their appropriate strengths and balance. Alas, while there are several developmental theories of the differentiation of the functions, which will be discussed below, none seems completely satisfactory and reliable.

As a cautionary note, be aware that, in theory, we are born with our true type latent and ready to come in on cue. Children are very different from one another almost from their first cry. While it is important to honor differences from birth, it would be unwise to draw conclusions from our observations of the very young. A better strategy is to act so as not to inhibit development or encourage inappropriate type differentiation. What is there in the child's nature will assert itself eventually, and we should welcome it with acceptance and support. Developmental hypotheses are most valuable to us when they are kept in the back of our minds as we observe the young, and the data we gather should not be forced to fit them.

Grant's Hypothesis

The most important theory of type development was proposed by W. Harold Grant and his colleagues in *From Image to Likeness*, an approach to Roman Catholic spirituality using the MBTI. Rather than developing four parallel spiritualities (in a Christian context) using the cognitive function pairs, Grant focuses on the single functions of Sensing, Intuition, Thinking, and Feeling, using as a point of departure the Great Commandment of Jesus for loving God with your heart (F), soul (N), mind (S), and strength (T).[3] Each of these four functions comes into its own on a schedule, so that after age fifty, people may employ all four in an integrated way as appropriate for the situations they face.

Until age six, children live in an undifferentiated way typologically, but between six and twelve, they begin to function in their dominant with its attitude, either Extraversion or Introversion. Grant sees age six in "the Christian pastoral tradition as the beginning of the use of reason."[4] This development is a "spontaneous emergence," as though it had been preordained and not the result of experiences in the first six years.

Age twelve is the time of rites of passage in religions around the world. It is not surprising that this is when the auxiliary function emerges with the attitude opposite from that of the earlier dominant. To expect this rather abrupt change of pace for the adolescent years might be comforting for parents for whom this shift can be disorienting. An interesting variation introduced by Grant here is his association of the perceiving functions (S and N) as "to receive from life" and of the judging functions (T and F) as "to contribute to it." In a sense, this might describe why some teens become hardworking and serious citizens (J), while others seem to fall apart into long sequences of experimenting (P). However, it is important to avoid using this contrast in a pejorative way.

Grant becomes more controversial in his treatment of the adult stages, ages twenty to thirty-five and ages thirty-five to fifty. In the former stage, we bring in the tertiary function, and by midlife the inferior function "finds its place in our conscious investment in life." This means that from age fifty, the first five stages have been completed, and in our "second childhood" we are able to use the four cognitive functions in a differentiated way, whereas in the first childhood it was undifferentiated. Grant contrasts "childlikeness" (Matthew 18:3) with the "childishness" we have left behind.[5]

Grant's six-stage schema seems too neat and tidy to me. People mature at different rates, and what we call "late blooming" may mean a delayed differentiation of the functions. Particularly at midlife, the issues can be far more complex and chaotic than Grant allows for, especially around the operation of the inferior function and the unconscious, often taking us beyond the explanations of typology into a larger dynamic. His six stages of type development will be most useful as a reference point for discovery, not as a hard-and-fast guideline.

Duniho's Hypothesis

Counselor Terence Duniho traces fourteen "chronological changes in seven-year cycles." Each cycle has the attitude opposite from the one before, beginning with introverted "unconscious wholeness," from birth to age seven. He calls ages seven to fourteen the "literal years," when we emphasize the Extraverted preference. For Introverts this means the auxiliary will be the first function to come in. Ages fourteen to twenty-one he calls "trying on different hats," where the introverted function comes in response to the question, Who am I? Ages twenty-one to twenty-eight is "paying our dues" (E), ages twenty-eight to thirty-five, "owning who we really are" (I), thirty-five to forty-two, "changing who we are" (E), forty-two to forty-eight, "taking off" (I), and forty-eight to fifty-six, "conscious wholeness" (E). Six additional cycles follow, but it is in the eighth stage—ages forty-eight to fifty-six—that the inferior function becomes integrated with use of the other three. When this is accomplished, we move on to "confronting self and 'Old Age,' " and various tasks of elderhood and letting go follow in the last six cycles if we live that long.[6]

Duniho's labels for each period and their correlation with the MBTI scales certainly seem to be in accord with developmental psychology in general and Jungian meanings in particular, but the task for the individual aspirant to identify each cycle with the content of his or her own life story seems daunting. I recommend the same general approach as for Grant's scheme—to take it all under advisement to the extent that it is useful. For the most part, the basis for both theories is clinical and anecdotal, useful but not authoritative.

Robert and Carol A. Faucett, Catholic lay ministers, see "a much less ordered development than this [Grant's] theory suggests." They believe that the dominant and auxiliary functions are developed by midlife, and after midlife the tertiary and inferior functions are developed if all goes well. Even here the goals of wholeness and freedom are never "finally" reached.[7] Jung himself was concerned with differentiation and individuation through compensatory balancing along the way. There is no final goal, and indeed, stasis is a negative. The goal of spiritual growth is never exhausted. It is ever greater depth and breadth in a fulfillment of our natures, an ultimate form of adaptation in an ever-changing situation.

⟲ EVALUATIONS FOR MEN AND WOMEN

Most references to the four sets reported in the Jungian personality framework are presented as follows:

E – I
S – N
T – F
J – P

Whether Isabel Briggs Myers intended it or not, Loren Pedersen, the Faucetts, and others have pointed out that the left side is the historically archetypal—or, at least, socially reinforced stereotypical—male, and the right side is an historically and socially reinforced archetype of an ideal female. The center four MBTI types shown earlier in figure 1 are the "gentlest" types (ISFP, INFP, ESFP, ENFP), and the most "tough-minded" types are on the four corners of the chart (ISTJ, INTJ, ENTJ, ESTJ). Historically, society has positively reinforced women whose types are at the center of the figure and men whose types are at the corners, negatively reinforcing the reverse.

So subtle can these reinforcements be, as unnoticed as the air we breathe, that those whose preferences match their gender stereotypes might need to find ways to gain the perspective essential for bringing balance into their lives. Those whose preferences are opposite the stereotypes will require a patient process of listening to the social shoulds and oughts implanted in the persona and ego consciousness, gradually letting them go, and releasing their own true type into its freedom.

In the discussion of the Thinking–Feeling scale in chapter 1, I mentioned that 41 percent of men are Sensing Thinkers and 47 percent of women are Sensing Feelers. An additional 20 percent of men are Intuitive Thinkers, and an additional 20 percent of women are Intuitive Feelers. Only 13 percent of men are Intuitive Feelers, the opposite of the stereotype, and only 9 percent of women are Intuitive Thinkers, opposite of Sensing Feeling.[8] This imbalance, reinforced by social norms and gender-role expectations, has been with us since age six or seven, through the peer pressure of our teen years, and young adulthood, until we begin to discover the implications for our development in preparation for spiritual growth.

There are times when the expectations on us are so great that we become "turntypes," people who cannot yet manifest their true type on the MBTI inventory or in an interview because of powerful influences from family, school, ethnic neighborhood, or work, internalized and reinforced.[9] This whole issue needs careful evaluation before we will be ready for authentic spiritual growth.

⤶ AT MIDLIFE

An important part of your own evaluation is the recounting of your own life story, matching key events, experiences, and transitions with theories outlined in this chapter. Are you on schedule, and if not, what were the special pressures and detours in your childhood, youth, and young adulthood? What have been the expectations of others at home, school, and work? Have the pressures reinforced preferences opposite to your own on one or more of the four MBTI sets, and if so, where have you given yourself some room to be yourself? Or have pressures so strongly reinforced your own preferences that you have ridden your own type hard and cannot adapt to use the opposite preferences so as to bring balance into your personality? You can be so successful at being your type that you miss coming into your full humanity. For many, integration of the tertiary and inferior functions, in particular, is a critical issue at midlife.

Open yourself to your own life story. Write it down. Put it on tape. Ask for input from those who know you well. Find a friend to share with you this journey of self-discovery and growth, for your mutual progress. You will soon have a much more satisfying answer to the question, Where am I on the path so far?

CHAPTER THREE

PREPARATIONS

TZU-KUNG ASKED SAYING, WHAT DO YOU THINK

OF ME? THE MASTER SAID, YOU ARE A VESSEL.

TZU-KUNG SAID, WHAT SORT OF A VESSEL?

THE MASTER SAID, A SACRIFICIAL VASE OF JADE!

Analects of Confucius, trans. Arthur Waley

THE SPIRITUAL JOURNEY ALWAYS TAKES place in a context, even when the pilgrim walks alone. All branches of the spiritual tradition around the world ask those about to begin their travels to steer a new and rigorous course in preparation for the journey. They are asked to regulate their bodies and their minds and to set their worldly affairs in order before embarking. Practices vary widely, but the principle that preparations are needed is universal.

As a shorthand, for physical and social preparations, I will use the term *ethical preparation*; for the mental/spiritual preparations, *philosophical preparation*; and for the third preparation, *the spiritual tradition*.

ETHICAL PREPARATIONS

Hindu culture divides life into four chapters: student (brahmacharya), householder (grihastha), and two associated with the spiritual journey (vanaprastha and sannyasin). When the decision is made to embark on the spiritual path, a socially sanctioned bon voyage is preceded by the settling of one's affairs. If you are married and have children, plans must be made for a new balance of support in the family, for both body and mind, after you have departed, whether the departure involves physical leave-taking or simply the absence of the old level of attention and care. Jesus disappointed the rich young ruler when he responsed to the question "What shall I do to inherit eternal life?" with "Sell all that you have and distribute to the poor."[1] For this man, the journey had ended before it began. While this example is extreme, there is wisdom in the observation that the manner of our departure from the past will add its coloration to the quality of the beginning of the new. We carry our past always into our present.

Jesus, so far as we know, had spent a considerable period in his twenties apart from society, incubating his spirituality before he emerged into his public ministry. He had a sense of detachment worked out between himself and his mother and siblings, which he maintained throughout, even to the extent of his controversial words to a disciple who sought leave for his father's funeral: "Let the dead bury their own dead."[2] The Buddha left his wife and children in the early dawn, in the opulent environs of his father's court. He never returned. Mohammed was married to a wealthy businesswoman. He was free to travel at will back and forth between home and his mountain retreat where portions of the Koran were revealed to him. Amos was a "hewer of sycamore trees."[3] While his people allowed him only one sermon, which did not please them, we have a feeling his spirituality and his work were compatible. There is no one way to prepare for the spiritual journey. We only know that a preparation must be made.

In addition to settling our affairs, we need to settle down the cauldron of our own passions and behaviors as well so that we will have a stable ethical platform as a basis for spiritual deepening. The Buddha recognized this preparation in a famous exchange with his disciple Ananda:

> Ananda, good moral habits have no-bad-conscience as their goal and good result; no-bad-conscience has delight as its goal and good result; delight has joy; joy has calm; calm has ease; ease has contemplation; contemplation has knowledge and vision of what has really come to be; knowledge and vision of what has really come to be has dispassion due to disregard (of empirical knowledge); dispassion due to disregard (of empirical knowledge) has knowledge and vision of freedom as its goal and good result. Thus, Ananda, good moral habits gradually go on up to the highest.[4]

The ethical platform consists both in physical behavior and mental attitudes, which flow together in gradual stages of awareness and control. In early Buddhism (NT), the latter are superior to the former, bringing the physical along until the chaos of appetites is quelled and freedom for higher growth is achieved.

This general view is shared in classical Hinduism. In the Indian sage Patanjali's *Yoga Sutras* (second century B.C.) the disciplines rest on five restraints (yama) and five observances (niyama). The *yama* involve our social relationships, and the *niyama* involve inner cultivation of our own character.

B. K. S. Iyengar translates verse II:30 as: "Non-violence, truth, absten-tion from stealing, continence, and absence of greed for possessions beyond one's need are the five pillars of yama." In his translation, Charles Johnston gives the verse a Western cast, not unlike several verses in Exodus: "The Commandments are these: non-injury, truthfulness, abstaining from steal-ing, from impurity, from covetousness."[5]

Iyengar translates verse II:32: "Cleanliness, contentment, religious zeal, self-study, and surrender of the self to the supreme Self or God are the niyamas." Johnston gives it a more ST cast: "The Rules are these: purity, serenity, fervent aspiration, spiritual reading, and perfect obedience to the master."

There is some disagreement about whether obedience to God (Isvara) is intended here, as indicated by Iyengar, or ishitva, "to have divine powers," "to be like a god," as it is interpreted by Alain Danielou.[6] Tamil scholar S. V. Ganapati believes that Patanjali did not subscribe to a personal God,[7] and this is generally backed up by the reliance of the Yoga tradition of Patanjali's generation on the older Samkya orientation of religious naturalism. It is easy to be sidetracked by the biases of translators. Common to all views is the importance of establishing a constancy in our personal and social ethics on which to build our spiritual practice.

By comparison, in the oldest levels of religious traditions around the world there is very little mention of ethics as a separate practice at all. In the original pagan religious traditions of Europe, ritual in itself was seen as a heal-ing and orienting activity. If you were right in your ritual, your behavior would follow of its own accord, implying a doctrine of grace. With the advent of neo-pagan thought in our time, this proclivity has continued,[8] and only now is the movement, most prominently with the leadership of Starhawk, beginning to differentiate an ethical orientation and a social program.

Likewise in the Vedic period in India, harmony and integration were real-ized through ritual experience. The ritual act brought into being the ethical balance through one's essential participation in the order of the world. Ethics was undifferentiated from affirmation. The literature of Hinduism shows a gradual differentiation of works (ST) from the older levels of devotional acts (SF), until two distinctly different pathways to spiritual fulfillment were estab-lished—karma yoga (ST) and bhakti yoga (SF). Both as they have developed require the same five yama and five niyama mentioned previously.

Native American culture likewise does not differentiate ethics from the upbringing of a traditional culture. The puberty rites include a vision quest, where the young person experiences being apart from the traditional rou-tines long enough to find a personal, separate vocation or orienting symbol for their life. It is necessary to differentiate oneself apart to find an idea or symbol (NT or NF), ritual practice (SF), or duty (ST) that gives one an individualized mission in life. In societies that are pluralistic, on the other hand, puberty rites need to initiate the young person into commitments to social rules and values that in traditional societies are already internalized and secure. The need for ethics per se therefore tends to evolve in diverse and pluralistic societies, where the individual knows there is more than one truth and multiple ways to live rightly. There must be a stable platform for the vision quest of the spiritual life to spring from into deeper levels of practice, awareness, and cosmic participation.

We see the remains of an earlier social unity even in such an advanced and sophisticated ethical religious system as Confucianism. In the quotation at the beginning of this chapter, Confucius, referring to the oldest level of Chinese ritual practice, identifies a disciple as having reached an exemplary status, having become as a sacrificial vessel of jade, the highest compliment for a person's social and cosmic participation. In Chinese society, an individual seldom identifies him- or herself as a "Confucian," a "Taoist," or, later, a "Buddhist" apart from the others. Speaking of the two older religions in China, Joseph Politella summarizes:

> In an ideal sense, the two religions supplement each other, and of this no one seems to have been more conscious than Confucius himself....The precepts and the commandments come first—first, the clean and the pure life—and then mysticism and esoteric knowledge.[9]

There is a built-in polarity of social ethics on the one hand (Confucian) and natural ethics on the other (Taoist). When we are able to coordinate these two, then spiritual growth begins.

Western ethics has a broad spectrum of ethical orientations, ranging from mortification of the flesh and social isolation to pragmatic approaches such as that of Benjamin Franklin. In his *Autobiography*, Franklin recalls his experiment for "arriving at moral perfection" in which he listed thirteen virtues to be developed in ascending order: temperance, silence, order, resolution, frugality, industry, sincerity, justice, moderation, cleanliness, tranquility, chastity, and humility. He credited his political and economic success to the cultivation of these virtues, though somewhat short of "perfection." As a likely Extravert, he must have found the admonition "Silence—speak not but what may benefit others or yourself; avoid trifling conversation" arduous. Order, resolution, frugality, industry ("Lose no time; be always employed in something useful; cut off all unnecessary actions"), justice, cleanliness are all mainstream Sensing Thinking guideposts. Franklin leaves the best for last: "Humility—imitate Jesus and Socrates."[10]

There are two principal attitudes in ethical preparations for spiritual deepening—that which quells or neutralizes the energies of life and that which enlists and actualizes them. The advice of the Buddha to Ananda is an example of the first principle. The approaches of Confucius and Franklin are examples of the second. While there is evidence of the practice of what Albert Schweitzer calls the asceticism of "world and life negation" in religions originating in India, there is also evidence of "world and life affirmation" in them as well.[11] It is not necessary to go to the extremes of withdrawal from the world in order to establish a base for spiritual work. Find an accommodation appropriate for you that does not deny completely any of the four cognitive functions (S, N, T, F) and four attitudes (E, I, J, P).

Finally, consider the injunction of Jesus, "Judge not, that you be not judged."[12] There is the problem of projection, where the inferior in your own personality—that which you neither understand well nor control—is projected onto someone else who has your inferior function as his or her dominant. The speck in your eye becomes the stick in the other's. While the person may be fully competent in her use of her dominant, it is something in yourself that provokes fear and distrust. And, thus, you judge it, push it away, deny it as undesirable in others. Shouldn't everyone agree with our preparations for spiritual growth? And shouldn't they be pursuing our journey, and our superior way?

A positive manifestation of this phenomenon, but as treacherous in its own way, is the dictum "Opposites attract." We see the strengths in others as the complement and fulfillment of the weaknesses in ourselves. This can often happen when couples fall in love. For a time, they enjoy a wonderful sense of completion and unity. The four functions and the four attitudes are together in full measure. But in time, they come to realize that dependency is involved. They dare not separate from each other, for a great lack in themselves becomes apparent when they do. They must patiently learn the lesson that ultimately there can be no substitute for growth and obtaining greater complementarity within themselves. If they are wise, they learn from each other and give their mutual support, allowing for "spaces in our togetherness," as Kahlil Gibran put it, and continue along pathways to spiritual growth with each other's blessings.

It is important to distinguish between the ethical as preparation for the journey and continued ethical deepening and sophistication as an aspect of the spiritual journey itself. The ethical dimension is essential in the reintegration process as the journey connects with the continuing cycle of life, a theme we will return to in chapter 9, under "Faith Development."

⟲ PHILOSOPHICAL PREPARATIONS

It is important that we know we are not embarking on a spiritual journey for ourselves alone. We walk because it is in our nature to reach for a larger, greater spirituality, and we walk that the fortunes of life on the planet may be extended. It makes a difference in the world that we deepen our lives.

There are many givens in the universe, laws of gravity and leverage, strength of materials, the first and second laws of thermodynamics, the emergence of galaxies, revolutions of the earth around the sun and the moon around the earth, the evolution of life on the planet. Although the big picture appears orderly, we know that harmony is not an inherent quality in being as such. Order and chaos coexist and flow together. If perfection were the goal and larger reality, stasis would reign, tomorrow would be completely predictable, and life would be monotonous. Our gratitude, then, is directed toward change, variety, and the unknown, the adventure that awaits us each new day. Life consists in dynamic adaptations to change, the balancing of forces internal and external, the re-forming of our awareness and understanding, and acts of creation in the world.

In this context I see three major fields for human purpose. So far as we know at present, we are the only beings endowed with conscious intelligence as we conceive it. We have added to biological evolution a cultural evolution as well. Human purpose therefore involves our intelligent powers to understand more, to integrate that knowledge in greater synergies of creation, to monitor, to solve problems as they arise, and to build up this neighborhood of space. R. Buckminster Fuller expresses this in the context of his "design science."[13] A sense of an essential cosmic purpose for the human emergence on this planet motivates participation in this evolving ethical/spiritual presence.

Jungian and MBTI research and use, including its interface with cognitive psychology, certainly will be an important part of this overall purpose for the human experiment on this planet, for we must understand and effectively develop our own psychological and spiritual functioning and be helpful toward the same end for our neighbors if we are to integrate our lives with and participate in this larger purpose.

A second purpose gives us perspective from a different direction, as proposed by analyst Lawrence Jaffe in a Jungian context. We are here to expand the human consciousness as far as possible, for this affects the unconscious cosmos. It is the actualization of God in the world. He quotes Edward Edinger: "Individuation is the ongoing incarnation of God for the purpose of divine transformation."[14] In other words, we have here an inner psychological parallel for the first purpose, which is a purpose with reference to the outer world. In the first, God unfolds as a syntropy to compensate for the entropy of the world. In the second, God emerges into a conscious spiritual presence.

Our third purpose on the planet is our covenant with life itself. We live in spiritual connection with all life, to be considerate of it, to love it, to care for it. To the extent that earth's ecology reaches healthy balance, the human soul can obtain peace. Short of the well-being of the whole, individuals must attempt their separate negotiations and connections as near as possible to that peace. Part of our covenant with all of life is our obligation to fulfill ourselves, to enjoy and to employ our natures.

When we are aware of the context and purpose of our living, we begin to form a sense of our particular unique contribution to the story of the world and the story of human emergence on the planet. Essential in the spiritual journey is the sense that we are living a story that is part of a larger story. Our struggles, deepenings, the reports of our learnings, and our wisdom make a difference. Engaging deeply in the spiritual journey brings our past up for review. We discover the impact of others on our development and our influence on those around us. We remember epic events, turning points, critical experiences.

These discoveries come when we take the time for reflection, in the Introverted preference, or in the give-and-take of dialogue or sharing, in the Extraverted preference. It is important not to lose the data, insights, and even the narrative of our personal stories that we will discover as we embark on the spiritual journey. It is essential that we maintain some form of regular meditation during or after, in which the story of our participation in the world's purpose is set down in creative form. The journey needs a diary, markers to flag what you have learned for when you revisit your experience, to nurture your future participation in the ongoing story.

ᕦ THE SPIRITUAL TRADITION

On mountaintops, under salt water, hidden in dense jungles, buried beneath drifting sands are many hundreds of thousands of ancient temples and shrines, with many millions of god and goddess images—silent testimony to the centrality of religion. The rain dance and the evening song of chimpanzees encourage us to surmise that we come by our worship naturally.[15] Neanderthal humans carefully buried their dead with cherished artifacts.[16] The caves of Lascaux and El Castillo inspire us today as sacred places. At the Paleolithic temples in Malta, monolithic rocks are formed and arranged with as much precision as a Japanese vase of flowers. One is a three-story temple underground, carved by hand for the sleeping goddess. The earliest known architect for any of these magnificent religious centers was Imhotep, creator of the Step Pyramid complex in Saqqâra, Egypt, circa 2800 B.C., where earth meets sky in an awesomely dramatic spiritual effect.

Such are examples of what is known about the origins of our spiritual inheritance. When we set out on our own pilgrimage, we walk in their company. To simplify this discussion, I have consolidated the many branches of religion into four groupings: Western, Asian Indian, Far Eastern, and the nature-centered traditions. Today's pilgrims need to claim their inheritance from each.

The Western Tradition

Western culture has two major sources: Greco-Roman and Middle Eastern. Christianity is a synthesis of large portions of both. A philosophical tradition continued from Greek origins blossoming during the Renaissance, Enlightenment, and the emergence of science. From Persian-Sumerian-Egyptian origins, the Zoroastrian, Jewish, and Islamic traditions evolved. Among the founders are examples of all Four Spiritualities: Socrates (NT), Mohammed (SF), Moses (ST), and Jesus (NF).

The Asian Indian Tradition

The god Shiva has been found in images dating from circa 2700 B.C. in Mohanjo-daro, seated in the classic yoga meditative position.[17] Jains, Buddhists, and Hindus continue numerous variations of yoga as a spiritual discipline today. From the *Vedas/Upanishads* through the Bhagavad Gita, the medieval poets Kabir and Tulsidas (as well as Nanak, founder of the Sikh religion) to thriving traditions today, Hindus practice a form of active religious tolerance quite different from that to which the Enlightenment West is accustomed, equally valid and vigorous. India rebelled against colonial rule, achieving independence from the British in 1947, but never removed the statues of Queen Victoria that grace its big city public parks. Likewise, the very oldest and the newest spiritual practices remain side by side in perhaps the most complex living religious mosaic on the planet.

In Hinduism, the Four Spiritualities have a direct parallel in the four classic forms of yoga, which have been singled out for special attention in a section of each of the next four chapters. For the Journey of Unity the parallel yoga is jnana yoga; for the Journey of Devotion, bhakti yoga; for the Journey of Works, karma yoga; and for the Journey of Harmony, raja (and integral) yoga. Although the yogas are in a Hindu context, they will help to deepen insights for those practicing in other religious traditions as well.

The Far Eastern Tradition

Religious humanism in many forms has been a continuous tradition in the Far East for perhaps four thousand years. The dialectic of Confucianism (ST) and Taoism (NF) with the later influence of Buddhist forms (NT and

SF) has produced a rich and varied humanist–naturalist culture. Not only the scriptures but also the landscape paintings, poetry, sculpture, music, and architectural forms are expressions of a deep spiritual tradition. Of the major centers of spirituality, the Far East is probably the most neglected today, seldom taken in its fullness and balance.

Nature-Centered Traditions

By nature-centered traditions, I mean all tribal religions in Africa, Polynesia, and Australia; pre-Christian northern European traditions; the widespread shamanic forms; North, Central, and South American Indian traditions; and the oldest continuous living spiritual practice today among the !Kung bushmen of Southwest Africa. When I use the word *pagan*, I will confine my attention to Celtic practices originating in Ireland, Britain, and France.

↶ WHICH SPIRITUALITY FOR YOU?

The next four chapters present the Four Spiritualities. Honor the importance of each, and reflect on your own home-base spirituality until you become comfortable with your version of it. Included in each chapter are numerous quotations from representative examples around the world. Take these as an invitation to delve deeper when you find one of them particularly attractive. This can be done at various points along your journey.

Following this will be a chapter that explores ways to deepen the journey already under way, and a final chapter, Destination, places your return into the context of your life. Spiritual growth occurs at various junctures in the life cycle and therefore will affect the contexts in which you live and work, including the temple or religious community in which you are engaged and that you will influence. Your spiritual journey has great import for those who surround you and share the planet with you!

II.

JOURNEYING

CHAPTER FOUR

THE JOURNEY OF UNITY

I HAVE GONE INTO THE HEARTS OF ALL.

FOR ME COME MEMORY,

KNOWLEDGE, REASONING.

I AM WHAT IS TO BE KNOWN

BY ALL THE VEDAS,

AUTHOR OF THE VEDAS' END

AND VEDA-KNOWER.

Bhagavad Gita, trans. Ann Stanford

EACH OF THE FOUR SPIRITUALITIES tends to gravitate to compatible settings for fullest support. While dovetailing with the other spiritualities, sharing spaces, programs, and spiritual practices with them, each also needs special contexts that accentuate its unique approach.

The Journey of Unity is likely to require the least adorned setting for spiritual practice: a Zen garden, a quiet grove, a white room with clear-paned windows, a simple chapel. Decoration is added to educate or to focus the attention. Imagine a small dome-shaped room with Doric columns at the doors and windows. The focal point is at the center, an arrangement of flowers, a bell. The leader welcomes you, perhaps gives a commentary on the reading of the day. The group may engage in discussion of the theme. Ritual practice may include a chant sung by the group, accented with the clear bell tones, followed by silent meditation. Perhaps there will be a profound truth or principle presented, or even a single word or picture that adds clarity to your life. You feel a sense of balance and symmetry, note a cogency of ideas linking the elements together. There is an educational component, and you leave feeling more centered, engaged, and informed.

⟨⟩ THE NT PERSONALITY

Variations of this picture, more or less elaborate and taking many forms around the globe for the Journey of Unity, are likely to appeal most to two Intuitive types with Thinking (INTJ and ENTP) and two Thinking types with Intuition (INTP and ENTJ). Before examining the outlines of this native spirituality, it is useful to have in mind a concept of the NT personality.

As Children and Youth

Have you noticed how some children at an early age will from time to time seem to be intrigued by an idea very large or very far away? These are the children who sometimes invent their own toys. Or they enjoy solving problems that no one else seems to notice. They will often excel in one subject: math, reading, biology. From time to time, they will focus on an issue such as the school dress code or grading system, and they may succeed in changing the system.

NT youth value their independence and work very hard to establish their competence in whatever challenge they decide to tackle. They desire respect from adults and peers but may feel somewhat awkward or aloof in some social situations. In responding to rules or academic subjects or parental authority, they are likely to ask why, and will either be satisfied with the response they receive or set out to improve upon it or to rebel against arbitrary answers.

As Adults

As adults, NTs have vision, either intensely concentrated or extensively comprehensive. They thrive on solving problems, impersonally analyzing situations, finding the possibilities inherent in the patterns and the logic they discover. They love to exchange ideas, engage another mind, test their own competency, and be stimulated to new efforts. They focus on the task, the goal, and on the discovery, exploration, and interpretation needed to reach understanding. They seek intellectual clarity, the underlying organizing principles, the big picture. NTs love speculative theories, models, systems thinking, macro logic or analysis that leads to predictability or control, global concepts, a synthesis that can explain everything in a unity.

They are the foremost change agents and strategic planners. They are comfortable with abstractions, ideas that have no reality in the present. While they are cognizant of past and present, they are not attached to them and are rarely satisfied with things as they are. Being good critics, they are sometimes quicker to see what is wrong than what is right. They can be rather compulsive in their quest for perfection and high standards. Thus, they are sometimes misunderstood and can be perceived by others, particularly SFs, as uncooperative or stubborn or as having a superior attitude. Because of their NT orientation they may neglect the physical (S), emotional (SF), and interpersonal (F) sides of their lives. Often we see attention to these as a part of an overall spiritual strategy when NTs enter the spiritual pilgrimage of their adult lives.

ᗢ NT NATIVE SPIRITUALITY

Of the Four Spiritualities, the Journey of Unity is the most efficiently described, dividing into just four comprehensive aspects. For each individual these four overall manifestations will assume different proportions: (1) organizing principles operating throughout life and nature; (2) truth that can be global, honest, and clear; (3) social justice as the aim and context for our involvement, including opposition to ignorance with education; and (4) clarity as the basis of spiritual enlightenment.

Organizing Principles

The quest for great organizing principles that bind life and nature into one unity is a central focus of the Journey of Unity. A classic experience of this guiding light of NT spirituality is told by Albert Schweitzer:

> Lost in thought I sat on the deck of the barge, struggling to find the elementary and universal conception of the ethical which I had not discovered in any philosophy. Sheet after sheet I covered with disconnected sentences, merely to keep myself concentrated on the problem. Late on the third day, at the very moment when, at sunset, we were making our way through a herd of hippopotamuses, there flashed upon my mind, unforeseen and unsought, the phrase, "Reverence for Life." The iron door had yielded: the path in the thicket had become visible. Now I had found my way to the idea in which affirmation of the world and ethics are contained side by side. Now I knew that the ethical acceptance of the world and of life, together with the ideals of civilization contained in this concept, has a foundation in thought.[1]

It was important to Schweitzer that thought be the force knitting together both a worldview and an ethic in one unifying principle.

The Journey of Unity always tries to boil complexity down into simplicity, whether it be broad principles, honesty, or clarity. It operates in both theological and humanist–naturalist contexts. A classic statement comes from the nineteenth-century American theologian William Ellery Channing:

> That unbounded spiritual energy which we call God, is conceived by us only through consciousness, through the knowledge of ourselves. . . . The Infinite Light would be forever hidden from us, did not kindred rays dawn and brighten within us. God is another name for human intelligence raised above all error and imperfection, and extended to all possible truth. The same is true of God's goodness. How do we understand this, but by the principle of love implanted in the human breast? . . . Men, as by a natural inspiration, have agreed to speak of conscience as the voice of God, as the Divinity within us . . . the universe, I know, is full of God.[2]

Here is the NT global view from which human participation is seen as coordinated with larger principles of order in the universe. The closing lines of Albert Camus' novel *The Stranger* give this same vision of the reflection of human patterns with cosmic realities in a humanist context:

> [G]azing up at the dark sky spangled with its signs and stars, for the first time . . . I laid my heart open to the benign indifference of the universe. To feel it so like myself, indeed, so brotherly, made me realize that I'd been happy, and that I was happy still.[3]

In these two readings we see reference to both Sensing (S) and Feeling (F) values, but in an NT context. Channing established goodness and love as global NT principles rather than as F values. This often happens when an F-composed value is adopted as a principle by Thinking types. It is an important distinction, for principles have very different dynamics in the inner life. They take on the nature of premises in logical systems rather than values interacting with other values as the Feeling function navigates and composes appropriate responses to life in an SF or NF context.

Truth

In the search for truth, Intuitive Thinkers can be either philosophical realists or idealists. The latter intentionally ignore the input of the senses to substantiate a principle. Socrates, for example, in Plato's *Republic*, summarizes his epistemology thus:

> True knowledge is concerned not with the physical world of the senses but with the qualities, the realities, that are inherent in the everyday world — with Beauty, not with beautiful sounds and colours. The changing world of the senses is the object of opinion, but the unchanging world of realities is the object of true knowledge or wisdom, and it is this wisdom that true philosophers love.[4]

In a famous exchange between the American social reformer Margaret Fuller and the British historian Thomas Carlyle, she said, "I accept the universe," and he replied, "By Gad, she'd better."[5] Her announcement is completely understandable in an NT context. Nothing is taken for granted. She had to consider the issue from the beginning. She came down on the side of philosophical realism in the debate as expressed theologically in her memoirs (1828):

> I believe in Eternal Progression. I believe in a God, a Beauty and Perfection to which I am to strive all my life for assimilation. From these two articles of belief, I draw the rules by which I strive to regulate my life. But, though I reverence all religions as necessary to the happiness of man, I am yet ignorant of the religion of Revelation. Tangible promises! well defined hopes! are things of which I do not *now* feel the need. At present, my soul is intent on this life, and I think of religion as its rule; and, in my opinion this is the natural and proper course from youth to age.[6]

The worldview of modern science has a powerful NT bias. Although there have been some NTs who have not adopted it, the idea of evolution (a refinement of Fuller's "Progression") has replaced older, more static principles and truths that proposed absolutes as their premise. Now macro theories of life and nature build in change and most recently accommodate chaos as well. In the Journey of Unity, the search for truth itself is often as satisfying as its conclusions at any given point.

Julian Huxley calls religion "a way of life." He sees us as living in a unity, a continuity of the living and the nonliving, mind and matter. This continuity is "one ultimate world-substance." In his words,

> all reality then consists, as Whitehead put it, of events. The events are all events in the history of a single substance. The events looked at from outside are matter. Experienced from inside, they are mind.[7]

The philosopher Michael Polanyi agrees with Huxley that the world has within it a theme of emergence. Life is emergent, and we are part of a community of emergence, which Polanyi calls "a Society of Explorers."[8] What exists now was contained in the previous world as possibilities, as what he calls "the tacit dimension." Possibilities in nature may later emerge into expression. Buckminster Fuller calls the more that comes into being *synergy*. When we add up our experiences, our scientific testing, our celebrations and our joy, we have more than a mere sum of the parts. More is always emerging.

Some may be surprised that a number of those traveling the Journey of Unity are secular when viewed from some spiritual traditions. A rapprochement is made by the theologian Martin Marty, who identifies a form of Introverted NT spirituality he calls "wintry spirituality." He quotes the novelist Lars Gustafsson:

It was gray, pleasant February weather, fairly cold and hence not too damp, and the whole landscape looked like a pencil sketch. I don't know why I like it so much. It is pretty barren and yet I never get tired of moving about in it.[9]

This scene is in contrast to what Marty calls the exuberance of "summery piety." Marty, from his perspective as a Protestant Christian theologian, considers himself a wintry sort and feels that this whole perspective is neglected for good reason. He continues:

The wintry sort of spirituality, let it be remembered, stakes out its place on the landscape next to persons who have seen God excluded from their horizons. That exclusion is the signal of their wintriness. They have not given up on the search for God. They remain committed to the Christian meanings, and they find many occasions to worship and affirm. That is the sign of their spirituality. . . . They cannot satisfy their hunger by reading the descriptions of summery piety. They have to find their Yes on the colder, more barren landscape.[10]

Marty devotes much of his book to the Psalms, where he finds numerous examples of "wintry spirituality." His message to us is clear: Within the major traditional religions, there are many ways to journey. You can take the hot southern path (largely SF)—dramatic, charismatic, exciting. Or you can look out at the vast grayness of the northern pathway (largely NT)—contemplative, rational, skeptical, simple, even stark; unpretentious, focused on a search for truth wherever it may lead. This pathway does not bask in public favor, but it is a legitimate search for the spiritual life.

Social Justice

Along with principles and truth (either static or emerging), NTs on the Journey of Unity must have justice. Prometheus is an early prototype, stealing fire from the gods because the world needed balancing. Justice deals with issues of power and control in society in a systemic way. The nineteenth-century American clergyman Theodore Parker made a distinction between "palliative Charity" and "remedial Justice," extolling the superiority of the latter.[11] Charity would be an SF commitment, reform an NT imperative. NTs want permanent, long-range change and may neglect the immediate human need right before them. SFs may be so tuned in to the tangible hurts and hopes that they will not call time-out to formulate a long-range plan.

The image of the plumb line employed by the prophet Amos—"Behold, I am setting a plumb line in the midst of my people Israel"[12]—could be either ST or NT. But the content of this new standard is an exceedingly early example of the direct opposition of NT and SF spiritual practice. Amos believed that the devotional practices of the people had become hollow and distracting, that the corruption of their behavior had consequences. Whether his cause-and-effect logic was accurate, of course, has been a theme of religious debate for millennia. But his is the classic statement of the issue:

> I hate, I despise your feasts,
> and I take no delight in your solemn assemblies.
> Even though you offer me your burnt offerings
> and cereal offerings,
> I will not accept them,
> and the peace offerings of your fatted beasts
> I will not look upon.
> Take away from me the noise of your songs;
> to the melody of your harps I will not listen.
> But let justice roll down like waters,
> and righteousness like an everflowing stream.[13]

His style was blunt and tactless. At one point, he characterized worshipers as "you cows of Bashan,"[14] hardly a way to win hearts and effect change. But he did get their attention, and his message has endured.

Frequently, concern with justice and social reform takes indirect forms. NTs are often architects, building temples and landscapes in such a way that human behavior is reformed. When I saw the Step Pyramid complex, it was clear to me that it was unique. The design was unlike anything else in Egypt. Imhotep, as well as being the earliest known designer of a stone monument, may be the earliest known NT.

Pharaoh Akhenaton, too, in moving the entire court and administration of Egypt into a newly designed city, reformed religion, taking the celebration of religion from the priesthood of Luxor and placing it in the hands of the people:

> When thou sendest forth thy rays,
> The Two Lands (Egypt) are in daily festivity,
> Awake and standing upon their feet
> When thou hast raised them up.
> Their limbs bathed, they take their clothing,
> Their arms uplifted in adoration to thy dawning.
> Then in all the world they do their work.[15]

This is an early religious revolution. Rolfe Gerhardt observes that most major religious reform is initiated by Intuitives. Intuitives are present "at the changing points of religion," Sensing types "in its stable structured expression."[16] While this is generally true, I believe there are brilliant exceptions: Confucius (ST), Moses (ST), and Mohammed (SF).

Another indirect means of religious reform is through education, which addresses the NT concern that ignorance is at the root of evil in the world.

If people could be exposed to truth, in the marketplace of ideas, truth and right would prevail. In the words of the Indian Buddhist philosopher Ashvagosha,

> the confused mind is a hindrance to thought and darkens the original wisdom of the True Reality. Ignorance is called the hindrance of wisdom, and darkens the natural wisdom of the world.[17]

And from another Buddhist source, the *Itivuttaka:* "I see no other single hindrance such as this hindrance of ignorance, obstructed by which mankind for a long long time runs on and circles on."[18]

The great Islamic theologian al-Ghazali sees us as born in ignorance, "devoid of knowledge of the worlds subject to the Creator," but gradually we rise through four stages of perception, remarkably similar to Jung's four functions (S, F, T, and N, respectively). First, "each of his senses is given him that he may comprehend the world of created things." At age seven we receive "the faculty of discrimination," then "reason," and, finally, what he calls "inspiration," such as is discerned in dreams and ecstasy:

> [C]ertain rationalists reject and deny the notion of inspiration. It is a proof of their profound ignorance; for, instead of argument, they merely deny inspiration as a sphere unknown and possessing no real existence.[19]

Horace Mann, who is credited with setting in motion the system of universal public education in America, placed education in the context of the spiritual journey that he called "rational piety":

> How can a man who is ignorant of God's laws be God's ambassador or representative? Get knowledge, then, my young friends, get wisdom, and with all thy gettings, get understanding. Get science (which is nothing but a knowledge of God's laws) as a religious duty. Before you can obey, you must know. Knowledge, then, is essential to a rational piety.[20]

In Far Eastern Buddhism, one of the four great bodhisattvas is the Great Bodhisattva of Boundless Conduct, who expresses confidence in the centrality of education in classic NT fashion: "However limitless the Buddha's teachings are, I vow to study them."[21]

Clarity

With principle, truth, and justice, the Journey of Unity strives to attain clarity of mind, clarity of spiritual enlightenment. NT meditation has as its distinguishing quality an intellectual mysticism, and in its more intense forms (I) is practiced in solitude, often in silence, often with great discipline.

The twentieth-century American mystic Thomas Merton, an INTJ, was a brilliant student, but spiritually restless, visiting churches, taking

Communion daily. He exercised his mind not only in his Ph.D. studies but also in writing literary reviews and teaching. He felt a need for uninterrupted reading and thinking, which he finally found in his recuperation time after an operation. He began an application to the Franciscans (SF), but discovered the alternative tradition of the Trappists in a Holy Week retreat. He describes his experiences in a chapter called "True North":

> The embrace of it, the silence! I had entered into a solitude that was an impregnable fortress. And the silence that enfolded me, spoke to me, and spoke louder and more eloquently than any voice and in the middle of that quiet, clean smelling room, with the moon pouring its peacefulness in through the open window, with the warm night air, I realized truly whose house that was, O glorious Mother of God![22]

After his retreat was over, life outside seemed strange, the busy pace of people in the city appeared "futile," and he knew "there was only one place where there was any true order."[23] A major change for his life seemed imminent. He opened up his Bible and the first verse that greeted him was "Behold, thou shalt be silent" (Luke 1:20):

> I was almost as ignorant as I was before, except for one thing.
>
> Deep down, underneath all the perplexity, I had a kind of a conviction that this was a genuine answer, and that the problem was indeed some day going to end up that way: I was going to be a Trappist.[24]

In the intervening time, the distance widened between him and college teaching, friends, and family. His brother was killed in World War II. He had crossed a boundary:

> I read a story in the *New Yorker* about a boy who, instead of becoming a priest, got married, or at least fell in love or something. And the emptiness and futility and nothingness of the world once more invaded me from every side. But now it could not disturb me or make me unhappy. It was sufficient to know that even if I might be in it, that did not compel me to have any part of it, or to belong to it, or even to be seriously begrimed with its sorry, unavoidable contact.[25]

Merton chose the course of rejecting the outside world for a life of solitude, discipline, and even humiliation in an effort to break through into clarity. Life outside had been increasingly self-defeating for his search:

> My God, it is that gap [between us] and the distance which kill me. That is the only reason why I desire solitude—to be lost to all created things, to die to them and to the knowledge of them, for they remind me of my distance from You. They tell me something about You: that You have made them and Your presence sustains their being, and they hide You from me. For I knew that it was only by leaving them that I could come to You: and that is why I have been so unhappy when You seemed to be condemning me to remain in them.[26]

He returned to the monastery: "So Brother Matthew locked the gate behind me and I was enclosed in the four walls of my new freedom."[27]

Merton had exercised a thoroughgoing discursive meditation known as Thomistic prayer (after St. Thomas Aquinas), whereby one sets before oneself an issue involving truth, integrity, or one's own shortcomings and wrestles with it until it is analyzed, resolved, and acted upon. In his case, it resolved itself in a kind of reconversion.[28]

Twentieth-century British mathematician and philosopher Bertrand Russell did not leave the world, but in his "Free Man's Worship" faced its toughest elements, again with central themes of the Journey of Unity: principle, truth, justice, clarity, and freedom:

> The life of Man, viewed outwardly, is but a small thing in comparison with the forces of Nature. The slave is doomed to worship Time and Fate and Death, because they are greater than anything he finds in himself, and because all his thoughts are of things which they devour. But, great as they are, to think of them greatly, to feel their passionless splendour, is greater still. And such thought makes us free men; we no longer bow before the inevitable but we absorb it, and make it a part of ourselves. To abandon the struggle for private happiness, to expel all eagerness of temporary desire, to burn with passion for eternal things—this is emancipation, and this is the free man's worship.[29]

Russell stated in positive terms what the Buddha expressed subtractively in his famous Fire Sermon. Russell sees us burning in a transcending of our attachments in an embracing global affirmation. The Buddha sees our consciousness becoming neutral and the world as such holding no future meaning for us beyond present experience:

> The eye, O Bhikkhus, is on fire; forms are on fire; eye-consciousness is on fire; . . . The ear is on fire; sounds are on fire . . . the nose is on fire, odours are on fire; . . . the tongue is on fire; tastes are on fire; . . . mind-consciousness is on fire; impressions received by the mind are on fire; and whatever sensation, pleasant, unpleasant or indifferent, originates in dependence on impressions received by the mind, that also is on fire.[30]

When a disciple perceives this and the means by which the fire burns in the passions, an aversion for all forms of fire is cultivated.

> And in conceiving this aversion, he becomes divested of passion, and by the absence of passion he becomes free, and when he is free he becomes aware that he is free; and he knows that rebirth is exhausted, that he has lived the holy life, that he has done what it behooved him to do, and that he is no more for this world.[31]

The German philosopher Martin Buber (1878–1965) places the issue in a theological context. In clarity, the preference of the Journey of Unity for systems and knowledge is itself transformed. We move beyond even ideas to unity.

All real living is meeting.

The relation to the Thou is direct. No system of ideas, no foreknowledge, and no fancy intervene between I and Thou. The memory itself is transformed, as it plunges out of its isolation into the unity of the whole. No aim, no lust, and no anticipation intervene between I and Thou. Desire itself is transformed as it plunges out of its dream into the appearance. Every means is an obstacle. Only when every means has collapsed does the meeting come about.[32]

The quest for clarity in the Journey of Unity can bring us to the limits of the mind and knowledge: to an encounter with the limits of life itself, to a renouncing of the world, a neutralizing of the world, or to a communication with God. All have a common awareness that we are truly ourselves and that we live in true freedom.

⌦ JNANA YOGA

The most direct parallels to the Four Spiritualities, explicit in an existing tradition, are the yoga practices of Hinduism. Jnana yoga, bhakti yoga, karma yoga, and raja yoga correspond readily to the Journeys of Unity (NT), Devotion (SF), Works (ST), and Harmony (NF), respectively. Thus, they are singled out for special mention in this and the other three journey chapters, 5 through 7.

The goal of jnana yoga, the path of knowledge, is to hear about, mull over in the mind, sort, and ultimately realize the bliss of identification in Unity:

Jnana-yoga is an all-out effort to overcome the subject-object division by realizing the subject in its true form—as the transcendental Self, which is permanent, indivisible, and inherently blissful. Jnana, or gnosis, is both the goal and the medium of jnana-yoga.[33]

First, it is important to have a global understanding of universal laws for the physical world. Then one must concentrate inwardly to sort out the universal laws within. Finally, it is necessary to find the identity of all, to transcend these understandings for a more profound awareness of unity, which includes but is beyond them. The connection of this transcending of self with Self is identified as Brahman-Atman, the latter being the self/Self within:

As a lump of salt thrown in water dissolves, and cannot be taken out again as salt, so this great endless deathless Being dissolved is knowledge; He reveals Himself with the elements, disappears when they disappear; leaving no name behind.[34]

The mind tends to be attached to everything the nervous system is attached to: Spirit is attached to matter, purusha to prakriti. The process of jnana yoga aims to cross over in meditation to the state of bliss. From the transient we come to know the permanent. According to the innovations on this issue in the Bhagavad Gita, since prakriti is but another form of purusha, if one is successful in life the material (prakriti) falls away at death and the spirit (purusha) is merged, Brahman-Atman:

> But of those in whom this ignorance in the self
> Is destroyed by knowledge,
> That knowledge of theirs
> Causes the Supreme to shine like the sun.
>
> They whose minds are absorbed in that
>   (i.e., the Supreme),
> Whose selves are fixed on that,
> Whose basis is that, who hold that
>   as highest object,
> Whose evils have been shaken off by
>   knowledge, go to the end of rebirth.[35]

Alain Danielou itemizes seven stages of knowledge as they first appeared in the *Akashi Upanishad*: (1) good will, (2) reflection, (3) subtlety of mind, (4) perception of reality, (5) freedom from leanings toward the world, (6) the disappearance of visible forms, and (7) the entering of the unmanifest stage. It is clear that the tendency is from specific knowledge to unity, which he describes in this statement: "He remains for ever wandering in the delight of the knowledge of the Absolute."[36]

We sometimes find among jnana writers a tendency to see jnana yoga in a hierarchy, with jnana as superior. Swami Vivekananda, who is admired throughout India as one of the first to present Hinduism to the West, puts a unique spin on this issue. Bending over backward to treat the four yogas equally, he nevertheless places jnana last, as bringing us to a divine awareness that we are God. He reveals his real bias away from the senses by contrasting Introversion (or a form of INT) with Extraverted Sensing (ES):

> There is one set of ideas in our mind which is always struggling to get outside through the channels of the senses, and behind that although it may be thin and weak, there is an infinitely small voice which says, do not go outside. The two beautiful Sanskrit words for these phenomena are Pravritti and Nivritti, "circling forward" and "circling inward." It is the circling forward which usually governs our actions. Religion begins with this circling inward. Religion begins with this "do not." Spirituality begins with this "do not."[37]

An IN bias is common and dominates great quantities of spiritual literature, particularly in the Journey of Unity (NT).

⌖ MENTORS FOR THIS WAY

Although NTs make up only about 12 percent of the population, spiritual literature is replete with NT authors and NT subjects. Here I single out two.

The Buddha founded one of the world's great religions, and R. Buckminster Fuller was a spiritual genius of the present century.

The Buddha

The word *Buddha* is from the root *budh*, which means to awaken, to know. The Buddha is one who is awake. He was born in 544 B.C. as Siddhartha Gautama into the family of a wealthy king. His mother, Maya, died seven days after his birth, but he was raised in affluent and sheltered surroundings, where he remained even after he had married and had a son of his own. Soothsayers told his father that little Siddhartha would grow up to become either a great king or a Buddha. His father preferred his own calling and rigged the game in that direction, a lesson in the folly of deterring our children from their native type and journey. One day Siddhartha decided to see the town, so the charioteer brought him down one of the safe streets that his father had cleaned up. But an old man stepped out into view and Siddhartha asked, "What is old?" The next day, he saw a diseased man and Siddhartha asked, "What is sick?" And on the third day, they saw a funeral procession and Siddhartha asked, "What is death?" On the fourth day, he saw a holy man, and Siddhartha began to hear a deep call from a side of himself he had never listened to before.

His experiences of old age, sickness, and death had shaken the young prince's confidence, causing him to ask, What is life about? His father stepped up the distractions at court. There was a room full of dancing and feasting, but Siddhartha was so uninterested that he fell asleep. As if on cue, everyone in the room followed suit. Hours later, he woke up and was disgusted at what he saw around him on the physical plane—a stinking roomful of snoring, contorted bodies. He and his horseman saddled up, and at the river he gave his horse to his companion and told him that he would not be returning. He would lead an ascetic life in the forest. Seven years later he had gained considerable fame for his austerities (he was skin and bones), until one day he collapsed. A girl in the village gave him a bowl of porridge, and he began to regain his strength. He found he enjoyed food once again. This is the origin of his teaching of the Middle Path, nothing to excess, not too much, not too little: no gluttony, no ascetic deprivations.

He walked until he came to a pipal tree, called the bodhi tree, because this was the place he became the Buddha, the awakened one. This was the tree of knowledge and wisdom, the place of enlightenment. The soon-to-be Buddha approached the tree. He went to the north side, and the world ahead of him went up and the world behind went down. Lacking balance, he circled to the west, and the same strange thing happened, and then he walked to the south and it happened again. When he reached the east, the world stayed still, so he sat in yoga meditative posture facing east. This, of course, was the direction of the new day, the rising sun, and the Buddha acquired a golden halo, the solar sign. In circling the tree, he had drawn a circle of the four directions, a compass, the wheel around the hub of the world tree. It is the wheel of the Eightfold Path for attaining enlightenment, Buddhahood.

It was under the bodhi tree that Buddha endured the great temptations visited upon him by Mara, the tempter. He was first tempted by desire, by lust for experiences and greed for possessions. Then he was assaulted by the flip side of desire, fear of death. After resisting these, he was tempted by social duties, conventional expectations. Again the Buddha resisted the temptation, and the full force of enlightenment was now open to him. In the night, under the full moon, he moved through all knowledge of the four noble truths and attained the rapture of enlightenment. His last temptation occurred at this border: Would he accept nirvana, enter the void of nonbeing, or would he turn back? He hesitated at that point we call compassion, identification with the human condition of suffering. It was at this moment that the spiritual unity of humankind was affirmed. He felt compassion in his heart.

The Buddha spent the next fifty years teaching the Four Noble Truths. The first is *duhkha*, suffering, a state of pervasive "unsatisfactoriness."[38] Birth, decay, death, sorrow, grief, pain, desires, despair are all aspects of suffering none can avoid. One story that illustrates this truth is that of Kisa Gotami, whose son died. She brought him to the Buddha to be brought back to life. The Buddha told her to ask at doors everywhere to find a household that had known no death. When she found one, she was to ask them for a handful of mustard seed and she could bring it to him and he would bring her son back to life. She collected no mustard seed. When she returned she had buried her son and asked only for solace.[39]

The second noble truth is *anitya*, or impermanence. The more we grasp the world, the more it changes. We hold on tighter and tighter and everything dissolves in our hands. Avoid the two extremes: "Everything is" and "Everything is not." Everything gradually becomes something else. Nothing stays still. Don't be attached to things just as they are. Suffering or dissatisfaction is caused by our attachments, our cravings. The Buddha tells us we should not be attached to anything, even, at some point, life itself. He was moved to compassion for the human condition:

> The Enlightened One, because he saw Mankind
> drowning in the Great Sea of Birth, Death and
> Sorrow, and longed to save them,
> For this he was moved to pity.
> Because he saw the men of the world straying
> in false paths, and none to guide them,
> For this he was moved to pity.

Because he saw that they lay wallowing in the
mire of the Five Lusts, in dissolute abandonment,
For this he was moved to pity. . . .
Because he saw that though they longed for
happiness, they made for themselves no karma
of happiness; and though they hated pain, yet
willingly made for themselves a karma of pain:
and though they coveted the joys of Heaven,
would not follow his commandments on earth,
For this he was moved to pity.
Because he saw them afraid of birth, old-age
and death, yet still pursuing the works that lead
to birth, old-age and death,
For this he was moved to pity.
Because he saw them consumed by the fires
of pain and sorrow, yet knowing not where to
seek the still waters of Samadhi,
For this he was moved to pity. . . .
Because he saw them living in a time of wars,
killing and wounding one another: and knew that
for the riotous hatred that had flourished in their
hearts they were doomed to pay an endless
retribution,
For this he was moved to pity. . . .
Because some had great riches which they could
not bear to give away,
For this he was moved to pity.
Because he saw the men of the world ploughing
their fields, sowing the seed, trafficking,
huckstering, buying and selling: and at the end
winning nothing but bitterness,
For this he was moved to pity.[40]

The causes of duhkha, our attachments and cravings, bring us to consider the Buddha's resolution of the problem of causes, the third noble truth, *anatta*, non–ego attachment. With this prognosis we can begin to hope. The way through and beyond our suffering is to transcend our ego, to lose our attachments and to live instead, to be fully awake and present. Anatta is like a river: It is always there, but the water of which it is composed is never the same water. Anatta is like a dream: Once it is completed you do not carry it with you, at least in any tangible form. Where is reality? It is like a flame. It moves from candle to candle. Its very substance is continuous and not the same. And look at billiard balls: The energy can flow from one through another to another. Now you see it, now you don't. We must not be attached to any one thing, including some arbitrary and momentary notion of self. Self flows like a river.

In a dialogue with the wanderer Vacchagotta, the Buddha first had to ensure that his hearer was in his own frame of reference, which he did with a series of questions. They were calculated logically to bring Vaccha to the point of agreeing to subtract away cravings and attachments to the body, sensory objects, and interpretations of them, until a quiet state was reached:

"If there were a fire burning in front of you, would you know it?"

"Yes, good Gotama."

"If you were asked what made it burn, could you give an answer?"

"I should answer that it burns because of the fuel of grass and sticks."

"If the fire were put out would you know that it had been put out?"

"Yes."

"If you were asked in what direction the put-out fire had gone, whether to the east, west, north or south, could you give an answer?"

"That does not apply. Since the fire burnt because of the fuel of grass and sticks, then lacking sustenance, it went out."

"In the same way, Vaccha, all material shapes, feelings, perceptions, constructions, consciousness, by which a Truth-finder might be made known have been destroyed by him, cut off at the root, made like the stump of a palm-tree, so utterly done away with that they can come to no future existence. A Truth-finder is freed of the denotation of 'body,' and so on; he is profound, measureless, unfathomable, even like unto the great ocean."[41]

Not only all cravings, attachments, and intellectual theories, but even Buddha's way itself, the Dhamma, must eventually be dissolved as only a crutch and not the reality. A central metaphor in all branches of Buddhism is the raft (yana) that one uses to reach the other side, "the raft—for getting across, not for retaining."[42]

The Buddha spells out in the fourth noble truth his remedy: the raft itself, the way to eliminate life's unsatisfactoriness. It would bring you to the point he reached under the bodhi tree, one millisecond short of nirvana. The fourth noble truth is the Eightfold Path: right understanding, right-mindedness, right speech, right action, right living, right effort, right attentiveness, and right concentration. A Thai Buddhist catechism elaborates, citing the Majjhima-Nikāya as to how to proceed:

173. How should this Noble Eightfold Middle Path be practised?

All these eight parts should be practised together and not separately.

174. How is this Noble Eightfold Middle Path composed?

This Noble Eightfold Middle Path is composed of three elements, namely, the element of virtue, the element of concentration and the element of wisdom. The element of virtue embraces right speech, right action and right livelihood; the element of concentration embraces right effort, right attentiveness and right concentration, and the element of wisdom embraces right knowledge and right intention.[43]

Buddhism takes two forms at the millisecond before nirvana under the bodhi tree. The two forms are the Hinayana and the Mahayana. *Yana* means raft. How do you get from life as we know it to the undifferentiated state of nirvana? How do we traverse the flowing river? Hinayana, the small raft, tells us that by knowledge and wisdom, what the Buddha worked through under the tree of knowledge, we become disciples to the truth, arhats, and as individuals we develop toward nirvana. In the words of the *Dhammapada*:

> Clear thinking leads to Nirvana,
> a confused mind is a place of death.
> Clear thinkers do not die,
> the confused ones have never lived.
>
> The wise man appreciates clear thinking,
> delights in its purity, and
> elects it as the means to Nirvana.[44]

Mahayana, the larger raft, does not deny the validity of wisdom but transcends knowledge with compassion. The ideal is the bodhisattva, the Buddha who turns back from the edge of nirvana until all may enter together. Identification with the human condition, duhkha, Buddha's pity, is the very moment of unity with all creatures. The hand is raised to help others attain to the level of the bodhisattva.

In the fifteenth chapter of the Mahayana scripture, *The Lotus Sutra*, two ways of viewing the Buddha are graphically illustrated: (1) living as the Buddha lived in the direct experience of life on the planet, and (2) being as "buddha-nature," the eternal buddha. In this chapter, thousands of the latter, bodhisattvas, "springing up out of the earth," illustrated the need of the eternal to live in forms requiring ethical doing, and the need of the former to possess the perspective of knowing that the eternal is present always and equal.[45]

The question of arhat or bodhisattva is important. It is a question of whether we as individuals are independent or interdependent. Is there a synergy in our spiritual journey that requires us to travel in one another's company? And do we need to feel compassion above all knowledge? Is the knowledge of the cessation of suffering (bodhi) sufficient? Or is bodhi the means for reaching karuna, compassion? In this conflict the intensity of Introversion meets the embrace of Extraversion; nivritti, "circling inward," meets pravritti, "circling forward." And compassion itself in Buddhism meets with this challenge, to be an intense awareness or to turn back into action, touching old age, sickness, death, and the attachments of life.

At the edge of eternity is the prospect of nirvana. The Buddha developed an exquisite NT vision: At the center of self is emptiness.[46] In the words of the *Vigrahavyavartani*:

> All things prevail for him for whom emptiness
>   prevails;
> Nothing whatever prevails for him for whom
>   emptiness prevails.[47]

Rune Johansson, in his study of Buddhist psychology, listed forty-two semantic designations for nirvana, the most essential of which are pleasant, knowledge, liberation, permanent, attainable in this life, absence of desires, an experience, emptiness, freedom, peace of mind, freedom from rebirth, a state real, subjective, empirical, and psychological.[48] Reaching nirvana is a subtractive process. The bodhisattva pauses at the edge, but in an eternal state.

The Buddha lived to an old age and thus death presented him with the issue of succession and continuity for his teachings:

> I am now eighty years old, Ananda. The end of my journey has come. I drag my body along like a worn-out bullock cart, with great hardship.
>
> It is only when my thoughts are completely concentrated on the inner vision that has no bodily object that my body is at peace.
>
> Therefore, Ananda, be a lamp to yourself. Be an island. Learn to look after yourself; do not wait for outside help. . . .
>
> No, Ananda, no weeping. How often have I told you that it is in the very nature of life that what we love most must be taken from us?[49]

His instruction to his followers was to adhere to the Dhamma (way or teaching) and to the Sangha (monastic order). There would be no hierarchical clergy or successor and no deification.

Buckminster Fuller

Profound early influences on R. Buckminster Fuller were his great aunt Margaret Fuller, her brother (his grandfather), who was a Unitarian minister in Boston, his grandmother, who bought his beloved Bear Island as a family retreat, the U.S. Navy, and Einstein. Flunking out of Harvard twice and failing at business made important positive contributions, though they did not seem so at the time. For Buckminster Fuller was an original thinker who deferred to no one else's premises for his work. His great aunt wrote in 1842:

> Truth is the nursing mother of genius. No man can be absolutely true to himself, eschewing cant, compromise, servile imitation, and complaisance, without becoming original, for there is in every creature a fountain of life which, if not

choked back by stones and other dead rubbish, will create a fresh atmosphere, and bring to life fresh beauty . . . the spirit of truth, purely worshipped, shall turn our acts and forbearances alike to profit, informing them with oracles which the latest time shall bless.[50]

R. B. Fuller never read Plato, for example, and avoided the idealist–realist controversy in Western philosophy by developing his own original system. His biographer relates:

He neither affirms nor rejects Plato's allegory of the Cave; he merely submits the tetrahedron as the sole and proper path for its exit—for escape from non-conceptuality to the first stepping stone of Scenario Universe.[51]

An admirer penned a spontaneous verse that summarizes his vocation:

Fuller is a name
  For better or for worse,
Of two who grappled
  With the universe.
"I'll accept it,"
  Said the famous spinster.
"I'll explain it,"
  Said the bold Buckminster.[52]

When Fuller flunked out of Harvard, he took a job in a remote cotton mill in Sherbrooke, Quebec. Later, when he lost his job as president of a brick-making company, he saw no future and walked out onto a Chicago bridge, prepared to jump off:

Standing by the lake on a jump-or-think basis, the very first spontaneous question coming to mind was, "If you put aside everything you've ever been asked to believe and have recourse only to your own experiences do you have any conviction arising from those experiences which either discards or must assume an a priori greater intellect than the intellect of man?" The answer was swift and positive. Experience had clearly demonstrated an a priori anticipatory and only intellectually apprehendable orderliness of interactive principles operating in the universe into which we are born. These principles are discovered by man but are never invented by men. I said to myself, "I have faith in the integrity of the anticipatory intellectual wisdom which we may call 'God.' " My next question was, "Do I know best or does God know best whether I may be of any value to the integrity of universe?" The answer was "You don't know and no man knows, but the faith you have just established out of experience imposes recognition of the a priori wisdom of the fact of your being." Apparently addressing myself, I said, "You do not have the right to eliminate yourself, you do not belong to you. You belong to the universe. The significance of you will forever remain obscure to you, but you may assume that you are fulfilling your significance if you apply yourself to converting all your experience to highest advantage of others. You and all men are here for the sake of other men."[53]

His recovery from being beside himself in his inferior function could not have come at a more auspicious time. For the next two years, he took a vow of silence, resolved not to parrot the ideas of others but through thought to wrest an original relationship to the world. "Thinking is frequency modulation—tuning out finite irrelevancies into two main classes: micro-macro, which leaves residual defined system as lucidly relevant," he wrote.[54]

He modeled this reality of thinking as a "halo," for it has an inside and an outside, the "too frequent" inside, the "too infrequent" outside. Years later, he returned to the importance of original thinking when writing on education, advocating home schooling using computers as superior to schools with hundreds of students:

> When an individual is really thinking, he is tremendously isolated. He may manage to isolate himself in Grand Central Station, but it is despite the environment rather than because of it. The place to study is not in a school room.[55]

The halo could be seen as a model for Introversion and Extraversion, attraction toward the short-wave frequencies inside or the large-wave frequencies outside. There needs to be a balance. We need to be tuned in to both outside and inside, but in neither to the exclusion of the other. He defines halo as follows:

> The Halo is an omnidirectional, complex, high-frequency, Doppler-effected hypothetical-zone experience in an omnidirectional universal maelstrom of nonsimultaneous near and far explosions and their interaccelerating and refractive wave frequency patternings.[56]

Fuller may have prepared himself for his particular form of awareness in the first four years of his life. In this period, he was extremely farsighted and had never actually seen "a human eye or a teardrop or a human hair" until he was fitted with glasses at age four.[57] (What a preparation for a dominant Intuitive!) The halo of thought is not isolated. In a sense, it is part of a larger halo that embraces humankind.

His label for Atman or soul is "the Phantom Captain":

> This captain has not only an infinite self-identity characteristic but, also, an infinite understanding. He has, furthermore, infinite sympathy with all captains of mechanisms similar to his. What is this UNDERSTANDING? It consists in an intuitive, non-graphable awareness of perfection, or of unity, or of eternity, or of infinity or of truth. This awareness of perfection serves as a universal yardstick relative to which any sense experience may be measured, and by virtue of which CONSCIOUS SELECTION may be made.[58]

(Translating this to Jung's model of the self, the Phantom Captain is the self and the soul and in thought or understanding both the conscious and the unconscious are tunable.) Fuller rarely refers to the thought of others for his own expressions, but he does quote Einstein extensively in one of his early works, *Nine Chains to the Moon*. After rejecting any "anthropomorphic idea of God" and affirming "the cosmic religious sense," Einstein (INTP) reveals:

> [T]he individual feels the vanity of human desires and aims, and the nobility and marvelous order which are revealed in nature and in the world of thought. He feels the individual destiny as an imprisonment and seeks to experience the totality of existence as a unity full of significance.[59]

In his period of silence, Fuller purged his mind of vague vocabulary and culture-biased assumptions and came to a point of balance and understanding. He came to deeply admire the example of the yogis of India, "representing the high point of mental attainment of all time."[60] But he emerged from this intense experience himself with a third alternative for the dilemma faced by the Buddha at the moment of enlightenment. Shall it be nirvana or shall it be compassion, and, in compassion, shall it be an intense but cool awareness (NT) or an immersion in helping tangible suffering in the life around you (SF)? Fuller adds a third option (an exquisitely NT one). He called it *design science* and devoted his life to its development:

> I seek through comprehensive anticipatory design science and its reductions to physical practices to reform the environment instead of trying to reform humans, being intent thereby to accomplish prototyped capabilities of doing more with less whereby . . . chain reaction provoking events will both permit and induce all humanity to realize full lasting economic and physical success plus enjoyment of all the Earth without one individual interfering with or being advantaged at the expense of another.[61]

His work proceeded for half a lifetime before the evidence appeared that this strategy was not only noble but also essential and that it would work. In 1955 at United Nations meetings in Geneva, the evidence was "unequivocal":

> [F]or the first time in the history of man, it was in evidence that there could be enough of the fundamental metabolic and mechanical energy sustenance for everybody to survive at high standards of living—and furthermore, there could be enough of everything to take care of the increasing population while also always improving the comprehensive standards of living. Granted the proper integration of the world around potentials by political unblockings, there could be enough to provide for all men to enjoy all earth at a higher standard of living than all yesterday's kings, without self-interferences and with no one being advantaged at the expense of another.[62]

While Fuller called himself a "design scientist," his work was eminently ethical, religious, spiritual. It has far-reaching implications for the legitimation of social-justice strategies for equitable welfare, distribution of resources, and opportunities for all. He was unequivocal in his insistence that the planet could support all at a level of affluence, which he foresaw as the economy

shifted from "killingry" to "livingry."[63] As fewer workers are needed to produce a high standard of living for all, the primary purpose of life will come
more prominently into focus: "learning a living."[64]

Fuller always came at social policy from deep global spiritual visions,
weaving principle, material, and human purpose into one spiritual orientation. His biographer summarized his central focus:

> Fuller is utterly preoccupied with patterns of energy. He says it is the "fate of
> energy in the cosmic scheme to meander through eternity in persistent regen-
> erative bliss. . . . Energy is the capacity to rearrange elemental order." And it is
> the task of his synergetic geometry to identify energy with number, so it seems
> not only reasonable to him, but essential, to relate man's thought processes —
> his way of knowing — to the syntropic-entropic tidal flows of energy, the largest
> patterns in his cosmology.[65]

The only master of energy in the universe is the mind, which measures
light years in seconds.[66] Fuller's theology blends in with his estimation of the
purpose of the human mind:

> Yes, God is a verb,
> the most active,
> connoting the vast harmonic
> reordering of the universe
> from unleashed chaos of energy.
> And there is born unheralded
> a great natural peace,
> not out of exclusive
> pseudo-static security
> but out of including, refining, dynamic balancing.
> Naught is lost.
> Only the false and nonexistent are dispelled.[67]

It is beyond our purpose here to delve into his tetrahedronal geometry,
but he creates in it not only a rational metaphysics but also a fundamental
theory of relationships with profound consequences for an integrated ethical
spirituality.[68] Once when he spoke to a congregation of which I was minister, he summarized human purpose on the planet. Raising his arms in
a global arc and cupping his hands, he affirmed: "Problems, problems,
problems!"

He called his vocation "cosmic fishing." He believed that he was only a
vessel for such thought that has "its own integrity independent of the
thinker" and "does not belong to you." In his biographer's words, "our intuitive thoughts may be simply remote cosmic transmissions."[69] The critical
moment of Fuller's spiritual breakthrough occurred sometime in his two
years of self-imposed silence:

His listeners are vicariously compelled to share the lonely experience of his self-examination, a metaphor for the source of his commitment to humanity. Somewhere in the course of this transcendent spiritual crisis it is certain that Fuller visited a past or future landscape of astronomically remote philosophic distance.

It has always been my suspicion that some part of him remains in that alien country of his self-discovery, that he has never fully returned. . . .

Here was a bourn from which not only had traveler returned, but returned with a kind of cosmic zip code by which he could continue to receive messages. Here, at least, was a way of accounting for a recurring phenomenon in the course of writing *Synergetics*, when Bucky would say that he felt as if he were an agent for some transcendent or supernatural source of inspiration, as if he were merely an interceptor or transceiver of messages originating elsewhere.[70]

Whatever the sources of his inspirations, I trust his work will inspire the planet as we approach the millennium.

☙ UNDER STRESS, NEW LEARNINGS

Stress can activate the inferior function when the dominant and auxiliary are not competently managing the conscious situation. There are two sorts of benefits after such an episode begins to subside. As we have seen, R. Buckminster Fuller came out of his suicidal episode on the bridge to plunge into an intensely Introverted NT spiritual wrestling in his years of silence.

An alternative follow-through involves enlisting the tertiary and inferior (SF) functions in new spiritual practices. NT follow-through will always be accomplished in an NT way, even when SF values are very strong. Often a person will become attracted to rituals or practices in a formal religious setting and will participate from a need to rein in or discipline the Thinking or the Intuitive functioning. Quelling Thinking may be done in submission or obedience. To quell Intuition may be to focus and concentrate attention. Sensing Feeling values emerge in obedience, particularly when one feeds the poor, dresses the wounds of the ill, patiently educates the young in simple mathematics and recitation of the scriptures. These all involve direct, physical, humane, relationship-based activities, the sorts of emphases that balance the native strengths of the Journey of Unity.

Indeed, SF spirituality can be quite seductive, particularly, as is often the case, if one's early childhood was spent in an SF milieu. It is important that such an embrace of your polar opposite journey not permanently involve a rejection or abandonment of your native NT spirituality.

A remarkable example of new learnings is the tradition of Zen meditation. Chan or Zen Buddhism is a profoundly NT spirituality, but one that accentuates the S and F functions in an NT context. The goal of Zen is to relate to the world directly (S), without abstract symbols (holding N in abeyance), to apprehend suchness in its pure form.[71] Pictures of Bodhidharma, who introduced Chan (Zen) Buddhism into China from India, show in simple outline a person in meditation with sharp, bold, and penetrating eyes, one who sees directly.[72]

Zen enlightenment happens in most unexpected ways, strange and simple: "Once a monk asked Tung-shan: 'What is the Buddha?' Tung-shan replied: 'Three pounds of flax.' "[73]

In another encounter, an aspirant was enlightened by this experience:

When Banzan was walking through a market he overheard a conversation between a butcher and his customer.

"Give me the best piece of meat you have," said the customer.

"Everything in my shop is the best," replied the butcher. "You cannot find here any piece of meat that is not the best."

At these words Banzan became enlightened.[74]

One zen technique is pi-kuan, wall gazing, where one enters enlightenment by reason, meaning: "He will not then be a slave to words, for he is in silent communion with the Reason itself, free from conceptual discrimination; he is serene and not-acting."[75]

Zen involves integration through poetry, picture, simple philosophy, conduct, and direct experience. A wonderful metaphor is found in versions of the ten ox-herding pictures in which the herder looks for, rides, reflects upon the ox, and both disappear in moonlight. He reenters the city in one version "with Bliss-bestowing Hands."[76] There is no one way to find enlightenment or to determine what to make of it. You will know when it occurs, whether today as you walk to the store or after a lifetime of monastic routine.

☙ EDUCATION FOR THIS WAY

Preparation for all four journeys begins at the earliest age. The most essential elements of spiritual "In Forming" take place before age six or seven, when the functions are relatively undifferentiated. In his remarkable study of the rise and decline of cultures, neuroscientist Charles M. Fair calls this "the seeding of young minds . . . to become what we regard as fully human."[77] In his view, it is the function of the neocortex to organize the energies of the more elemental parts of the brain, the emergency and emotional aspects (the id, in Freudian terms) into a rational control. The seminal traditional ideas of the culture must be planted early, to remain beneath the surface of the soil until the sunlight and nurture of various developmental triggers can call them up from memory and enlist them in the formation of character, mind, and spirituality. Fair sees this process as the essential explanation for the rise and fall of cultures. In times of trouble the seeding process has not taken place. The basic ideas of what it is to be human are learned from story, from examples of people around the child, and from sincerely related precept. The child's mind must be impressed by the drama, genuineness, and honesty of input so that the memory remains until it can be utilized developmentally.

In later childhood, the bold outlines of typology begin to emerge in the personality. NT children will bring the seeds up for review, test them, synthesize them into working strategies in their life, particularly if reinforced by teaching approaches appropriate to NTs. The Intuition will be open to the unconscious, enjoying the play of imagination, even provoking stories and play that will actualize the seeds of culture. NT children use words and symbols freely and naturally, sometimes giving expression to concepts and principles they do not yet fully grasp in the flesh of experience. Encourage them, however, to advocate, challenge, and debate. Understanding comes only in the fullness of time.

The Journey of Unity becomes quite recognizable in youth by intellectual study, the search for truth, the passion for justice. Principles will be questioned and tested. Issues will be pursued in action and debate. There will be a need to achieve competence and, ultimately, clarity of orientation. Not only must these be encouraged, society also has an interest in instilling an appreciation and tolerance by NT youth of the other three spiritualities.

⟳ HOME AND TEMPLE

Mythologist Joseph Campbell recommends something dear to the hearts of all NT aspirants on the Journey of Unity, "a bliss station."[78] Each person needs a place and/or a time to which he or she can retire to think alone or to work on a personal project. You may be there with a book or your favorite music or a work of art to focus your thoughts. Or you may be seated on a cushion in the middle of a clear white room. Perhaps there will be windows revealing trees, mountains, desert, a stream, or cityscape just outside. Perhaps there will be no windows at all, only soft lighting. A more Extraverted NT might have three chairs, like Thoreau did: a chair for solitude, a chair for friendship, and a chair for society.[79]

NT spirituality often leads to the creation of temples to embody the truth or vision of that spirituality. In the West, the Greek temple, with its rational symmetries and balance (and the derivative of this form in the New England meetinghouse), exquisitely represents the Journey of Unity. Often the temple is established to teach the doctrine or truth the NT has created, such as Chartres Cathedral, with its highly sophisticated stained-glass-window themes. In the Far East, temples expressly connect the human realm with the larger spaces of heaven and earth. In the landscape of a temple, it is hard to know where the human-created part ends and nature begins. Frank Lloyd Wright had this same NT synthetic concern in the way he designed his churches and homes. Buckminster Fuller's domes are temples of "mind over matter" but employ the most central principles of geometry and physics.

ᙅ GIFT OF THIS JOURNEY FOR OTHERS

Introverted NTs, in particular, are engaged in spiritual research, producing a prolific literature of their observations. Extraverted NTs often excel as missionaries, polemical spokespeople, educators, organizers, and builders. Outstanding examples are Paul the Apostle and Emperor Asoka (perhaps ENTP and ENTJ, respectively).

Paul's great experience on the road to Damascus was an eruption of SF (his inferior functions) under the stress of his life as Saul the persecutor of Christians. His theology of the priority of faith, of Truth as a natural perception and of the principle of love are approaches of an NT mind combined with a strong extraverted emphasis on congregational life.[80]

Emperor Asoka in India inherited perhaps the most powerful empire in the world of his time (c. 274–232 B.C.) and expanded it in the early years of his reign. But he was appalled at the cost in violence, renounced it, and continued his long rule with a policy of nonviolence based in the teachings of the Buddha. Emissaries of his kingdom reached the West and Far East in an attempt to open up interfaith exchange. His policies can still be read on stone pillars, found scattered throughout India:

> Twelve years after my coronation I ordered edicts on Dharma to be inscribed for the welfare and happiness of the people, in order that they might give up their former ways of life and grow in Dharma in the particular respects set forth. Since I am convinced that the welfare and happiness of the people will be achieved only in this way, I consider how I may bring happiness to the people, not only to relatives of mine or residents of my capital city, but also to those who are far removed from me. I act in the same manner with respect to all. I am concerned similarly with all classes. Moreover, I have honored all religious sects with various offerings. But I consider it my principal duty to visit [the people] personally. I commanded this edict on Dharma to be inscribed twenty-six years after my coronation.[81]

Today it is often the NTs who will attempt interfaith peacemaking via attempts to synthesize the theologies of historically different religious traditions. A prominent example today in the West is Hans Küng, a Roman Catholic theologian at the University of Tübingen. He works with what he calls an "ecumenical world ethic" arrived at through dialogue. Having analyzed failed attempts by universal historians in the past, he prefers to honor parallel traditions, "the prophetic, mystical and wisdom religions," and to trace paradigm shifts each culture has experienced through the ages.[82] His principal focus, however, is on the prophetic (Judaism, Christianity, Islam) and leaves Indian and Chinese religion to one side, except for a particular attention to Christian–Buddhist dialogue.

Küng is straightforward about the limitations and obstacles to a world ethic, for example, the persistence of old paradigms through successive paradigm shifts in religious cultures. He leaves the question, In view of all the religious confusion on our globe, how can a global orientation be possible? He answers, only partially, that they all respond to human questions and that only a "world-wide approach will do justice to [world religions]."[83] However ambitious the attempts of the great NT synthesizers and "perennial philosophers," none has succeeded in even outlining the task in a way that can enlist all Four Spiritualities as equals.[84] And yet, as outlined here, the Four Spiritualities themselves are universal and provide a remarkable foundation for interfaith dialogue. The longing for the unity of truth and the universality of justice haunts and will always spur the NT synthesis. And Küng is completely justified as to its worth: "Those who carry on dialogue do not shoot."[85]

⟲ HOW NTs WILL USE THIS BOOK

Because NTs dominate in the comparative religion departments of the world's universities, it is an NT perspective that is most prominently represented in scholarly writing. It is what is most readily recognized by NTs in traditions other than their own. I therefore urge NT readers to read on. There is much more to the spiritual adventure of humankind than the Journey of Unity. Honor the affirmation of all four journeys in such sources of wisdom as the Bhagavad Gita:

> By meditation on the Self,
> see some the Self, by the Self.
> Others by the knowledge At-One-ment,
> others by the Action At-One-ment too.

> Others, indeed, thus not (themselves) knowing,
> having heard from others, (adoringly) attend.
> They also, too, transcend even death,
> that which is heard, (their) highest (goal).[86]

In these two verses we find affirmed first the Journey of Harmony, then the Journey of Unity and the Journey of Works, and finally in the second verse, the Journey of Devotion.

CHAPTER FIVE

THE JOURNEY OF DEVOTION

LOVE BEARS ALL THINGS, BELIEVES ALL THINGS,

HOPES ALL THINGS, ENDURES ALL THINGS.

Apostle Paul (I Corinthians 13:7)

OF ALL FOUR SPIRITUALITIES, this one is the most readily tangible and specific, often involving direct experiences or highly prescribed behavior. Spiritual reality is present, approachable, personal, interactive. While this spirituality dovetails with other spiritualities and may share spaces, programs, and spiritual practices with them, unless the hands-on, direct, devotional life can be sponsored there, those attracted to this spirituality will migrate to a more compatible environment.

For example, you may enter a space rich in stimulation, perhaps washing your hands and face at the fountain by the door. You remove your shoes to place you in direct contact with and to honor the earth. You sit or kneel for the rituals. No one gives you instructions, for the steps of speaking, singing, standing, and bowing are repeated each time and known. There are candles in the prayer area for lighting at the conclusion of the first fruits offering. The brilliant light and pungent odor of the incense add to the auspicious feeling. To one side is an impressive mural depicting the story of this holy site, the gratitude felt by the population when evil was vanquished. Ever since, a major feast day and festival have been held each year, when a large car has been taken from its shrine on a journey to the village and back, accompanied by music, dancing, and exultant singing. Acrobats, firecrackers, spontaneous theatrics, and tossing of bright-colored flowers completes the rejoicing. You feel a great loyalty to this place that extends over a lifetime.

⟲ THE SF PERSONALITY

Infinite variations around the world of this picture of the Journey of Devotion are likely to appeal to two Sensing types with Feeling (ISFJ and ESFP) and two Feeling types with Sensing (ISFP and ESFJ). Before examining the outlines of this native spirituality, it is useful to have in mind a concept of the SF personality.

As Children and Youth

Some children are gentle and cooperative from the beginning. They are often born cute, and start trying early on to smile and to please. They only need to be loved and to have their space respected, for they like to keep their rooms neat and their school notebooks organized. SF children flourish when expectations are clear; they try to please others, avoid conflict, and move toward harmony. They have many friends and are generous and kind to them. When a friend is hurt or treated badly, they feel the pain and try to help. They love to make gifts for friends and adults they know. Pets can be important for emotional balance, expression, and care.

They learn methodically, step by step, trying very hard not only to please the teacher but also not to miss any intermediate steps, for if they do they will feel frustrated and perceive the situation as unfair. SF children like to feel they are on the right track, to be reassured, and they need to be rewarded for good performance in a supportive atmosphere. They thrive in a well-structured, conventional household and classroom. Their learning and their relationships are immediate, tangible, trusting, and caring. Whether Introverted or Extraverted, they are attached to people.

If they are supported appropriately in their childhood, SFs find youth a good experience. However, males may feel a need to overcompensate for their F values among their peers, acting tough. They may take awhile to settle down, particularly if there is no clear vocational goal for them to deal with in a direct, tangible way. Introverted SFs may be outside the mainstream in their teen years, with a few compatible friends. Some SF teenagers, particularly Extraverted SFs, may engage in volunteer activities that directly help people, especially if the activity is shared by peers and they have fun working together. ESFPs particularly like to have fast-moving ways to care for others, with plenty of laughs.

As Adults

When SF youth grow up and all goes well, they may specialize in personal helpfulness, practical down-to-earth support for people. They are sensitive, friendly, loyal, and caring. In young adulthood, they are likely to marry, have children, and live responsibly as parents and citizens. In neighborhoods and congregations, they are the ones who initiate bringing a meal to the family of a sick person or who send flowers when a child is born or an elder dies. In short, they are devoted to serving others in direct, tangible, personal ways.

Those on the Journey of Devotion are the polar opposite from those on the Journey of Unity. In contrast to NT global past and future time, here we attend to the immediate present. Instead of the cosmic, the tangible task at hand is the focus. It is reported that Einstein (INTP) once had his mind on matters of such magnitude that he forgot to put his pants on when he left for a meeting.[1] In contrast, SFs will see that every detail is accounted for; they like to keep almost everything intact, traditional, harmonious. Clothes should not only be on but also appropriate and pressed, homes should be neat and clean, with fresh flowers on the dining room table. Above all, the setting they are in should be congenial for supporting happy, warm, and friendly people.

SFs live for sociability, and interpersonal considerations are never far from their thoughts, whether it be working on gifts for others, sharing appreciation of others (and expecting it from others as well), and helping or being helped. Personal reciprocity in relationships at home and at work is essential, and SFJs especially can feel like martyrs if the care and rewards are always one-way and nothing comes back to them. Being Sensing types, they are interested in facts, but about people, not so much about things.

They will prosper most in structured settings. SFJs require them for support; SFPs may use them as a reference point for their spontaneity. They work within traditional values in practical, concrete, cooperative ways. SFJs especially will be culture bearers, stressing continuity and propriety. This is the framework within which they will reach out to care for others and give tangible support to make households, neighborhoods, and institutions effective for people. SFPs have a spontaneous approach and are likely to loosen things up to bring service and assistance where it is most needed.

Their conversations are likely to begin with a warm smile and a friendly greeting. In their communications you are unlikely to hear much symbolic or abstract reasoning, but rather anecdotes, stories, and tangible references. They will respond to people as they are now, noticing how they feel, their body language and facial expressions—cues that Intuitive types are likely to miss. Often they speak most eloquently simply by doing for others rather than talking—if they are Extraverts, doing as they talk.

⮌ SF NATIVE SPIRITUALITY

The native spirituality for the Journey of Devotion engages life in eight ways, manifesting themselves in different proportions for different individuals:

(1) the importance of pilgrimage, (2) the attraction of heroes, (3) the agency of stories, (4) a direct hands-on approach to the spiritual life, (5) the appearance of archaic forms incredibly old in human experience, (6) the centrality of personal experience, (7) the importance of simple things, and (8) action on the world through direct service.

The Importance of Pilgrimage

For nine centuries (3600–2500 B.C.), a Paleolithic temple culture thrived on Malta, producing the most exquisite centers of ancient SF piety on the planet.[2] Hagar Qim, Ggantija, the Hypogeum, and Tarxien are pilgrimage sites of human gratitude, created with loving, devoted hands. There seems to have been nothing abstract or complex about their function; they were associated with birth, regeneration, and death. The birth celebrations tended to be found to the east and the death celebrations to the west.[3] The presence of altars and paraphernalia for slaughter point to animal and vegetable sacrifice, ongoing present-focused concerns. The temples are anthropomorphic in shape and centered on the womb and bountiful features of the goddess.

The world has numerous pilgrimage cities: Mecca, Medina, Isfahan, Jerusalem, Stonehenge, Rome, Assisi, Glastonbury, Calcutta, Vrindavan, Puri, Bodh Gaya, Lhasa, Angkor Wat, the T'ien-shen-t'an complex near Beijing. The St. Sargius Church in Old Cairo is on the site where the holy family, it is said, stayed in Egypt. In the shadows, kneeling pilgrims meditate, kiss ancient icons, view the "blooding" pillar and icon of Mary. The experience is tangible, intense, and founded on story.[4]

In France, Lourdes is a center for healing, with an atmosphere of hallowed peace and the quiet intensity of piety. There is a steady stream of earnest pilgrims, lighting candles, learning the story of St. Bernadette as portrayed in stained glass, and participating in the many opportunities for worship and guided contemplation. One has a feeling that much sickness falls into remission here. In 1858 a fourteen-year-old shepherd girl in the town of Lourdes saw eighteen apparitions of the Virgin Mary in a six-month period and was told to drink from a health-giving spring, hitherto hidden, and to build a chapel on the site.

Bernadette's visions are all tactile: "I heard a sound like a gust of wind. . . . I saw a Lady dressed in white, wearing a white dress, a blue girdle and a yellow rose on each foot."[5] Born into poverty, having suffered from cholera and tuberculosis, Bernadette Soubirous became a nun shortly after her experiences, devoted herself to the sick and to children, and died of an asthma attack at age thirty-five. The whole sanctuary today remains true to her memory and vocation.

Powerful experience followed by a confirmatory form of dedication assists SFs in overcoming feelings of victimization by the circumstances of their lives.

The Attraction of Heroes

Very often the Journey of Devotion takes up themes of heroes. The story of Daniel tells of a devoted Jew in the Babylonian Captivity who is schooled in the court of King Nebuchadnezzar and rises to a position of considerable administrative importance[6] (which often is the case for SFJs). However, he refuses to eat the rich food of the court, keeping a kosher diet. He opposes idols out of fidelity to his god (*Daniel* means "judge of the god") while interpreting the king's dream. He is thrown into a fiery furnace but is saved by a miracle from death. Keeping a literal faith to the last, he is vindicated when the Babylonian kingdom is conquered by the Persians. The bumper sticker "Let Go, Let God," might have been Daniel's apocalyptic motto.

Other heroes (SP) may take a long and dangerous journey, encountering difficulties, temptations of good and evil, dragons to slay, rainbows pointing to elusive treasures, deep rivers to ford, oceans to cross with whales to devour the adventurer. But usually the hero perseveres, finds the object of the divine quest, and gives humanity a great boon. There is a great trust that he or she can hold on, that the world, or God, will clear the hero's path, so that he or she may return to journey in a new reality. Sometimes the hero dies, or ascends to heaven, or comes back to retire quietly as a hermit in the forest or an elder in outwardly ordinary circumstances.

The Agency of Stories

The Journey of Devotion can assume extreme pathos and even melancholy if practice is combined with powerful story. Former minister to the U.N. from Pakistan, Muhammad Asad, witnessed how Shiite Islam can be expressed in Iran:

> [T]heir religious feeling itself, so unlike that of the Arabs, bore a strong tinge of sadness and mourning: to weep over the tragic happenings of thirteen centuries ago — to weep over the deaths of Ali, the Prophet's son-in-law, and Ali's two sons, Hasan and Husayn — seemed to them more important than to consider what Islam stood for and what direction it wanted to give to men's lives.
>
> On many evenings, in many towns, you could see groups of men and women assembled in a street around a wandering dervish, a religious mendicant clad in white, with a panther skin on his back, a long-stemmed ax in his right hand and an alms-bowl carved from a coconut in his left. He would recite a half-sung, half-spoken ballad about the struggles for succession to the Caliphate that

followed the death of the Prophet in the seventh century—a mournful tale of faith and blood and death. . . .

And the chanted ballad would bring forth passionate sobbing from the listening women, while silent tears would roll over the faces of bearded men.[7]

Religious practice and story have a close relationship in the Journey of Devotion. Apuleius' second-century novel, *The Golden Ass*, was created from his profession of oral storytelling and contains remarkable descriptions of worship of the goddess that stretch back millennia before him. At the full moon Lucius, the subject of the story, waded into the ocean seven times, uttered a prayer in which he asked for a boon, and then witnessed the goddess rising from the waves in a glorious apparition, telling him exactly how his miracle could take place. In the procession of the festival of first fruits of the sea the next day, he was to be transformed in full sight of the priests and he was later initiated into the order of priests of the goddess Isis.[8] Most prominent in Apuleius' descriptions are the exacting practices, followed sequentially at appointed times, for example, in the festival procession, using pipes and flutes, torches, candles, mirrors, fans, rattles, garlands of flowers, hymns, dancing, priests and initiates dressed in precise garb, symbol-inscribed bowls, wands with serpents, milk containers shaped like nipples, moon shapes, wine urns, and a sacred cultic box. Around the structure of the parade revolves great spontaneous joy and ecstasy, giving the other side of the coin, the SFP accompanying the SFJ aspects of the Journey of Devotion.

SF spirituality often has a female voice. Apuleius described the goddess thus:

[T]he apparition of a woman began to rise from the middle of the sea with so lovely a face that the gods themselves would have fallen down in adoration of it. First the head, then the whole shining body gradually emerged and stood before me poised on the surface of the waves. . . .

Her long thick hair fell in tapering ringlets on her lovely neck, and was crowned with an intricate chaplet in which was woven every kind of flower. Just above her brow shone a round disc, like a mirror, or like the bright face of the moon, which told me who she was. Vipers rising from the left-hand and right-hand partings of her hair supported this disc, with ears of corn bristling beside them. Her many-coloured robe was of finest linen; part was glistening white, part crocus-yellow, part glowing red and along the entire hem a woven border of flowers and fruit clung swaying in the breeze. But what caught and held my eye more than anything else was the deep black lustre of her mantle. She wore it slung across her body from the right hip to the left shoulder, where it was caught in a knot resembling the boss of a shield; but part of it hung in innumerable folds, the tasseled fringe quivering. It was embroidered with glittering stars on the hem and everywhere else, and in the middle beamed a full and fiery moon.

In her right hand she held a bronze rattle, of the sort used to frighten away the God of the Sirocco; its narrow rim was curved like a sword-belt and three little rods, which sang shrilly when she shook the handle, passed horizontally through it. A boat-shaped gold dish hung from her left hand, and along the upper surface of the handle writhed an asp with puffed throat and head raised ready to strike. On her divine feet were slippers of palm leaves, the emblem of victory.[9]

Such massive Sensing detail is in striking contrast to the stark lack of detail in earlier mother-goddess images, which were often nearly as round and fertile as the earth itself, with little or no detail in the face and limbs. The mother-goddess was the body of birth and death, sleeping in the winter, reviving in the spring birthing, growing large in summer, receiving the dead in late fall. She was the all-embracing OM, womb to home to tomb. While in the earlier images the detail is not there, the SF realities and values are quintessential.

Long before Apuleius, the matrifocal had given way to a patrifocal society and, hence, the change in the appearance of the goddess. The evidence at Catal Huyuk, one of the last matrifocal cities in the Middle East, gives the impression, according to William Irwin Thompson, that the traditional social structure of "the intimate rule of custom and maternal authority"could not cope with the size and complexity of the new order. To summarize what might have been the end of the traditional, pure SF, organic society:

> Catal Huyuk was the supernova of the old religion, for the agricultural surplus not only supported a conservative priesthood of women, it also enabled the hunting band of men to shift their activities to trade and warfare. As the process of military development grew, the contradiction would grow, until eventually the conservative religion of the Great Goddess would be surrounded by a new culture. Catal Huyuk was a brilliant achievement, but it also represents the maximum development of traditional, matrilineal society.[10]

Gradually, we see the absorption of the goddess tradition into the new religions. Numerous temples to the goddess became Christian churches—from Assisi and Rome to Argos and Athens. The cathedral of the city of Syracuse is a former temple to Athena from 480 B.C. with a Norman baroque facade.[11] Likewise, the old goddess traditions entered Buddhism and remain as Tara or Kuan Yin.

A Direct Approach

Ramakrishna (1836–1886), one of the great gurus of modern India, was a devotee of the goddess Kali in Calcutta.

O Mother, make me mad with Thy love!
What need have I of knowledge or reason?[12]

In his view, "God reveals Himself in the form which His devotee loves most."[13] Spiritual experience is personal. Ramakrishna wrote:

God is both personal and impersonal. It is difficult to conceive an impersonal God, so, to begin with, God has to be thought of as a person. Can anyone think of the white colour without thinking of a white object? One can look at the morning sun, but not at the midday sun. Similarly, when God is manifest in a person we know what God is like, otherwise God is impersonal and beyond thought and speech.[14]

Ramakrishna was intensely on a Journey of Devotion. Almost illiterate, he absorbed all his learning from the many thousands of people who surrounded him. He would listen, meditate upon what he had heard, and filter it through his austerities of experience as a priest in the Kali temple of Dakshineswar in Calcutta and then as founder of the Ramakrishna Order. At first, his work as a priest was perfunctory; then he entered into the practice of bhakti. He was likely ESFP, a whirlwind of activity, always with people and needing little privacy, deeply caring, powerfully perceptive, drawn to variety and novelty, actively open to the world and others. He wrote:

God cannot be seen with these physical eyes. In the course of spiritual discipline one gets a "love body," endowed with "love eyes," "love ears," and so on. One sees God with those "love eyes." One hears the voice of God with those "love ears." One even gets a sexual organ made of love. . . with this "love body" the soul communes with God.[15]

Swami Nikhilananda describes Ramakrishna's first vision of Kali:

To the ignorant She is, to be sure, the image of destruction; but he found in Her the benign, all-loving Mother. Her neck is encircled with a garland of heads, and Her waist with a girdle of human arms, and two of Her hands hold weapons of death, and Her eyes dart a glance of fire; but, strangely enough, Ramakrishna felt in Her breath the soothing touch of tender love and saw in Her the Seed of Immortality. She stands on the bosom of Her Consort, Siva; it is because She is the Sakti, the Power, inseparable from the Absolute. She is surrounded by jackals and other unholy creatures, the denizens of the cremation ground. But is not the Ultimate Reality above holiness and unholiness? She appears to be reeling under the spell of wine. But who would create this mad world unless under the influence of a divine drunkenness? She is the highest symbol of all the forces of nature, the synthesis of their antinomies, the Ultimate Divine in the form of woman. She now became to Sri Ramakrishna the only Reality, and the world became an unsubstantial shadow. Into Her worship he poured his soul. Before him She stood as the transparent portal to the shrine of Ineffable Reality.[16]

In his early years, Ramakrishna engaged in numerous dialogues with followers of the Brahmo Samaj, religious liberals central to the origins of the modern Hindu renaissance and to Indian nationalism.[17] But their profoundly NT approach provoked in him a longing for deep, nonintellectual forms of devotion:

> There is no need for much reading of the Scriptures. You would be inclined to argue and debate. What you gain by repeating the Name of God with love ten times is the very essence of the Scriptures. Be mad for God, truly be athirst for God, the Divine Intoxication. Love, the key to Knowledge, opens all doors.[18]

The argument that God must resemble the human form for it to be possible to know and relate to God is carried a step further at times in the Journey of Devotion. A human teacher, such as Ramakrishna, or Jesus of Nazareth, becomes the living God in the presence of his disciples. Experiential discipleship, spiritual guidance, and apprenticeship—whether the teacher/guru is perceived as God or as a remarkable human—is often found to be essential in the Journey of Devotion. Traditions are transmitted personally; the faith is made flesh.

When we discuss the various manifestations around the world of the Journey of Devotion, it is essential to recognize that SF devotion is a cognitive process, not a description of behaviors. This is the crux of the difference between Jungian typology and temperament theory as represented by Keirsey and Bates and others.[19] It is true that the distinction between SPs and SJs is useful and readily observable in external behavior. But what St. Bernadette, Daniel, Ramakrishna, and, as we will see, Nicodemus, Mohammed, St. Francis, and others have in common is the combination of Sensing and Feeling. SF spirituality is a deep internal orientation, and the wide variety of behavior can all be connected to these inner patterns.

For example, remember the impatience of Jesus with Nicodemus in the Gospel of John. Jesus had described with considerable eloquence the process of spiritual transformation, in some of the most poetic Intuitive language in the New Testament. When he had finished, Nicodemus had said, "How can this be?"[20] This four-word question is a classic SF response to mystic NF ruminations. Nicodemus was not ready for spiritual rebirth, certainly not until he was clear about the details. But he did not forget the teachings of Jesus. They had attached themselves to something deep within him that for the time being he was not ready to bring up to his conscious attention. But at the end of the Gospel of John, we once again meet Nicodemus, who, in the intervening years, has undergone a transformation toward his native spirituality. The time had come when he became ready to grow spiritually, and he had remembered those sayings that would be most help-ful for his progress. Now he had become one of the central figures in the inner circle. It was he who took hold of the situation, tangibly and lovingly anointing, wrapping, and burying the teacher after his crucifixion.[21]

Archaic Forms

A most archaic form of SF experience, hypothetical but convincing, is pro-posed by Yeats scholar Dudley Young, in *Origins of the Sacred*. Looking at beginnings of religion in the early Paleolithic, Young traced the evolution of the dancing circle, from one where the men danced around the women (as primates do), until the women and men together danced around an empty center. Here the dance reenacts the hunt, the very being of the buffalo at the center, until in the ecstasies the buffalo is there, present to them, and the magic of the buffalo, its permission, is received for the hunt. Meanwhile, the leading male has been studying the buffalo firsthand, from a tree or rock, learning minutely and utterly the behavior of that fearsome beast. At the peak of the dance, the leader—now shaman—pounces into the circle. He dances until he fills the emptiness with the essence, the very presence of the buffalo. The dance continues, in total rhythm with the sympathetic magic of the moment. But the ursurper has violated the unspoken, hard-won (by the women) equality of the dancing circle. The balance is disrupted. And so when he stumbles slightly and breaks the perfect incarnation of the buf-falo, spontaneously the circle closes and he is torn apart and eaten. The magic empowers, animates, and is carried in the hot blood of union. The awesome implications sink in only later, to be incorporated in the cultic milieu of society. It becomes the foundation and legitimation of the body politic.[22]

Young quotes Coleridge's "Kubla Khan":

And all should cry, Beware! Beware!
His flashing eyes, his floating hair!
Weave a circle round him thrice,
And close your eyes in holy dread,
For he on honey-dew hath fed
And drunk the milk of Paradise.

Orgiastic mysteries are repeated throughout emerging human culture. We see them in Dionysian festivals and Christian communion. Incarnational presence of the divine in the flesh and blood of real existence, the animated present, is fundamental in the Journey of Devotion.

The Centrality of Personal Experience

Bill Moyers asked Joseph Campbell, in the *Power of Myth* television series, what myth is. Campbell responded, "Myths are clues to the spiritual potentialities of the human life." And he expanded this definition:

> I think that what we're seeking is an experience of being alive, so that our life experiences on the purely physical plane will have resonances within our own innermost being and reality, so that we actually feel the rapture of being alive.[23]

This "experience" and "rapture of being alive" are exactly the goal of the SF spiritual quest. We see experience-based spirituality in the early shamanic poetry of China, for example:

> I have washed in brew of orchid, bathed in sweet scented,
> Many-coloured are my garments; I am like a flower.
> Now in long curves the Spirit has come down
> In a blaze of brightness unending.
> Chien! he is coming to rest at the Abode of Life;
> As a sun, as a moonbeam glows his light.
> In dragon chariot and the vestment of a god
> Hither and thither a little while he moves.[24]

Much SF spirituality is experienced not in sacred dance, mass or temple sacrifice, or poetry, but rather in homes, fields, and neighborhoods. Such is the context for the touching story of Martha and Mary. While Martha served her guests, Mary sat at the feet of Jesus to listen and to anoint his feet with oil. Martha became jealous, but Jesus reassured her. Both activities were important, but Mary's happened to be "the good portion."[25] Martha's work could be either ST or SF; Mary's was SF devotion.

Spiritual growth in the Journey of Devotion is grounded in personal experience. God is not a far-off, impersonal principle but rather a personal and approachable entity. God is love; the individual soul, through inwardly felt piety, sometimes through charismatic experience, takes on the qualities of that which it loves. As a river flows into the sea, so also does our love of God flow into a state of grace. What the Journey of Unity might call idolatry, the devotee would call images to focus true relationship. God is seen as a master, a friend, a parent, or a lover. Faithfulness is living, step by step, with appropriate emotional tones, sometimes in joy and ecstasy, sometimes in measured practices of every day. While at times endowed with magic or beatific vision, and often lived inside the context of story, there is nothing of the abstract or speculative.

The Importance of Simple Things

When life is lived to one's satisfaction, and one's household, vocation, and social connections are in good order, one feels a comfort and peace that are expressed in a most delicate, powerful, and beautiful way by the Shaker hymn:

'Tis the gift to be simple,
'Tis the gift to be free,
'Tis the gift to know
just where we want to be,
And when we find ourselves
in the place just right,
'Twill be in the valley
of love and delight.

When true simplicity is gained,
To greet all as friend
we shan't be ashamed.
To turn, turn, will be our delight,
Till by turning, turning
we come 'round right.

This hymn is suggestive of one of the oldest collections of poetry in the world, the *Confucian Odes*. Set in the context of Chinese naturalism, this collection of songs is deeply Sensing, a celebration of both SF and ST spirituality. For example, the following poem is a family benediction, depicting blessings all would wish, the goal of simplicity, good living, the beneficent household:

May heaven guard and keep you
in great security,
Make you staunch and hale;
What blessing not vouchsafed?
Give you much increase,
Send nothing but abundance.

May Heaven guard and keep you,
Cause your grain to prosper,
Send you nothing that is not good.
May you receive from Heaven a hundred boons,
May Heaven send down to you blessings so many
That the day is not long enough for them all.

May Heaven guard and keep you,
Cause there to be nothing in which you do not rise higher,
Like the mountains, like the uplands,

Like the ridges, the great ranges,
Like a stream coming down in flood;
In nothing not increased.[26]

Such simplicity of aspiration, grounded in networks of relationship, influenced one of the few major SF sages before the advent of Buddhism in China, Mo-Tzu. Moism posits a heaven with personal characteristics, a heaven that "loves the world universally and seeks to bring mutual benefit to all creatures." In a remarkable chapter called "Explaining Ghosts," Mo-Tzu justifies the sacrificing of millet and wine to the ghosts, whether or not they actually exist:

> Now when I perform sacrifices it is not as though I were pouring the wine in a sewage ditch and throwing the millet away. Above I am seeking the blessing of the ghosts and spirits, while below I am gathering together a pleasant group and making friends with people of the community. And if the ghosts and spirits really exist, then I am able to provide food and drink for my father, my mother, and my elder brothers and sisters. Is this not beneficial to the whole world?[27]

After Buddhism came to China, so did the ascendancy of the great goddess Kuan Yin. Beginning as the bodhisattva Avalokitesvara, in India this figure came under the influence of Tantric Buddhism, where compassion takes a male form and wisdom a female form,[28] and by the tenth century in China the figure had been gradually transformed from a male to a female goddess. She in turn absorbed large quantities of folk traditions to become a multidimensional figure. She is goddess of mercy, patron of the afflicted and distressed, bestower of children or "lady who brings children,"[29] mediator of the forces of nature, sponsor of purity and wisdom. The most popular image of her shows her flowing over clouds, or seated on a rock before a waterfall, majestic and graceful, in a white robe, often with a child on her arm or holding a lotus or a box containing "the nectar of immortality." She still carries on the quality of Avalokitesvara, presiding over Providence.[30] In Sanskrit, she is Padma-pani, "born of the lotus," and in Chinese, "She who always observes or pays attention to sounds"; "she who hears the weeping world"; "she who hears prayers."[31] Kuan Yin (or Kannon in Japan) became the most important daily focus of SF spirituality in Chinese religion. It is as if she were transparently created by the culture to concentrate the genius and values of the Journey of Devotion.

One of the four great bodhisattvas found in the *Lotus Sutra* is the Great Bodhisattva of Pure Conduct: "However inexhaustible the passions are, I vow to extinguish them,"[32] brings the commitment of the bodhisattva to refuse nirvana until all sentient beings may enter, together with the SF emphasis of exacting devotion combined with service to others.

Direct Service

For the Journey of Devotion, piety leads naturally to service and service to devotion. Often the line between them is not demarcated. To begin the day with prayer, focused on the spiritual context of our relationships, placing oneself into this frame, leads seamlessly into acting toward others with compassion, kindness, and genuine care for serving the human needs present to you. The bodhisattva itself in the SF context is a devotee of the Buddha while being a servant of humanity.

Many on the Journey of Devotion are attracted to monastic orders that unite prayer life with teaching, nursing, and serving the poor. For every Mother Teresa known to the world, there are many thousands of anonymous others who roll up their sleeves with mercy and helpfulness in the context of a spiritual vocation and many millions who reach out in much the same way from their households to neighbor and community. It is done in the name of Christ, the Buddha, Allah, or to honor the family ancestors. Service to others is service to God in many traditions, often felt in terms of a relationship. Even as the divine being loves the devotee and servant, so also are all our neighbors loved, person by person, in a network of relationship in which all humans come as equals before God. In the words of Mother Teresa:

> Love cannot remain by itself—it has no meaning. Love has to be put into action and that action is service. Whatever form we are, able or disabled, rich or poor, it is not how much we do, but how much love we put in the doing; a lifelong sharing of love with others.[33]

"The Story of the Other Wise Man" encapsulates in fable the values inherent in the Journey of Devotion. Artaban, a Zoroastrian magus of Parthia, is late for his rendezvous with the other three wise men because he stopped to help a man in the road who would surely have died had Artaban not felt pity and delayed his journey. He despairs, "Only God the merciful knows whether I shall not lose the sight of the King because I tarried to show mercy." He reaches Bethlehem after the holy family has fled to Egypt and uses the second of his three jewels brought for the Christ child to protect an infant from death at the hands of Herod's soldiers. The child's mother blesses him. He travels to Egypt and spends decades helping the poor and oppressed. Finally, as a failing old man, he enters Jerusalem just as Christ is being nailed to the cross. Artaban walks toward the Damascus Gate. Suddenly he stops to rescue an orphan girl who is being carried away into slavery. She grabs his feet and pleads for her life. He takes the third jewel and with it buys her freedom. He now has no gift for the King and knows his mission has failed. Just then the ground shakes, the sky is darkened, a tile from a roof falls on his head, and he sinks to the ground with a mortal wound. He hears a voice affirming his compassion and service as the greatest gift of a life. He had fed the hungry, given drink to the thirsty, clothed the naked, comforted the sick and the prisoners. The voice (of Christ) concludes: "Verily I say unto thee, inasmuch as thou hast done it unto one of the least of these my brethren, thou hast done it unto me."[34]

It is interesting to contrast this delicate and moving story with the rather wooden demeanor of the three wise men in Matthew.[35] Whereas Artaban is a gentle, warmhearted, responsive man, who despite his regal bearing enters into the lives of all he encounters, the other three are unable to bridge the gap, to connect. Their response is to respect and worship the infant in the manger and to present to him gold, frankincense, and myrrh (rather cold gifts for a newborn). They had followed the map, followed correctly the procedures that do honor to a king, and exercised responsible caution in avoiding Herod on the return trip. The other three had not waited for Artaban to join them in Babylonia; after all, he knew the arrangement for their rendezvous and they had to leave to keep their appointment. For them the structure of the situation needed to be honored (ST). What if everyone were late? How could the world continue on its course? Artaban, on the other hand, allowed himself to be deterred by human need as it arose before him (SF). When confronted by suffering and need, he turned from the royal path. Ultimately, devotion to people becomes the highest form of devotion to the divine. Every act of kindness and helpfulness in a lifetime of service becomes illumined as eternity in that one moment before Artaban's death, in peaceful resolution, at the Damascus Gate.

☙ BHAKTI YOGA

Bhakti yoga is devotion through love to a God who is "the geyser of love."[36] The practice of responding to God's love, and directing love in a relationship to God, gradually transforms the devotee from one who experiences the bliss of love occasionally to one who has it constantly accessible as a "sacred emotion."[37] When we "fall in love," the world is transformed for a time, and when we "fall out of love" the world turns drab again. The bhakta (worshiper) concentrates toward a constancy of love so that a truly lasting transformation can be fulfilled. The ego fears loss and fears losing its own centrality, falling out of love into concern with its preservation, but beyond this "primal fear" (bhaya) is the more basic human nature that is bliss or happiness (ananda), love.[38] The Bhakta seeks to live in that awareness.

Bhakti yoga approaches God through relationship. The focus is Ishvara, a divine personality, not Brahman-Atman, the impersonal absolute. Most writers identify the two as one, somehow, but the goal is not union with God, only the unselfish pleasure of adoration. Vivekananda summarizes:

"Who cares to become sugar?" Says the Bhakta, "I want to taste sugar." Who will then desire to become free and one with God? "I may know that I am He, yet will I take myself away from Him and become different, so that I may enjoy the Beloved."[39]

Love is realized in relationship. It is what we in our natures can experience firsthand. According to the God-intoxicated sage, Narada in his *Bhakti Sutras*, there are eleven basic forms of the divine relationship:

Love of the glorification of the Lord's blessed qualities

Love of his enchanting beauty

Love of worship

Love of constant remembrance

Love of service

Love of him as a friend

Love of him as a son

Love for him as that of a wife for her husband

Love of self-surrender to him

Love of complete absorption in him

Love of the pain of separation from him.[40]

In the great Indian epics the *Ramayana* and the *Mahabharata*, various heroes epitomize each of these qualities.[41] Hanuman, the monkey god–hero, is an example of "Love of service." When he identified the God, Rama, in the forest coming to enlist his help:

To clasp Rama's Feet then Hanuman fell,
What words his heart's rapture can tell.
His body thrilled, no speech he found,
As at the Lord he gazed spell bound.[42]

This is a typical verse in Goswami Tulsidas' *Ramayana*, one of the great achievements of the golden age of bhakti devotional poetry. It is read, sung, and danced throughout India today.

Similarly, we see the use of allegory in the stories of the God, Krishna, and the Gopi girls, a tradition quite different from the role of Krishna posing as Charioteer in the *Mahabharata*. Poetry and drama proliferated over the courtship of Krishna and one of the Gopis, Radha, portrayed everywhere in embrace, with Krishna playing his flute (the call of God). A steamy story symbolizes sublime meanings:

Radha, it was held, was the soul while Krishna was God. Radha's sexual passion for Krishna symbolized the soul's intense longing and her willingness to commit adultery expressed the utter priority which must be accorded to love for God. If ultimate union was symbolized by romantic love, then clearly nothing could approach such love in ultimate significance.[43]

Images of this couple are everywhere in the Hindu cultural milieu to bring the straying attention to focus via the concrete on the reality playing beneath.

It is reported that Ramakrishna, in his development on the Journey of Devotion, took up powerful imitations of gods to experience the different forms of relationship to God, "with his usual shocking literalness and singleness of purpose."[44] He identified with Radha, Hanuman, Krishna as Charioteer, and others. When living as Hanuman,

> he subsisted on unpeeled jungle roots and fruits, and passed his time jumping and swinging through the canopy of an adjoining forest. His eyes became restless just like those of a monkey and, incredibly, his coccyx grew of its own accord over an inch in length, forming a kind of impromptu tail.[45]

A variety of expressions of bhakti devotion were catalogued in observing Bengal Vaishnavism (Vishnu worship): intense love of Krishna, dancing, rolling on the ground, singing, loud crying, twisting of the body, shouting, yawning, profusion of sighs, disregard of popular opinion, foaming at the mouth, loud laughter, giddiness, and hiccuping.[46] In context, we read in the Bhagavad Gita:

> A leaf, a flower, a fruit, (a little) water—whatever
> one offers to Me with devotion, that love-offering
> of the striving-soul I taste and enjoy.

> Whatever thou doest, whatever thou enjoyest,
> whatever thou sacrificest, whatever thou givest,
> whatever energy of tapasya, of the soul's will
> or effort thou puttest forth, make it O Kaunteya,
> an offering unto Me.[47]

One technique for concentrating bhakti is called *japam*, or repeating the name of a god as a mantra. A popular twentieth century guru, Sri Sri Sitaramdas Onkarnath, for example, recommends that the following words be repeated exactly in this fashion when writing the name of Rama:

Sri Rama Rama Rama Sri Rama Rama Rama Sri Rama Rama Rama
Sri Rama Rama Rama Sri Rama Rama Rama Sri Rama Rama Rama
Sri Rama Rama Rama Sri Rama Rama Rama Sri Rama Rama Rama
Sri Rama Rama Rama Sri Rama Rama Rama Sri Rama Rama Rama
Sri Rama Rama Rama Sri Rama Rama Rama Sri Rama Rama Rama
Sri Rama Rama Rama Sri Rama Rama Rama Sri Rama Rama Rama

Sri Rama Rama Rama Sri Rama Rama Rama Sri Rama Rama Rama
Sri Rama Rama Rama Sri Rama Rama Rama Sri Rama Rama Rama
Sri Rama Rama Rama Sri Rama Rama Rama Sri Rama Rama Rama
Sri Rama Rama Rama Sri Rama Rama Rama Sri Rama Rama Rama
Sri Rama Rama Rama Sri Rama Rama Rama Sri Rama Rama Rama
Sri Rama Rama Rama Sri Rama Rama Rama Sri Rama Rama Rama

Sri Rama Rama Rama Sri Rama Rama Rama Sri Rama Rama Rama
Sri Rama Rama Rama Sri Rama Rama Rama Sri Rama Rama Rama
Sri Rama Rama Rama Sri Rama Rama Rama Sri Rama Rama Rama
Sri Rama Rama Rama Sri Rama Rama Rama Sri Rama Rama Rama
Sri Rama Rama Rama Sri Rama Rama Rama Sri Rama Rama Rama
Sri Rama Rama Rama Sri Rama Rama Rama Sri Rama Rama Rama
Sri Rama Rama Rama Sri Rama Rama Rama Sri Rama Rama Rama
Sri Rama Rama Rama Sri Rama Rama Rama Sri Rama Rama Rama
Sri Rama Rama Rama Sri Rama Rama Rama Sri Rama Rama Rama
Sri Rama Rama Rama Sri Rama Rama Rama Sri Rama Rama Rama
Sri Rama Rama Rama Sri Rama Rama Rama Sri Rama Rama Rama
Sri Rama Rama Rama Sri Rama Rama Rama Sri Rama Rama Rama

Sri Rama Rama Rama Sri Rama Rama Rama Sri Rama Rama Rama
Sri Rama Rama Rama Sri Rama Rama Rama Sri Rama Rama Rama
Sri Rama Rama Rama Sri Rama Rama Rama Sri Rama Rama Rama
Sri Rama Rama Rama Sri Rama Rama Rama Sri Rama Rama Rama
Sri Rama Rama Rama Sri Rama Rama Rama Sri Rama Rama Rama
Sri Rama Rama Rama Sri Rama Rama Rama Sri Rama Rama Rama
Sri Rama Rama Rama Sri Rama Rama Rama Sri Rama Rama Rama
Sri Rama Rama Rama Sri Rama Rama Rama Sri Rama Rama Rama
Sri Rama Rama Rama Sri Rama Rama Rama Sri Rama Rama Rama
Sri Rama Rama Rama Sri Rama Rama Rama Sri Rama Rama Rama
Sri Rama Rama Rama Sri Rama Rama Rama Sri Rama Rama Rama
Sri Rama Rama Rama Sri Rama Rama Rama Sri Rama Rama Rama

Sri Rama

However, if your japam is to be spoken, Onkarnath recommends what he calls "the Mantra of Mantras" to be repeated in this form many times:

Hare Krishna Hare Krishna Krishna Krishna Hare Hare
Hare Rama Hare Rama Rama Rama Hare Hare.[48]

Very likely, such detail in the teachings of one guru is far less important than the full relationship a disciple has with the teacher. The Narada *Bhakti Sutras* lists three key ways in which a bhakta advances: "By uninterrupted loving-service; by hearing and singing the glory of the Lord, even while engaged in the ordinary activities of life; through the grace of great souls." It emphasizes how difficult is the relationship of disciple to guru:

> But it is extremely difficult to come into contact with a great soul and to be benefited by his company; the influence of such a one is subtle, incomprehensible, and unerringly infallible in its effect.
>
> Nevertheless it is attainable by the grace of God and Godmen alone.[49]

While this passage avoids fundamentalism by focusing on the effect in the person rather than on the perfect authority of the guru, the intent is quite unequivocal that the guru–disciple relationship set the norm and standard for the bhakti yoga tradition.

As with other yoga traditions, there are some who believe that bhakti yoga may be the superior path among the four. English yoga practitioner James McCartney believes the Bhagavad Gita teaches the superiority of bhakti to jnana and the other yogas, citing 7:17 among others:

> [O]f them all, the Bhakti would appear to be held in the highest esteem. The seeker after knowledge, the Jnani, is attracted by the Immutable aspects of the Divine, the Karma Yogi is the man of works, whose efforts are largely concerned with the cause and effect of worldly affairs, relating these to their spiritual equivalents. The Raja Yogi aims at achieving Union through austerities and mental powers, but the Bhakti's sole aim is Union with the Divine through devotion and service, living with thoughts of the Divine ever before him, imagining the Divine as dwelling in the heart.[50]

McCartney does little more in this listing of NT, ST, NF, and SF yogas than to reveal his preference for the bhakti approach. Even the verse he cites could as easily point to jnana as to bhakti. As might be expected, Narada agrees with him: "But the Supreme Divine Love described before is also something more than Karma, Jnana and [Raja] Yoga. For, it is of the nature of the fruit or result of all these."[51]

Joseph Politella feels that bhakti is so popular and permeates so extensively into all Indian religious expression that it forms "the very heart of other forms of Yoga." Even though the chief emphasis of bhakti yoga is the devotee–Ishvara relationship rather than Brahman-Atman, Politella, unlike Vivekananda and others, believes that the goal is union itself: "The soul takes on the qualities of the thing it loves, until its very nature becomes love. Then there is no longer subject and object; the lover becomes one with the beloved."[52]

∽ MENTORS FOR THIS WAY

As the Journey of Devotion represents 38 percent of humanity, it should not be surprising that Mohammed, the founder of one of the world's major religions, was an SF. In contrast to what seems to be Mohammed's introverted preference, Francis of Assisi gives us an extraverted SF spirituality which also exerts great influence today.

Mohammed

Ubu'l-Kassim, later known as Mohammed, was born in 571 into a prominent Mecca family. Custodian of the Kaaba, a revered building in Mecca said to have been built by Abraham, Mohammed's grandfather died when he was eight, making him already an orphan, destitute. Something of a dreamer as a child, given to quiet reflection, such traumatic beginings had a lasting impact. Sura 93 in the Koran may be autobiographical:

> Did he not find thee
> An orphan and give thee
> Shelter (and care)?

> And He found thee
> Wandering, and He gave
> Thee guidance.

> And He found thee
> In need, and made
> Thee independent.[53]

In his youth, he joined caravans journeying to trading centers in Syria, gradually absorbing impressions of Christian and Jewish lore and practices. Arab culture focused spiritually on a multitude of divinities, each tribe cultivating a tribal poet who could recite the traditions. In Mecca, the goddesses El-Lat, El-'Uzza, and Manat were prominent.[54]

Mohammed underwent a long period of incubation before his spiritual life became a public ministry. He absorbed the contrasts between the spirituality of his home city and what he saw at destinations of the caravans. In his public life he was a serious young man, in business diligent, honest, intelligent, and caring toward the unfortunate. When Mohammed was twenty-five, the owner of a caravan for which he worked, the widow Khadija, admired his industry and his stature and in a short time proposed marriage to him, which he accepted. She was somewhat older than he and they had six children (only one, Fatima, lived longer than the prophet).

For the next fifteen years Mohammed had the leisure to engage in protracted spiritual vigils, often journeying to Mount Hira to engage in prayer and fasting under the stars or in a cave there. It was during this period that his devotional life was established and that he formed for his monotheism an opposition to the religious corruption and social injustice that he had so long observed. He was an exceedingly sensitive man (likely ISFJ), and he internalized all the tensions in his society, wrestling with them late into the night.

At age forty, in a dramatic dream, he received his call to be the prophet. According to an eighth century compiler of traditions, Ibn Ishak, Mohammed reported these events at Mount Hira:

> One night Gabriel came to me with a cloth as I slept and said: Recite! I answered: I cannot recite! So he choked me with the cloth until I believed that I should die. Then he released me and said: Recite (Iqra)![55]

As Mohammed could not read or write, this was a remarkable command. (Later he would appoint a Jewish scribe, Zaid ibn Thabit, to be his personal secretary, who under the first caliph, Abu Bakr, collected and edited the Koran as recited by the prophet to various of his followers.)[56] Mohammed awakened only to be plunged into a vision (reported by Ibn Ishak):

> I awoke from my sleep, and it was as if they had written a message in my heart. I went out of the cave, and while I was on the mountain, I heard a voice saying: O Mohammed, thou art Allah's Apostle, and I am Gabriel! I looked up and saw Gabriel in the form of a man with crossed legs at the horizon of heaven. . . .[57]

He came out of this experience shaken, shivering uncontrollably, with "the knowledge that a Book had 'come down' into his heart."[58] His recitations would continue for the next twenty-three years until his death.

The Koran declares itself to be the last of the four great revelations from God. The four sources of revelation are the Tawrah (Torah), the Zabir (Psalms), the Injil (Gospels), and the Qur'an (Recital). The understanding Mohammed had was that these were the direct revelations to Moses, David, Jesus, and to himself, not the secondary writings of others. He felt that his work purified the religion of the Peoples of the Book, Christians and Jews, bringing them back to their true origins, while he was bringing to the Arabs the religion of the same God. As were Abraham, Moses, and Jesus before him, he was only a prophet, the messenger of God.

Mohammed propounded a practical, down-to-earth, highly structured spirituality. The word *Islam* means peace and submission.[59] Islam is that practice of complete and uncompromised surrender to God which brings perfect peace. The word *Moslem (Muslim)* means "one who submits." Allah is "wholly other" and complete in every way, but at the same time sees, hears, and apprehends every action and thought.[60]

In Islam, no detail of everyday life is insignificant or overlooked. You know in a powerful SF way exactly what you have to do. There are clear and precise guidelines. The core spirituality of Islam is Feeling and Sensing, as, for example, the Five Pillars all Moslems must perform: belief in one God, prayer, alms giving, fasting, and pilgrimage.[61]

1. *Monotheism.* "There is no God but Allah, and Mohammed is his Prophet." This is the Shahada testimony of Islam, recited at the begining and end of all prayers. The oneness of God is so wondrous and overwhelming that all else in life falls into place as a result. Since God is the Creator, the creation is good; nature and human nature are just as they should be. We are created as free moral beings, all equal in the sight of God and therefore equal in society. All of life—social, economic, political, domestic—all thoughts, all relationships, all possessions are part of one whole, one way of life, subservient to the will of God. There is no realm of life that is not equally the concern of God. Religion is in our acting and submission to God in all aspects of living. God is ever present, ever fair, merciful, loving, and exacting.

2. *Prayer.* In Islamic countries when the call of the muezzin, "Ahadun, ahadun" (One, one) drifts out over the city from the minarets, everyone hesitates, and many, at least among the men, prepare themselves, roll out their prayer rugs or something clean, and begin the rakatin, "bendings." While it is better to do it with others in congregation, you may pray wherever you are. At the mosques, the imams (prayer leaders) will kneel in front, then rows of men behind them, and where women are present they participate in the back, out of modesty. The complex ritual is performed with high precision five times each day. The high points include reciting first the *Allahu akbar*, "God is most Great," and the Shahada, then the first sura in the Koran, called the *Fätiha*, then they glide to their knees, then hands and face to the ground, then knees, back on their heels, then forward to the ground again, several times, and then at the end they recite the Shahada, "There is no God but Allah, and Mohammed is his Prophet." Why this exacting, tangible (SF) ritual? It is an act of gratitude and supplication, a reminder of the context and perspective of all we do each day.

3. *Charity.* Every Moslem is expected to give or is taxed to provide for widows, wayfarers, orphans, and the poor. Mohammed's personal childhood experience gives this act of service, zakat, a deep, passionate concern. There is the general expectation that you will be hospitable to strangers and guests. "All that I have is yours" is a common greeting.

The *Sunna*, or sayings of the Prophet, expresses it thus: "The best of almsgiving is that which springeth from the heart, and is uttered by the lips to soften the wounds of the injured."[62]

4. *Fasting.* For one month each year, the month of Ramadan, every Moslem fasts from first light to last light each day. When Ramadan falls in the summer, in a country like Egypt or Saudi Arabia the days can be sixteen hours long. The day begins and ends when you can distinguish a black from a white thread in the light. Fasting gives self-discipline, reminds us of our dependence, and sensitizes our compassion for others.

5. *Pilgrimage.* The hajj is the trip to Mecca, where one performs the rituals of that most sacred place once during one's lifetime. All pilgrims wear two plain, unsewn sheets and a shaven head, and thus there are no distinctions of wealth or class, simply a million and a half people each year entering the Great Mosque, performing rituals of purification, gazing at the black stone, and visiting other sites nearby, all in highly prescribed ways. It is a personal reenacting of the great story of Islamic origins.

In the Journey of Devotion it can be comforting to put yourself in the hands of unambiguous tradition. Islam provides spiritual disciplines, and moral, social, and legal rules that encompass all of life (appreciated by all SJs). It derives from the Koran, then the Sharia, traditional practices based on the Hadith, sayings and doings of Mohammed. All of life is circumscribed with guidelines. Bankers may not charge interest. Architects must blend their buildings and landscape in with Islamic principles. Marriage must be undertaken in certain ways. Force and weapons must be used only for defensive purposes to preserve the integrity of society. Tolerance of non-Moslems is prescribed. There must be no racism in any aspect of life. Islam has no clergy, no saints, no hierarchy, no sacraments.

Mohammed shows no tendency to plan in such a way as to solve social problems in a systematic NT or even NF fashion. In his biography, Tor Andrae points to the prophet's focus as always intensely direct, toward the individual and the relationship he or she has to the problem before them of an orphan, a widow, or a beggar, and in the context of devotion to Allah:

> Mohammed certainly felt a real and sincere concern for the poor and neglected. But we find in him no real indignation concerning their hard lot, and still less did it occur to him to attempt to abolish poverty. Pious gifts are not made for this purpose. Alms are given for Allah's sake because they are pleasing to Him, or they are given for one's own benefit, for the "cleansing" of the soul, to eradicate the effects of sin committed, or to prevent accumulated wealth from becoming a damning burden on the Day of Judgment, or to store up good works with which to earn Paradise.[63]

The act of service is immediate, personal, and devotional.

To understand the appeal of Islam, it is important to see how the heart takes precedence over the forms and legalisms often assumed to be at the center. In the *Sunna* there is this anecdote:

> When the child (of Zainab) was brought to Muhammad, dying; its body trembling and moving; the eyes of the Apostle of God shed many tears. And S'ad said, "O Messenger of God! What is this weeping and shedding of tears?" Muhammad replied, "This is an expression of the tenderness and compassion, which the Lord hath put into the hearts of His servants; the Lord doth not have compassion on and commiserate with His servants, except such as are tender and full of feeling."[64]

This is what Arabic scholar H. A. R. Gibb calls Mohammed's "largeness of humanity"[65] and Andrae summarizes in what can be seen as a nutshell description of a vigorous ISFJ spirituality:

> At first he seems to be dominated by a native shyness which is not uncommon in an introvert type of temperament. Such a person often possesses a richly developed emotional and imaginative life, but suffers from a certain fear of action, or rather, from a fear of direct contact with brutal reality. This shyness is not identical with weakness of character and will, and it has nothing to do with a pathological paralysis of the will. On the contrary, people of this type may have exceptionally strong will-power, the ability to carry out a plan with stern indomitable consistency, and an amount of energy by which the noisy and reckless daredevil temperaments are ultimately put to shame.[66]

Mohammed's life in many respects follows the classic SF hero's journey: the turning point of his call to the journey; the night on Mount Hira, in 610; a dozen bleak and tortured years in Mecca, where he was ridiculed and despised by all but his few followers; the exciting escape; the Hijra, the migration from Mecca to Medina during which he and Abu Bakr hid in a cave from pursuers; his sojourn in Medina, followed by the Battle of Badr, where 300 led by Mohammed, who had never handled a sword before, defeated a superior force of 1,000; and eventually his ascendancy back in Mecca in 630, and death in 632 after all of the Arabian Peninsula had been won for Islam.

Out of this experience comes a tight-knit Islamic brotherhood combined, paradoxically, with a broad and thoroughgoing tolerance of other faiths. In the third sura the new Islamic unity is affirmed:

> Hold you fast to God's bond, together, and do not scatter; remember God's blessing upon you when you were enemies, and He brought your hearts together, so that by His blessing you became brothers.

And in suras 2 and 109:

No compulsion is there in religion.

To you your religion,
and to me my religion.[67]

SF spirituality is practiced in the groves of northern Europe, in the mountains of Tibet, and in the deep jungles of the tropics. But nowhere has it achieved a greater intensity than in the searing deserts of the Middle East, with their omnipresent heat and sunlight, wide horizons, and deep night skies. Desert images are felt with immediacy and impact, as in this Hadith: "Where are those who love one another through My glory? Today I shall give them shade in My shade, it being a day when there is no shade but My shade."[68] The particular character of Mohammed's SF spirituality can be appreciated most by keeping in mind the landscape in which he lived. Muhammad Asad in *The Road to Mecca* captured this essence (italics mine):

> We ride and Zayd sings: always the same rhythm, always the same monotonous melody. For the soul of the Arab is monotonous—but not in sense of poverty of imagination; he has plenty of that; but his instinct does not go, like that of [the European] after width, three-dimensional space and the simultaneity of many shades of emotion. Through Arabian music speaks a desire to carry, each time, a single emotional experience to the utmost end of its reach. To this pure monotony, this almost *sensual* desire to see *feeling* intensified in a continuous, ascending line, the Arabian character owes its strength and its faults. Its faults: for the world wants to be experienced, emotionally, in space as well. And its strength: for the faith in the possibility of an endless linear ascent of emotional knowledge can in the sphere of the mind lead nowhere but to God. Only on the basis of this inborn drive, so peculiar to people of the desert, could grow the monotheism of the early Hebrews and its triumphant fulfillment, the faith of Muhammad.[69]

St. Francis

Francis of Assisi was born Giovanni di Bernardone in 1182, son of an affluent cloth merchant in the city. He is described as an exuberant, carefree, but decent, popular child, who loved variety and adventure. He dreamed of becoming a famous knight. In his youth when Assisi and the neighboring city of Perugia fought a war, Giovanni joined in, was knocked from his horse, and taken prisoner. He was a perpetual optimist, even in this ordeal. On his return home he became ill and had to part company with his would-be knight companions, who had scoffed at him for not being of nobility. On resuming his trip, and now alone, his mood was somewhat more sober, and when he spied a leper walking along toward him, his feelings overwhelmed him. He saw his fear as a challenge, so he dismounted and kissed the leper— an act of compassion and courage. Serving lepers became a major theme in his life, for he "saw the face of the suffering Christ" beneath the deformed features of this leper.[70]

In his *Testament*, written just before his death, he looks back at this formative experience:

> The Lord granted me, Brother Francis, grace to begin to do penance, for while I was living in sin, it seemed a very bitter thing to look at lepers; but the Lord Himself led me among them, and I showed pity on them. And when I left them the thing that had seemed so horrible to me was transformed into happiness of body and soul for me. After this I delayed awhile, and then renounced the world.[71]

Until this moment on the road home, which marks the beginning of his ministry, his childhood and youth appear to have contained all the elements of the ESFP personality type.[72] Even with the disciplining and polishing of his vows and vocation, his spontaneity and love of association with people continued.

Shortly thereafter, an experience of great significance for Francis' Journey of Devotion occurred in the Church of San Damiano. In 1206 he wandered into a neglected, abandoned chapel, and sat in prayer before the crucifix at the altar. In the midst of his reflections the crucifix spoke to him: "Vade Francisce et reparadomum meam! Go, Francis, and repair my falling house!"[73]

Of course, for some time Francis took this command literally and actually went about repairing churches. His lifework gradually made him aware of the larger meaning, that in his century the church was in a decrepit and corrupt condition. The monastic orders he was to found and the life he was to lead contributed greatly to a spiritual revival at the center of Catholic life.

Poverty, or what he called "Lady Poverty," was his central value.[74] He divested himself of all worldly possessions, for he did not want to be possessed by them. A tour guide summarizes the central (SF) symbol of the Franciscans, portrayed in numerous ways in Assisi: "Poverty, not laziness nor escape from action but voluntary and heroic renouncement of possession, the tyrant of man, Poverty as source of charity and love."[75]

Francis' father, Pietro di Bernardone, was not pleased with his son's decisions and denounced him before the city council. He demanded that Bishop Guido order his son to return any money of the family (so that it would not go into repairing churches!). The bishop obliged, and Francis not only handed the Bishop his money but also gave his father his clothes. A naked Francis made public his religious vow before the congregation in a rather striking and SP way!

In 1210 he founded the Friars Minor, gaining approval for the Rule of the Order from Pope Innocent III. He and his first disciples, the Poverello, gathered in a small abandoned church given to them in Portiuncula. They all dressed in single-piece gray cross-shaped tunics, wrapped about their bodies and secured at the waist with a cord. They had renounced the world, affirming certain core values that are summarized by Francis in his *Praise of the Virtues:*

> Hail, O Wisdom, O Queen!
>   The Lord keep thee and thy sister holy and pure Simplicity.
> Hail, O holy Lady Poverty!
>   The Lord keep thee and thy sister holy Humility!
> Hail, O holy Lady Charity!
>   The Lord keep thee and thy sister holy Obedience.[76]

Two years later, a major coup occurred when the daughter of Count Favarone, Clare of Assisi, heard Francis preach in the cathedral and, "inflamed with the love of Jesus," knelt before him with the desire to take a vow of poverty and enter the religious life.[77] Soon afterward, in 1212, arrangements were completed for the establishment of the Poor Clares, a second Franciscan order.

Next we see Francis journeying to attempt peaceful conversion of "the Saracens" (Arabs) in Egypt and Palestine. While that effort was unsuccessful, he did experience a remarkable pilgrimage to the revered religious sites in the Middle East. Even in the years remaining in Italy after his return, a constant restlessness is present. Francis preached to congregations and street crowds in villages, was a troubadour to birds and animals, journeyed several times to Rome, tended lepers and the sick, made the arduous climb to his hermitage just outside Assisi, never ceasing to introduce variety into his life, even during self-imposed solitude, as in his famous forty-day and forty-night fast, when all he ate was a half loaf of bread. Bertrand Russell mentions the hot-and-cold reactions of the popes to Francis' "enthusiastic and anarchic impulses."[78] Francis was not a staid institutionalist but a charismatic and spontaneous leader. His Franciscan order became widely popular, and the pope required him to sequester himself and to write new rules to keep the movement in bounds. His first draft in 1221 was rejected, and two years later, after what must have been the most difficult period of his life, he finally produced an acceptable set of rules.

Important themes in Francis' life were his arbitrary affirmation of "secular priests" out of his awe for the responsibilities of their office, and his nearly obsessive concern that liturgical books be kept off the floor in safe places and that the elements of the Eucharist be stored in clean receptacles, served on clean altars and in appropriate ways. He wrote letters to the clergy as part of what is called his "Eucharistic Crusade."[79] In his last *Testament* he wrote:

> I wish the most holy Sacrament to be honored above all things, and venerated and reserved in precious places. And wherever I find writings containing God's most holy Name and word lying in unfitting places, I gather them together and put them in a seemly place.[80]

Such energy must have been irritating to those in the population for whom this much attention to detail was not customary.

An oft-told story of Francis' charismatic presence took place in Greccio, where on Christmas Eve he sang the Mass and preached on the meaning of the nativity. The manger scene in the church contained a wooden Christ child. When Francis took it up into his arms as he was speaking, it seemed to many in the congregation as if the statue had become animated, stirring in his arms.[81]

Two years before his death, Francis climbed Mount La Verna with several of his closest disciples for an intensive retreat:

> While rapt in prayer on the mountainside, he saw a Seraph with six fiery wings come down from the skies. Then he saw Christ Crucified amidst the wings. Francis fell into ecstasy and was filled with joy and sorrow: joy because Christ looked at him with such love, sorrow at compassion for Christ's sufferings. As the vision disappeared, his heart was all aglow with love, but—wondrous to behold—his hands and feet were pierced with nails and his side bore a wound, as if pierced by a lance.[82]

These wounds, known as the stigmata, represent the last stage in the recapitulation in his life of features in the life story of Christ.

Today, Francis is most revered as "the ecological saint," although in the Christian sense of all life and nature deriving from the Creator. Pope John Paul II designated him as "the heavenly patron of those scientists and students who are concerned with the physical wellbeing of planet Earth and indeed of the universe itself."[83]

In the Basilica di San Maria degli Angeli in Assisi, and at the Eremo delle Cemeri, there are statues of St. Francis where nests are maintained in the palms of his hands for white doves. These derive from a story of his rescue of two caged turtledoves a young man was carrying to the village to be slaughtered:

> My young man, I beg you to give me them. Birds so meek are likened in the Scriptures to chaste and faithful souls. They ought not to fall into the hands of cruel people who will kill them.[84]

When Francis was ill in the last year of his life, in the garden of the Poor Clares' convent he composed his famous *Canticle of Brother Sun*, a celebration of the sun, moon, stars, wind, cloud, water, fire, sister bodily death and "our sister Mother Earth Who sustains and directs us, And brings forth varied fruits, and coloured flowers, and plants."[85]

St. Francis is best known for an oft-quoted devotional prayer:

Lord, make me an instrument of Thy peace.
Where there is hate, may I bring love
Where offense, may I bring pardon;
May I bring union in place of discord;
Truth, replacing error;
Faith, where once there was doubt;
Hope, for despair;
Light, where was darkness;
Joy to replace sadness.
Make me not to so crave to be loved as to love.
Help me to learn that in giving I may receive;
In forgetting self, I may find life eternal.[86]

⟲ UNDER STRESS, NEW LEARNINGS

There is no question that a strong NT bias exists, particularly in the Western branch of human culture. The universities are dominated by it, as are the scientific worldview and the idea of "progress" itself. It is estimated by R. Buckminster Fuller that

> 99% of all the important work now being done . . . relating to our evolutionary advance is work going on in the areas above and below the tunable range of man's direct optical or other sensorial participation in the electromagnetic spectrum.[87]

He sees us going from "being muscle and reflex machines" to developing our "mental and intuitive faculties."[88] The NT preference is favored, though "muscle" and "machines" do not represent SF values.

When NT pursuits get the attention and resources of a society, other strengths also important for our social well-being and balance are depreciated. NT work becomes the wave of the future, and SF work is undervalued. Although we could not survive or maintain a humane civilization without SF participation, nevertheless a sense of social obsolescence creeps in, creating a feeling of inadequacy and generalized social stress. It is not that SFs should not be computer programmers or electronic engineers, for example, but rather that early childhood educators, nurses, clergy, youth workers, counselors, full-time parents, landscape designers, and receptionists who work with the public are exceedingly valuable participants in society as well.

Under such chronic generalized stress, many SFs find prospects for socially rewarding work depressing or even catastrophic. It is tempting to give up on oneself, even to feel victimized.

So, too, SF spirituality is looked down on by some as common or even anachronistic. Those who feel assurance that lighting a candle at the altar of Mary in deep devotion will grant them the strength to endure the vicissitudes of motherhood, for example, often have floundered in an arid and skeptical age. SF spirituality seems in retreat in modern Western culture, whereas in most branches of religion it has been the most prominently visible of the Four Spiritualities in the images and practices of the people. The great solace and comfort of religious piety is, tragically, a receding reality for contemporary Westerners.

It is important for those on the Journey of Devotion to find mutual support to become who they truly are, to feel comfortable in their native spirituality. There are many variations in the practice of SF spirituality all along the theological spectrum, from humanistic to theistic, and in practice from true simplicity to highly ornate and complex. To enter into the practice of devotion without apology and with assurance can be a great blessing to oneself and to all others.

ᥱ EDUCATION FOR THIS WAY

The paragraph introducing education in chapter 4 bears repeating here. Preparation for all four journeys begins at the earliest age. The most essential elements of spiritual "In Forming" take place before age six or seven, when the functions are relatively undifferentiated. Charles M. Fair calls this "the seeding of young minds . . . to become what we regard as fully human." In his view, it is the function of the neocortex to organize the energies of the more elemental parts of the brain, the emergency and emotional aspects (the id, in Freudian terms) into a rational control. The seminal traditional ideas of the culture must be planted early, to remain beneath the surface of the soil until the sunlight and nurture of various developmental triggers can call them up from memory and enlist them in the formation of character, mind, and spirituality. Fair sees this process as the essential explanation for the rise and fall of cultures. In times of trouble, the seeding process has not taken place. The basic ideas of what it is to be human are learned from story, from examples of people around the child, and from sincerely related precept. The child's mind must be impressed by the drama, genuineness, and honesty of input so that the memory remains until it can be utilized developmentally.

In later childhood, the bold outlines of typology begin to emerge in the personality. SF children wish to be good people and engage in appropriate behavior. They wish to please the culture bearers around them. The seeds of earlier inculcation come up into consciousness through a process of recognition. A sentimental poem, an Aesop fable, or a bedtime story will reactivate the seeds into memorable forms that will stay with children the rest of their lives. An SF child will cherish an experience of warm personal kindness or consideration as a memory to be invoked and emulated in similar situations the rest of his or her life.

Until the turn of the century, elementary education involved a great deal of memorization of poetry, maxims, and proverbs. Primers and literature texts from the time of Horace Mann onward included verse and stories based on the criteria of what aspects of character or what virtues and values they would inculcate. Students kept bound quotation books into which they wrote in their best penmanship important poems and sayings they were expected to remember or memorize.

Often SF education will have a strong oral component; what is to be learned will be learned to be recited or sung on appropriate occasions or to transmit to others. The tradition of black spirituals in American Protestantism was an oral tradition, transmitting by memory from generation to generation messages of solace, freedom, and dignity.

Mohammed, being illiterate, recited the Koran as he received it, and, in turn, a number of his followers who survived him had memorized the entire corpus of his recitations. As these survivors began to die, a panic set in for the young movement, and Caliphs Abu Bakr and Uthman saw to it that scribes listened to and recorded the authorized version of the Koran. Even today, young children learn the Koran by heart, as it was written primarily to be heard.

Content that is abstract, too removed from the present, and unconnected to relationships holds little value to the soul for SFs and is endured only when it has practical application. Education for the Journey of Devotion becomes deeply attractive and meaningful when it is laden with sentiment, story, the human context and landscape, focused on values of neighborhood, community, piety, benevolence, and service to others.

⟲ HOME AND TEMPLE

If "the body is the temple of the soul" for SF spirituality, so are the home, one's workplace, and the temple itself. In the foyer of the Buddhist house, retail establishment, or office, you will see a statue of Kuan Yin garlanded with fresh flowers or with a stick of incense burning. On the side lawn of a Roman Catholic home, surrounded by yellow chrysanthemums, is a porcelain Madonna. A picture of the Kitchen God is changed each New Year in Chinese homes. In the puja room in a Hindu home, rituals are conducted each morning for the goddess Durga, with a new dedication of sacred space, new garlands, and oblations of oil.

Prayer wheels are used by Buddhists, rosaries by Catholic and Orthodox Christians. Protestants sing favorite SF hymns such as "Joyful, Joyful, We Adore Thee" or "Nearer, My God to Thee." Moslems who use the Koran for daily readings are careful never to place it on the ground or floor. Jewish men wear yarmulkes and shawls when at prayer. Hindus and Moslems remove shoes before entering sacred spaces. Candles are lit on anniversaries before appropriate images. Flowers are arranged around the altar each Sunday and feast day. The colors and designs for vestments worn by priests are changed with the seasons and for special festivals. Celtic pagans build the altar with different symbols for each of the quarter and cross-quarter holidays.

The great religious festivals give a prominent place to the proclivities of the Journey of Devotion. Devotion is expended in detailed preparations for the fasts of Ramadan and Yom Kippur, finding the new Easter hat and decorating eggs with traditional Lithuanian designs, affixing garlands of flowers for the great image taken on the ratha or car in the processions of Durga Puja, making rice cakes for the Dragon-Boat Festival. Traditions are observed in every detail; true joy and ecstasy are experienced in participation. SFJs and SFPs together bring balance, as the one type makes sure everything is in proper readiness and the other makes sure the celebration is animated and lively. Ideally, they absorb each other's strengths and emerge stronger at the conclusion of festivities.

᧏ GIFT OF THIS JOURNEY FOR OTHERS

Often SF traditions in one branch of culture become attractive to onlookers in another and begin to take hold there, but appealing to non-SF types, usually Intuitives. NFs, for example, typically will move on to another mode of experimentation for their spiritual growth after a time. NFs, too, are notorious for adapting and changing the adopted practices until they may resemble the parent movement only faintly. For a successful transplanting from one branch of culture to another, SFs themselves will need to be brought on board, for they will give it continuity and integrity.

For this same reason, however, SFs tend to be traditionalists in their inherited cultural milieu. They learn early what is appropriate, and they like to please their early enculturators. They do their own traditions well, they enjoy and derive a sense of genuine spiritual participation from them, and see no reason for moving away from them. SF devotees tend to set the norm for popular spiritual practices, which other types attach themselves to from their own perspectives. Sensors give the traditions great staying power through the generations.

᧏ HOW SFs WILL USE THIS BOOK

Most SFs prefer direct experience over slogging through a book filled with abstractions and global conceptions. They would rather cut to the chase and find clearly and authoritatively spelled-out steps to take on the journey, and then push to get on with the actual walking.

Since SFs tend to dominate the popular practices and celebrations of the religious traditions, they are often unaware of the alternative forms of spirituality. In many ways they are the milieu in and from which the others must differentiate their own preferences. SFs, however, are capable of great sensitivity and patience when they understand they have been inadvertently overbearing. It would be beneficial for them to adopt as a mantra a saying such as this passage from the Bhagavad Gita:

> Some by the Yoga of meditation,
> and by the grace of the Spirit,
> see the Spirit in themselves;
> some by the Yoga of the vision of Truth;
> and others by the Yoga of work.

> And yet there are others who do not know,
> but they hear from others and adore.
> They also cross beyond death,
> because of their devotion to words of Truth.[89]

CHAPTER SIX

THE JOURNEY OF WORKS

HEAVEN CAN GIVE BIRTH TO CREATURES BUT IT

CANNOT ORDER THEM; EARTH CAN BEAR MAN UP

BUT IT CANNOT GOVERN HIM. ALL CREATURES

OF THE UNIVERSE, ALL WHO BELONG TO THE SPECIES

OF MAN, MUST AWAIT THE SAGE BEFORE THEY CAN

ATTAIN THEIR PROPER PLACES.

Hsüan-tzu, trans. Burton Watson

IT IS IMPORTANT FOR EACH spirituality to have its uniqueness reinforced in the environment. For the Journey of Works, order and a clear message presenting the purpose and operation of the center and expectations of participants are essential conditions. Everything is part of one whole, every person does his or her part to make it work, commitment gives religion stability.

Forms will differ around the globe, but steady support of each tradition is central for this journey. You might see yourself entering the sacred place through a door you had personally carved by hand. It has the same symbol on it that is found on all doors in centers of the faith. A stirring song is being sung, glorious in the story it tells and the invitation it sends to encourage faithful and upright living. This gathering is well run and knows exactly the mission it has in society. It is a bold and sustaining faith, going back before recorded history. You are grateful that the prayer is recited just as it was in your great grandparents' time. Even though you don't subscribe to every idea, the faith sustains lives and the world. You go on pilgrimage every ten years to the distant sacred birthplace of the founding sage, and your white skullcap gives you the special responsibilities incumbent on returning pilgrims. In a tragic world that often strays, your steadiness and fidelity will endure for posterity. Sometimes you feel like shaking things up so that everyone would know how important this spiritual center is.

⟲ THE ST PERSONALITY

There are many expressions of this journey around the world, likely to appeal to two Sensing types with Thinking (ISTJ and ESTP) and two Thinking types with Sensing (ISTP and ESTJ). Before examining the outlines of this native spirituality, it is useful to have in mind a concept of the ST personality.

As Children and Youth

Some children are always in motion. They have to test everything, even other children in a wrestling match to see where the limits really are. These children constantly ask why. They want to see the relationships of cause and effect, want to know what is really real, and want to get their hands on things and learn by experience. Their attachments are to inanimate things, how they work, their uses, and organizing them to accomplish tasks. Extraverted STs are particularly drawn to activities that are task-oriented, such as team sports, and they often will be leaders. STP children will sometimes be drawn to risky activities, such as racing their bicycles or high diving. STJ children will be quite conscientious about doing their chores around the house or tidying up at school. They are not swayed by the feelings of a parent or a teacher, however. They want to know why things are required, how things work, and they want to have them demonstrated on the spot so they can see it for themselves.

As teens, STs divide into two groups: the freedom lovers (STP) and the responsible ones (STJ). STPs like action, variety, challenges; STJs like organized activities with serious results, often lead student groups at their schools, need order and measurable outcomes. With hardly a ripple, they will continue into their young adult pursuits. It is the STPs who often become quite skeptical of book learning when they cannot see any direct practical relevance to their lives. Apprenticeship programs in hands-on skills are often helpful to them.

All STs are oriented around well-defined institutions—school, home, church, the Y—but STJs will help sustain them, whereas STPs will often honor them in the breach as they seek to respond to situations in the most direct way possible to solve whatever problems they are facing. All STs like clear definitions of exactly what they are dealing with.

As Adults

When they grow up, STs become the realists, always in touch with the facts, unbiased, accurate, objective, impersonal, giving full attention to all the relevant details. They organize the details in a straight linear way, reasoning from premise to conclusion. They experience the implications directly and look for clear-cut results from their efforts. They are skilled administrators, responsible, objective, consistent, efficient, careful, detached, analytical, and following procedures to the letter, even legalistically (STJ) or cutting through to the accurate decision efficiently, bypassing red tape (STP). The latter are known for their directness, even brutal frankness. And STs, particularly ESTJs, can be excellent negotiators, unbiased, not swayed by subjective feelings. Balance, prudence, duty, and, above all, fairness are their hallmarks.

The Journey of Works is practical and involves a lifetime of effort, a constant and responsible attention to leading a productive life. Work is the means for meeting all obligations and responsibilities. It gives life dignity, patiently earned, and the respect of solid citizenship. It is right to take one's turn, to discharge one's duties, whether they be to the high school alumni association or to the extended family of which one has become head. STs commit themselves to the building up and maintaining of institutions, reliably and loyally. In this way, their work can become service, but not in the SF sense of direct service to individuals; rather, indirectly to organizations that serve people.

STs prefer direct, experience-based, often physical activities, working with their hands or otherwise directly in situations, trying out procedures to see what works best, often preferring technical tasks to those requiring people skills. They learn best on the job, interacting with the problems and tasks as they actually arise in the situation. They will notice the relevant details. They will collect facts and verify them directly by the senses, extrapolating conclusions in a linear cause-and-effect way, comparing new data with past experience. They are most comfortable when they can relate their conclusions in a matter-of-fact, pinned-down, and documented fashion. Often STs will love their equipment almost as much as the uses they put it to; they often have machines, gadgets, and tools everywhere. Their opinions, based on their experience, will often be firmly held and based on common sense or Sensing realities.

Once a concept, solution, or procedure becomes clear, STs like to proceed with implementation. "Get on with it" could be their motto. If they believe they know what is right, or know what is true, then life becomes a matter of living in accordance with that reality. Sometimes an ST will learn at a very young age what is the right way to behave or what is true to believe, and these precepts are acted upon throughout the rest of life without new questioning. This is why some STs are seen as prejudiced or old-fashioned. Often they question such beliefs only when the outcomes have impractical or unfair consequences or directly clash with other beliefs they hold. A confusion of beliefs is intolerable for STs. They like to find a world in balance, with reliable structures that lead them toward the right way to go. Discerning a proper and efficient implementation then becomes the focus.

∾ ST NATIVE SPIRITUALITY

The native spirituality for the Journey of Works is divided into eight general manifestations, appearing in different proportions for different individuals: (1) the foundation of law, covenant, and order; (2) the strong sense of right and importance of righteousness; (3) the sense of responsibility and stewardship for personal, social, and natural resources; (4) clear-cut identity as essential for one's spiritual life; (5) work itself as life's aim and fulfillment; (6) a realist orientation; (7) a proclivity to administration in behalf of life; and (8) a sense, often a tragic sense, of justification.

Law, Covenant, and Order

Evidences of ST spirituality reach back to the origins of written history. Before history, there was generally a golden age of a perfect social order. The king ruled fairly and presided over a peaceful and prosperous world. Then dissolution and chaos entered in, often through disobedience or unfaithfulness. To bring order out of this new chaos, some kind of law or covenant needed to be imposed. Regulation of society through wisely administered covenants and ethical understandings, defining how relationships should be mutually rewarding, is the province of the Journey of Works.

The Code of Hammurabi, a king of Babylon (2067–2025 B.C.), is remarkably detailed in the proscriptions of its 282 paragraphs. Numerous areas of conduct are enumerated, with punishments for not acting rightly. The purpose of the Code is spelled out unambiguously in the Prologue: "When Marduk sent me to rule men, and to promulgate justice, I put justice and righteousness into the language of the land, and promoted the welfare of the people."[1] Hammurabi here shows a classic ST interest in the regulation of society.

ST rulers often manifest a genuine concern for their people akin to the attitude of parents for their children, tied in as well with a theology of destiny being fulfilled through them. Marduk, of course, was the supreme god of Babylon, shepherd and guardian of the order, God of Kings.

Righteousness

This theology can be played out in God working through either a king or a prophet. The prophet Zoroaster (circa 1500 B.C.) presents the need for ordering of society in a broader, less narrowly legal context of worship:

> Through good mind and through rectitude and through the deeds and words of wisdom, we come near unto Thee.
>
> Grant, O Mazda, for this life and the spiritual life, that we may attain to fellowship with Thee and righteousness for all Time. Thou the good king of us, men and women. We dedicate ourselves unto Thee, of good renown, the adorable one, the possessor of truth.[2]

Here a theology of righteousness is combined with worship of God as king. Zoroaster believed we are needed in the cosmic scheme as collaborators with the forces of good and order (asha) in opposing the forces of evil and disorder (druj), an important innovation in the history of ethics. Ahura Mazda (the Wise Lord) needs human participation.

Good behavior is rewarded, and evil behavior is punished. "I am on the side of those who preserve order, not on that of those who create disorder," says Ahura Mazda.[3] In the Indian *Laws of Manu*, this notion is accompanied by warnings that the rewards and punishments may not be immediate nor easily recognized.

> 172. Unrighteousness, practiced in this world, does not at once produce its fruit, like a cow; but, advancing slowly, it cuts off the roots of him who committed it. . . .
>
> 174. He prospers for a while through unrighteousness, then he gains great good fortune, next he conquers his enemies, but (at last) he perishes (branch and) root.[4]

In Judaism this view came in with the Deuteronomic reforms under King Josiah in 621 B.C. Previously held by prophets on the outside, now the "lost book" of the law was "found" and became the official view inside society: ". . . you shall keep his statutes and his commandments, which I command you this day, that it may go well with you, and with your children after you. . . ."[5]

Ever since, there has been an element in Judaism, Christianity, and Islam that does not see religious laws as advisory ideas, the Ten Suggestions, but literal edicts to be obeyed, which will determine one's eventual destiny in the social and cosmic order of things. In the *Book of Deuteronomy* itself, chapters 12 to 26 spell out rather exactingly religious, humanitarian, civil, and political laws governing every reach of life. Canon law in the Roman Catholic, Orthodox, and Anglican communions, various schools of the Sharia in Islam, and others continue this emphasis. In the Journey of Works it is important to know exactly what is right and what is wrong, and the honoring of the right in one's behavior has consequences—sooner or later—of reward or punishment.

Whereas NT justice has a global, futuristic visionary component, ST righteousness is doing the right thing, yourself, for its own sake in the here-and-now and expecting others to do so as well. This sense that there is a right and a wrong in every situation may or may not be with reference to the authority of a divine revelation. The Chinese humanist and naturalist philosopher Lin Yutang (1895–1976), for example, cites the response of a Confucian friend to the issue of the absence of a God as the guarantor of ethics: "We should lead a decent human life simply because we are decent human beings."[6]

To give a contextual picture of such a statement: One of the many archetypal ST songs in the ancient Chinese *Book of Odes* shows clearly the sense of balance, order, and reciprocity that is the foundation of such an assurance. The poem is about King Wu, dating from the twelfth century B.C.:

> Great dignity had T'ai-jen,
> The mother of King Wen;
> Well loved was Lady Chiang of Chou,
> Bride of the high house.
> And T'ai-ssu carried on her fair name,
> Bearing a multitude of sons.
>
> He was obedient to the ancestors of the clan,
> So that the Spirits were never angry;
> So that the Spirits were never grieved.
> He was a model to his chief bride;
> A model to his brothers old and young,
> And in his dealings with home and land.
>
> Affable was he in the palace,
> Reverent in the ancestral hall,
> Glorious and regarded by Heaven,
> Causing no discontent, protected by Heaven.
> Therefore war and sickness did not destroy,
> Nor plague nor witchcraft work havoc.
>
> Without asking, he knew what was the rule;
> Without being admonished, he admitted.
> Therefore grown men could use their Inward Power,
> And young people could find work to do.
> The ancient were well content;
> And the doughty well employed.[7]

Edward Everett Hale (1822–1909), liberal Unitarian pastor in Boston's Back Bay for more than a half century, summarized the ST sense of social order and the role of all to make it work:

This true allegiance of man to the Infinite Law implies and involves more than verbal truth. It is the obedience of every act, so that the man does without concealment, without pretense, without exaggeration, the thing he undertakes to do. The errand boy does not loiter on his errand. The sentinel never misses a turn of his round. The screw-maker never puts one deficient screw in the parcel. We shall gain this absolute allegiance when the kingdom of God wholly comes. To gain it, to bring in that kingdom, is our present hope and duty.[8]

Hale was a prodigious author, orator, pastor, and organizer. One of his best-known projects was the Lend a Hand Clubs, for which he penned a classic ESTJ motto:

Look up and not down
Look forward and not back
Look out and not in
Lend a hand![9]

A related project organized children in Sunday schools into "Look-Up Legions," whose members pledged themselves to be "truthful, unselfish, cheerful, hopeful, and helpful."[10] Succinct mottoes, lists for guidance, and definite, even measurable standards to follow are core procedures for the Journey of Works, and inculcated most effectively very early in life.

This may be why the Golden Rule, the Great Commandment, the *Shema*, and the Lord's Prayer are so popular with STs. They give exact instructions:

Whatever you wish that men would do to you,
do so to them.[11]

You shall love your neighbor as yourself.[12]

And forgive us our debts,
  As we also have forgiven our debtors.[13]

A strong theme of fairness and reciprocity runs through ST human–cosmic relations. The world is in balance when everyone is doing his or her part.

There are things in life we do because we know they are the right things to do. That is really all we know. They make the world coherent; they are what make the world go around; they are right. To do right is our duty and the meaning of moral virtue. Gandhi defines civilization as:

Civilization is that mode of conduct which points out to man the path of duty. Performance of duty and observance of morality are convertible terms. To observe morality is to attain mastery over our mind and our passions. So doing, we know ourselves. The Gujarati equivalent for civilization means "good conduct."[14]

While one's performance of duty can be high-profile in the surrounding society, as a spiritual practice it becomes more private and humbly executed. In South India one of the oldest commentaries on the aims of life is a work of poetry, *The Kural*, which expresses one's responsibility as self-control:

Self-control takes one to the gods;
Its lack to utter darkness.

Guard self-control as a treasure;
There is nothing more precious in life.

Self-restraint taught by common sense
Leads to virtue and gains glory.

The steadfast self-controlled towers aloft
Taller than a mountain.

Humility, good for all,
Is an added richness to the rich.[15]

In the West, morality tends to be practiced from the interior conscience rather than primarily out of response to external standards. The expectations of society must be internalized early and be available for reference as situations arise. Of great appeal to ST spirituality in the West are lines from the General Confession in the Episcopal Book of Common Prayer:

We have offended against thy holy laws. We have left undone those things which we ought to have done, And we have done those things which we ought not to have done. . . .[16]

While not all forms of the Journey of Works involve the expiation of guilt— for example, it is wholly absent from Confucianism of the pre-Buddhist period—this is an integral hold for ST ethics in the Western branch of cuture.

Responsibility and Stewardship

One of the most popular icons of civic religion in post–Civil War America was U.S. Senate chaplain Edward Everett Hale's story "The Man Without a Country," about a navy officer who, while being tried in the Aaron Burr conspiracy, said before the judge: "Damn the United States! I wish I may never hear of the United States again!"[17] The judge granted him his wish, and for the rest of his life he was kept on various naval ships, which withheld from him all news and mention of his country. The sin, the judge, the naval procedures, and the author all epitomize an ST vision. There are things you do and don't do, there are civic duties akin to a sacred fealty, and there are boundaries beyond which your honor and very identity are violated.

Hale sees responsible participation in the "common life" as the center of the message of Christian history. He cites "No man liveth to himself, and no man dieth to himself"[18] and numerous other texts as the core contribution of Christianity to Western democracy. In his words:

It [the liberal church] says that that original Christian truth is the immanent presence of God—God living in man, and man living in him,—... and it is this common life of brethren, the life in common, in which all men are one.[19]

Hale centers his spirituality in works, in the duty to elevate all parts of our common life and our responsibility to uphold the entire social context as a spiritual whole that depends on the quality of our participation. But he centers his social participation in the life of worship.

Hospitality, education, charity, in the life of a church are all subordinate to worship. What is called in our time "Social Science" is a well meant and generally superficial effort to carry on education and popular improvement without personal consecration and surrender of the life to God. You might as well carry on a kaleidoscope without light; or the organ yonder without air; or a steam engine without steam.[20]

In the Bhagavad Gita, Krishna gives Arjuna, the ST archer, reasons for entering fully into his social responsibilities as a warrior.[21] Arjuna is in a situation where no matter whether he acts or does not act, he will destroy members of his own family and the balance of the world as he has known it since earliest childhood. The inevitability of change and destruction is especially troubling to an ST sense of order and tradition. Krishna has to convince him to go forward to do what he must attempt to do. First, Krishna appeals to his sense of duty: "Seeing thine own duty thou shouldst not shrink from it; for there is no higher good for a Kshatriya than a righteous war." Not to respond to his duty would bring him shame: "The world will for ever recount the story of thy disgrace; and for a man of honour disgrace is worse than death."[22] Acting is essential, regardless of victory or defeat:

Slain, you will obtain heaven;
victorious you will enjoy the earth;
therefore, stand up, O son of Kunti,
determined to fight.[23]

The spiritual level in the execution of his duty will lie in his ability to be objective, free from a bondage to self-interest in the outcome or to what might be lost in going forward:

Thy right is to work only,
but never to its fruits;
let not the fruit-of-action be thy motive,
nor let thy attachment be to inaction.[24]

In China the Journey of Works tends to be grounded in human nature and the social and natural order rather than in consecration to God or in nonattachment. In a remarkable poem by Po Chü-i (772–846 A.D.), a householder, weighed down by the burdens of his life, feels connected spiritually in his stewardship of a cluster of pines in the courtyard of his home. The concluding lines summarize:

> [T]he World called me mad—
> That a whole family of twice ten souls
> Should move house for the sake of a few pines!
> Now that I have come to them,
>   what have they given me?
> They have only loosened the buckles of my care.
> . . . Yet when I consider how,
>   still a man of the world,
> In belt and cap I scurry through dirt and dust,
> From time to time my heart twinges with shame
> That I am not fit to be master of my pines![25]

In seeking to live responsibly, the individual always needs to have a center and grounding to give the Journey of Works direction and legitimacy. Meng K'o (Mencius; 371–289 B.C.), for example, says: "The world, the state, the households; the world is rooted in the state; the state in the households; the households in the individual." And how do we build up the world? By starting with ourselves:

> If you love others, but they do not love you in return, reexamine your own love. If you would bring peace and order to [others], but disorder ensues, reexamine your own wisdom. If you are ceremonious with others and they do not return it, reexamine your own reverence. If your deeds are unsuccessful, seek for the reason in yourself. When your own person is correct, the whole world will turn to you.[26]

Even the leaders of government must be responsible to their calling. Confucianism twenty-five hundred years ago introduced the right of revolution, observed in the removal of "the mandate of Heaven," when the state fails to adequately shoulder its part of the world balance; for example:

> Mencius said to King Hsüan of Ch'i, "Suppose a subject of Your Majesty's, having entrusted his wife and children to the care of a friend, were to go on a trip to Ch'u, only to find, upon his return, that his friend had allowed his wife and children to suffer cold and hunger, then what should he do about it?"
>
> "Break with his friend."
>
> "If the Marshal of the Guards was unable to keep his guards in order, then what should be done about it?"
>
> "Remove him from office."
>
> "If the whole realm with the four borders was ill-governed, then what should be done about it?" The King turned to his attendants and changed the subject.[27]

Likewise, in the cosmic realm we see projected the need for stewardship and for a concerted effort to pursue the mission. One of the four bodhisattvas of the *Lotus Sutra* is the Great Bodhisattva of Steadfast Conduct. "However innumerable living beings are, I vow to save them."[28] Thus, the work of responsible ST guardianship is proceeding in the clouds as it would on earth.

Identity

There is a need in ST spirituality for identity and authority. After seeing a picture of a stole printed with symbols of the various religions of the world, an urbane taxi driver in Cairo, Mohamed Abd El Daim, asked:

> Is it not confusing? I give you an example. When a man calls and asks me to come in my taxi at two P.M. I say yes, I will come. Then if he calls me later and says, don't come, I don't come because that is the last thing I am told. Why are not your beliefs confused by mixing them all together?[29]

He was, of course, referring to the idea of progressive revelation. It was important that the last revelation took precedence over earlier ones, and that it was authoritative, to be followed.

For Martin Luther, the need for consistent and clear-cut beliefs was intense. The individual and the church needed to be in conformity. In his Short Catechism of 1529, Luther wrote:

> First, the preacher must above all things beware of and avoid the use of various and different texts and forms of the Commandments, Lord's Prayer, Belief, Sacrament, &c.; he must take one form and keep to it, and constantly teach the same, year after year. For the young and simple folk must be taught one definite text and version, else they will easily become confused, if to-day we teach thus and next year thus, as though we wanted to improve it, and so all our labour and toil is lost.[30]

The conflict between church practice and church theology (and, more fundamentally, scripture itself), caused him to nail his Ninety-Five Theses to the door of the Wittenberg Castle Church. And later, appearing before the Diet of Worms, he refused to recant his beliefs:

> [M]y conscience is captive to the Word of God. I cannot and I will not recant anything, for to go against conscience is neither right nor safe. Here I stand. I cannot do otherwise. God help me. Amen.[31]

Often the Journey of Works is accompanied by a dramatic sense of the importance of what holds one's commitment, sometimes of epic or cosmic proportions. There are clouds of glory, power, strength that will prevail to save the world. Perhaps the most striking ST hymn ever penned is "Battle Hymn of the Republic" (1862) by the American reformer Julia Ward Howe:

Mine eyes have seen the glory
　of the coming of the Lord;
He is trampling out the vintage
　where the grapes of wrath are stored;
He hath loosed the fateful lightning
　of his terrible swift sword;
His truth is marching on.[32]

The concluding portion of the Lord's Prayer was very likely an ST-inspired addition: "For thine is the Kingdom, and the Power, and the Glory, for ever and ever."[33]

Work as Life's Aim

People on the Journey of Works will see their work itself as the fulfillment of their spirituality. It is the other side of the coin from the sense of destiny and glory that holds their loyalty in the larger arena of the world. The particular work that they do, from nine to five every day, even mundane and routinized activity, will have an importance for the integrity of the world order. It must be done and often also is their vocation, life dedication, or enduring avocation. Running a household, a farm, or a store every day for sixty years, through the exercise of careful and ceaseless commitment can become holy offices. The most routine task faithfully and thoughtfully executed can be transformed into a holy ritual attuned to the eternal.

Hsün-tzu, in a chapter called "Improving Yourself," emphasized the importance of paying attention to being centered and persistent even in the midst of drudgery. Even going to the market or to the well for water should be entered into without procrastination or discouragement.

> If he keeps putting one foot in front of the other without stopping, even a lame turtle can go a thousand li. . . .
>
> Though the road is short, if you do not step along you will never get to the end; though the task is small, if you do not work at it you will never get it finished.[34]

A woman expressed the same ST wisdom at a Baptist prayer meeting in Farmington, Maine, in the late nineteenth century: "With patience and perseverence any snail can reach Jeruzalem."[35]

Perhaps because, unlike NTs and SFs, STs have their preferred functions, one in each sphere of the neocortex, extra precautions have to be put in place if the judging function is to ride herd on the perceiving function.[36] Therefore, from earliest childhood the pattern needs to be established whereby an ST person will pause after discerning what is, with the Sensing function, to wait for the Thinking function to process perceptions and to render its judgments. This pattern of built-in patience needs to be reinforced and faithfully kept throughout life. "Work before play" is one such pattern, particularly for STPs. Life could become chaotic without the regulation of this and other such understandings. A patient spiritual discipline is a major means for fulfilling the Journey of Works.

Spiritual growth takes place for STs as work gradually becomes a sacred ritual, or if not work, then the routine responsibilities that are seen as the most important appointments of every day. Brother Lawrence (1605–1691), a Carmelite monk in Paris, carried on a dialogue with God through his daily work in a kitchen, in what he called "The Practice of the Presence of God":

> [I]n his business in the kitchen (to which he had naturally a great aversion), having accustomed himself to do everything there for the love of God, and with prayer upon all occasions for His grace to do his work well, he had found every-thing easy during fifteen years that he had been employed there.[37]

Given the ST attention to detail, it is important that the discipline include not only things of major importance but minor works as well.

> That we ought not to be weary of doing little things for the love of God, Who regards not the greatness of the work, but the love with which it is performed. That we should not wonder if in the beginning we often failed in our endeav-ours, but that at last we should gain a habit which will naturally produce its acts in us without our care and to our exceeding great delight.[38]

"The Practice of the Presence of God" was a continual conversation, until the coordination between the self and its work was complete, absorbed in its larger purpose and mission:

> That in the beginning of the spiritual life we ought to be faithful in doing our duty and denying ourselves, but after that unspeakable pleasures followed; that in difficulties we need only have recourse to Jesus Christ and beg His grace, with which everything became easy.[39]

Realism

This same rootedness in the tangible, the task, the reality of supporting and sustaining life, and the spiritual corollary of fealty to the divine or natural world order are seen in the pragmatism so important to STs. Theology and spiritual philosophy must be practical and verifiable in the here-and-now and in experiences from the past.

According to Lin Yutang, in China "one is born a realist." He lists qual-ities of his culture that, while not as aggressive as ST qualities may be in many other places, are nonetheless predominantly ST in orientation:

> If we review the Chinese race and try to picture their national characteristics, we shall probably find the following traits of character: sanity, simplicity, love of

nature, patience, indifference, old roguery, fecundity, industry, frugality, love of family life, pacifism, contentment, humor, conservatism, and sensuality.[40]

Of course, some of these, for example, "love of nature," can be expressed in each of the Four Spiritualities, but in the context of this list it has an ST positioning. To give an example from Chinese music, a recording of ancient Chinese music lists the song titles (in translation):

Four Tokens of Happiness, Spring Thoughts at Han Palace, The Bird's Song, Sound of the Temple, The Great Ambuscade, Yearning on River Shiang, The Flowing Streams, In Remembrance of an Old Friend, and The Elegant Orchid.[41]

The sounds are made to mimic as realistically and directly as possible what is described by the titles. Likewise, when Arthur Waley came to translate the *Confucian Odes*, he arranged them into the following topics:

Courtship, Marriage, Warriors and Battles, Agriculture, Blessings on Gentle Folk, Welcome, Feasting, The Clan Feast, Sacrifice, Music and Dancing, Dynastic Songs, Dynastic Legends, Building, Hunting, Friendship, Moral Pieces, Lamentations.[42]

Confucius saw the *Odes* as "a text-book of personal morality."[43] They depict the spiritual life as very much conducted in the tangible context of everyday forms, hallowed and elevated through tradition and observance.

Perhaps an insight into the linkage of realism and spiritual tradition can be gained from Hsün-tzu's discussion of "Rectifying Names":

When one, on hearing the names, can immediately understand the realities they refer to, then names are fulfilling their practical function. When they are combined to create pleasing forms, then they are fulfilling their esthetic function. He who can use names in such a way that they are both practical and esthetically pleasing may be said to have a real understanding of them.[44]

When you truly say what you mean, the practical is transformed into spiritual understanding.

Administration

In the Journey of Works we see the importance of administration as a way to protect the traditions of a people and, ultimately, to protect the world order. Everything is interrelated; as the rectification of names sorts and clarifies, the ST journey goes on to protect and manage. While all STs have this sense of order and balance maintained through enlightened administrations, for men we discover an archetype of the king or paternal elder here more than for any other type.

Chief Seattle, the leader of the Dwamish and allied tribes of Puget Sound, operated out of this frame in his famous response to the United

States government in 1857. He was presenting the sense of social and natural order from a Paleolithic cultural perspective:

> This we know: the earth does not belong to man, man belongs to the earth. All
> things are connected like the blood that unites us all. Man did not weave the
> web of life, he is merely a strand in it. Whatever he does to the web, he does to
> himself.[45]

This is a profoundly conservative statement of the organic integrity of
humanity and earth. Seattle introduces a very basic ST sense of tragic reality later in his letter. Predicting that White culture will inevitably supplant
his own and feeling justified in his idea of right, he records his hope that
what he believes, what he knows, will, against all observable odds, be
remembered and preserved:

> When the last Red Man has vanished with his wilderness and his memory is
> only the shadow of a cloud moving across the prairie, will these shores and
> forests still be here? Will there be any of the spirit of my people left?[46]

One of the central spiritual leaders at the founding of the United States
was George Washington, surely an STJ. He contributed a sterling character,
a sense of fairness and propriety, and a patient and steady hand on the helm
of the ship of state. In his years as a general, he was not particularly good at
strategy (though the very survival of his army was a major accomplishment);
he lost more battles than he won, but his great strength was the reassuring
quality of his spiritual presence. He accomplished this not by any outward
signs of piety (theologically he was a Deist), but by a kind of nobility of person, a fairness and confidence, communicating that the war and the new
country were a fulfillment of all that was decent and right in civilization. He
lived the liberty of personhood that was the cornerstone of the new democracy. We can see this spiritual presence in his Farewell Address:

> Observe good faith and justice towards all nations; cultivate peace and harmo-
> ny with all. Religion and morality enjoin this conduct; and can it be that good
> policy does not equally enjoin it? It will be worthy of a free, enlightened, and,
> at no distant period, a great nation, to give to mankind the magnanimous and
> too novel example of a people always guided by an exalted justice and benevo-
> lence. Who can doubt that in the course of time and things the fruits of such a
> plan would richly repay our temporary advantages which might be lost by a
> steady adherence to it? Can it be, that Providence has not connected the per-
> manent felicity of a nation with its virtue? The experiment, at least, is recom-
> mended by every sentiment which ennobles human nature.[47]

Washington strongly believed that the moral order in a democratic society
should reflect the general order of nature, and that "nature's God" in some
way intended and effected this coordination of the world order.

The Old Testament hero Gideon, an early judge in Caanan, seems in many ways to be a mirror opposite of Washington, for he excelled in his exploits as a military leader but failed to fulfill his contract with the world order in his efforts as a political leader in the consolidation period after the war. He began with an ST understanding of what the order of things should be, an unequivocal judgment of the right. He provided inspirational leadership (of an ESTP nature) as head of his little army. In staccato fashion he made decisions and deployed his resources to score brilliant victories over the Midianites. But his judgments after victory were harsh, not magnanimous, and in a pragmatic compromise he violated the religious motivations of his work, creating an ephod with the spoils of war.[48] While both Washington and Gideon were men of action, the former (STJ) excelled in administrative leadership and the latter (STP), a local hero, in a subordinate form that implemented incisively the larger order.

In many ways, we are reminded of the king in the literature of the current men's movement. Jungian analyst Robert Moore and mythologist Douglas Gillette discuss the work of psychotherapist John W. Perry in identifying the king as the "central archetype":

> [T]he good King is at the Center of the World. He sits on his throne on the central mountain, or on the Primeval Hill, as the ancient Egyptians called it. And from this central place, all of creation radiates in geometrical form out to the very frontiers of the realm. "World" is defined as that part of reality that is organized and ordered by the King. What is outside the boundaries of his influence is noncreation, chaos, the demonic, and nonworld.[49]

Poet and men's movement leader Robert Bly differentiates three forms for the king: "the upper Sacred King, the middle political king, and the third or inner king." The Sacred King, often represented in the images of Sun (king) and Moon (queen), guarantees the larger world order. The "earthly king" brings the authority of the heavens into the social order. The inner king brings a sense of vocation, "the fire of purpose and passion" in our lives.[50]

There is a spiritual struggle to coordinate these levels: the highest, or the mandate of heaven; the administrative in society; the inner in one's own motives and energy. Mencius, in the context of Chinese humanism, makes an important summary of the process:

> Great Man wishes to attain a firm hold upon right procedure by going deeply into its problems; he desires to attain it as a personal experience, and when that is achieved he feels himself dwelling securely in it. When he has it as a profound resource, he uses it as he comes upon it bubbling up on all sides. That is why Great Man wishes it to be a personal acquisition.[51]

When we have internalized the Way (Bly's sacred and inner kings), then we are ready to proceed to the ordering of the world through enlightened governance.

The strategist and strongest have never been conquerors of men. But if one knows how to support others, the whole world can be subdued. Nobody has ever become real king unless the whole world was submissive to him in its heart-and-mind.[52]

The Roman emperor and Stoic philosopher Marcus Aurelius (121–180 A.D.) meditates at length on the administration of the world in balance and order from his perspective of a concern for our mortality. He is established in his conservative view of a world order (the stars) and an apprenticeship to the best of the past:

In the writings of the Ephesians there was this precept: constantly to think of some one of the men of former times who practiced virtue. The Pythagoreans bid us look to the heavens in the morning that we may be reminded of those bodies which continually do the same things and in the same manner perform their work. . . .[53]

I find Marcus Aurelius and Washington to have remarkably similar spiritual orientations to their work and role in society. All that separates them is 1,600 years. Marcus Aurelius wrote:

Is my understanding sufficient for this or not? If it is sufficient, I use it for the work as an instrument given by the universal nature. But if it is not sufficient, then either I retire from the work and give way to him who is able to do it better, unless there be some reason why I ought not to do so; or I do it as well as I can, taking to help me the man who with the aid of my ruling principle can do what is now fit and useful for the general good. For whatsoever either by myself or with another I can do, ought to be directed to this only—to that which is useful and well suited to society.[54]

It is said that ESTJs will administer all in the world that is theirs to administer. The most enlightened find a spiritual milieu and sensibility grounded in a larger or divine order, a balanced character, a clear sense of right and wrong, and a sense of one's humble place as a person who journeys with discipline and propriety.

The Greek Stoic philosopher Epictetus (55–135 A.D.) reflected on his own approaching death:

What would you wish to be doing when you are found by death? I for my part would wish to be found doing something that belongs to a man, beneficent, suitable to the general interest. If death surprises me when I am busy about these things, it is good enough for me if I can stretch out my hands and say: the means which I have received for helping the world I have not neglected; I have not dishonored the world with my acts. That I have been given life, I am thankful. If I have used well the powers which are mine, I am content and give them back to the great life from which I came.[55]

Justification

Of course, not all STs find themselves in fortuitous circumstances when they reflect on the meaning of their life in the face of death. There is a strong tragic sense to be found in ST spirituality. The legendary Old Testament character Job presents us with a picture of a righteous man, grounded in the practical realities of prosperous herding and householding, who by all signs has pursued an exemplary Journey of Works, confronting a complete reversal of fortune into humiliation and poverty. His new condition flies in the face of the Deuteronomic assumption that the righteous will prosper and the evil will suffer misfortune.

Job's first reaction is to assume the attitude of patience. Surely, he will be justified if he waits for things to come around. He does not question the sovereignty of God, even though he does not perceive the logic of events. "Naked I came from my mother's womb, and naked shall I return; the Lord gave, and the Lord has taken away; blessed be the name of the Lord."[56]

His nonplussed sense of justification, and his confidence in patience and perseverance, are a steadfast ST reaction to times of trouble.

Job has no illusions about the constraints of the life cycle:

> Man that is born of a woman
> is of few days, and full of trouble.
> He comes forth like a flower, and withers;
> he flees like a shadow, and continues not.
>
> For there is hope for a tree,
> if it be cut down that it will sprout again,
> and that its shoots will not cease. . . .
> But man dies, and is laid low;
> man breathes his last, and where is he?
>
> But the mountain falls and crumbles away,
> and the rock is removed from its place;
> the waters wear away the stones;
> the torrents wash away the soil of the earth;
> so thou destroyest the hope of man.[57]

In the most Sensing-connected language, the author of Job fills in the parameters of the human condition.

Later, Job bargains, presenting arguments as if he were pleading his case in a court of law. He speaks of his ethical standards and conduct, obeying the covenant between God and his people and offering fourteen examples of his faithful keeping of the law:

> If I have walked with falsehood, and my foot has hastened to deceit; Let me be weighed in a just balance, and let God know my integrity! If my step has turned aside from the way, and my heart has gone after my eyes, and if any spot has

cleaved to my hands then let me sow, and another eat; and let what grows for me be rooted out.[58]

He argues here for fairness. After all, he has lost all respectability in the eyes of society and his tormentors. Only the fairness of God can now balance the scales of justice for his life. His condition is tragic and hopeless, but he retains an inner dignity and nobility.

The Book of Job ends without a resolution of his tragic condition. However, a later editor, who must have been a less patient ST than the hero of this poem, added a new epilogue with a happy ending: "And the Lord restored the fortunes of Job."[59] This addition reverts back to the Deuteronmic expectation, an example of the need of many STs for everything to come out as it should, a literal view of a moral order that rewards and punishes sooner or later in all cases. Most of the world's fundamentalisms derive from this literalism and legalism in religion. It may be that fundamentalism is a refusal to accommodate the reality of human tragedy.

An exception is Eastern Orthodoxy, which combines both. The Byzantine Christ, as portrayed in countless mosaics in Orthodox churches, is both a regal and a tragic image. With this is a thoroughgoing authoritarianism, which begins with the premise "Outside the church, even in the so-called 'christian' heresies, the inability of finding the whole Christ excludes the possibility of salvation."[60] The canonical concern with doctrinal boundaries between orthodoxy and heresy is combined with a deep and tragic spirituality.

In the ancient Byzantine images one can even detect a world-weariness, a sense that reality does not adhere to a progress in the world, that life goes ahead here but goes backward there. One must search for an alternative spiritual reality.

Charles Dickens wrote in A *Tale of Two Cities* (1859),

> It was the best of times, it was the worst of times, it was the age of wisdom, it was the age of foolishness, it was the epoch of belief, it was the epoch of incredulity, it was the season of Light, it was the season of Darkness, it was the spring of hope, it was the winter of despair. . . .

If we can be in touch with the tragic, we are likely to remain honest with ourselves. Tragedy never allows us to forget that there is always energy in the world to wear down and oppose our actions. If we push too far, the opposite will come in front of us and beside us and behind us and cut off our retreat back to our true center of humanity. The dust of the ground can swallow up our recklessness. Therefore, if we are going to defend the true order, if the traditions are to be available in the world, if our work is to bear fruit and we are going to leave our mark for good, all our actions must count. We must be constant and faithful to the end, deferring reward for our efforts.

A most powerful affirmation of this larger vision of the tragic bargain is found in the Book of Isaiah. The author explores the role of the suffering servant, who succumbs to the forces of the world, but, in dying, bequeaths to the future the testimony and healing of his or her life.

> [H]e was wounded for our transgressions,
>   he was bruised for our iniquities;
> upon him was the chastisement that made us whole
>   and with his stripes we are healed.[61]

And again:

> [A] bruised reed he will not break,
>   and a dimly burning wick he will not quench;
> I have given you as a covenant to the people,
>   a light to the nations,
>   to open the eyes that are blind,
> to bring out the prisoners from the dungeon,
>   from the prison those who sit in darkness.[62]

In the tragic bargain with life, what Isaiah calls our covenant, we may well be done in by the forces and circumstances of the world situation, but in our faithfulness to life itself, in the assertion of our lives, well lived, we place our hope in the posterity of humanity. Somewhere, sometime our faithful example, so far as we could live it, will take hold, grow, and prosper in other lives. Here we see placed in an ST context of covenant a positive manifestation of the inferior function, particularly for dominant Thinkers, which carries powerful meaning not only for STs open to their opposite preferences but also to SFs, who may acknowledge the importance of the structure and guidance of covenant.

The tragic sense in the Journey of Works always carries in it a sense of justification as well. The struggle, the challenge, the perseverance have an intrinsic worth and social benefit. Marcus Aurelius summarizes:

> Try how the life of the good man suits you, the life of him who is satisfied with his portion out of the whole, and satisfied with his own just acts and benevolent disposition.[63]

And the tragic consciousness in the Journey of Works coordinates with the west on the compass, with autumn, with the maturing of life into elderhood. In the words of Lin Yutang:

> I like spring, but it is too young. I like summer, but it is too proud. So I like best of all autumn, because its leaves are a little yellow, its tone mellower, its colors richer, and it is tinged a little with sorrow and a premonition of death. Its golden richness speaks not of the innocence of spring, nor of the power of summer, but of the mellowness and kindly wisdom of approaching age. It knows the limitations of life and is content.[64]

ᏸ KARMA YOGA

Karma yoga is disinterested action. To live is to act. We must act.

> For no one ever, even for a moment,
> remains without doing action;
> everyone is made to do action,
> through the constituents of Nature.[65]

But we are attached to the consequences of our action. We wish pleasure or gain (kama). If we fail, we become angry or plan new strategies of action. This continues our bondage (pravrithi) and impedes our progress to attain inner peace of mind (nivrithi).

Karma yoga is closely related to the concept of karma, the law of cause and effect whereby good deeds have good consequences and evil deeds have evil consequences. To make a cosmic law tangible by analogy, James McCartney points out that the situation of the Kurus and the Pandus behind the battleground setting of the Bhagavad Gita set in motion a situation where a certain inevitability of the conflict of good and evil was in place. There is no choice but to face up to the intrinsic tragedy of the situation and to move through it if there was to be any solution or peace of mind for Arjuna.[66]

To embark on the path of karma yoga is to act according to one's responsibilities but without being attached to any consequences redounding to one's self-interest. If we have performed the right action for us to do, that is all that matters, not whether we have succeeded or failed in the attempt. It is important that we do our duty, not someone else's:

> Better a man's own duty, though ill-done,
> than another's duty well-performed;
> better it is to die in one's own duty—
> another's duty is fraught with dread.[67]

Action must be undertaken as a sacrifice, yajna, our work dedicated to God, the equivalent of prayer. One of the best-known historical figures to be primarily a follower of karma yoga, Gandhi, said "work is worship." He believed yajna is a quality as old as humankind, connecting us with the gods and the gods with us in the mutual maintenance of the world order. Freedom consists of acting responsibly, and in that acting attaining freedom of the mind, all in a context of spiritual law, the order of nature and human nature, and the reality behind them. Sacrifice, yajna, guides us to know appropriate action in any given age. For example, Gandhi advocated "the yajna of spinning" in a time of British colonial imperialism in India.[68]

Karma yoga is the pathway taken by countless householders and merchants. It involves participation in economic life and in the networks of relationship that maintain families and communities. To amass wealth in a selfless manner requires great discipline. Gandhi reports how he began to study the spiritual classics after years of activism as a lawyer for Indians in South Africa. It was a turning point from his legal career to his eventual role as the Mahatma of Indian independence:

> I understood the Gita teaching of non-possession to mean that those who desired salvation should act like the trustee who, though having control over great possessions, regards not an iota of them as his own.[69]

Disinterested action, unencumbered by distracting attachments, can take on the qualities of stewardship of earth and life. In the words of Acharya Vinoba Bhave, a disciple of Gandhi, "The river takes no rest, the wind knows no fatigue, and the sun can only shine and shine for ever. The disinterested doer, too, cannot but render unremitting service."[70]

The stewardship theme is closely related to the responsibility to maintain the world order through one's actions. Krishna speaks in the Bhagavad Gita:

> These worlds would perish
> if I do not perform action
> and I will be the cause of chaos (or confusion)
> and destruction of all these people.[71]

The follower of karma yoga must take the initiative to be sure that order is preserved through the example of his or her own behavior:

> For whatever a great man does,
> others follow him.
> Whatever standard he sets up,
> mankind (or the world) follows the same.[72]

If we and others follow the standard, the world will head in the right direction. At some point unknown to us, defeat is turned around into a general tendency toward the just society. Even if we do not foresee this result and all may even look bleak, we must behave rightly to make it possible. There is a kind of sober hopefulness in this position, but it should be pursued even in a pessimistic age.

Work in itself can be a means of self-transcendence. Gandhi said that according to the Bhagavad Gita, " 'This world suffers bondage from work unless it is work done as yajna'; . . . In other words, any work dedicated to God helps one to attain moksha."[73]

In some ways, karma is the hardest road to pursue, for while you are aware of the goal (moksha), you are also making a difference in the practical world, earning a living for yourself and family, accumulating wealth, gaining recognition and career success, all the while trying not to be tempted to put these considerations before the disinterested sacrifice that is karma yoga. For this reason it is seldom proposed as superior in comparison to alternative yogas. However, its importance in the whole picture of society cannot be questioned, as amply demonstrated in the life of Gandhi and in its central role in the *Bhagavad Gita* itself.

ᑲ MENTORS FOR THIS WAY

Two major founders are singled out as mentors for this Journey representing approximately 38 percent of humanity. Moses can be credited with founding what came to be known as Judaism and profoundly influenced later Christianity and Islam. Confucius stands as the pillar at the center of Chinese religion. All future religious developments in China have been presented with reference to his contribution.

Moses

The earliest of the mentors we look to in the Four Spiritualities is Moses, who in all likelihood lived sometime before 1200 B.C. We can piece together a rather balanced picture of him, even though legend, myth, and symbolism are the medium of the traditions surrounding him.

It is thought he was born among the Ibri, or Hebrews, sojourning in Egypt but was raised in the family of the pharaoh's daughter. His name is Egyptian, Mose, meaning "a child," or "Aton-mose," meaning "child of Aton,"[74] and not meaning "drawn out of the water" as claimed in Exodus. Raised quietly in the royal family, he seems to have kept a consciousness of his connection with his captive people. Seeing an Egyptian overseer beating one of the Hebrews, Moses flew into a rage and killed him,[75] a rather dramatic beginning for a spiritual journey, to the land of Midian, to prepare for an epochal mission.

Professor of Hebrew Robert Pfeiffer summarizes the overall accomplishments of this founder of Judaism:

> Moses was unquestionably a great personality, a genius, one of the outstanding leaders in human history. His people were a group of uncultured tribes enslaved by cruel masters; he organized them in revolt; despite their complaints he led them to Kadesh to precarious freedom, and thereafter with fine sagacity, playing upon their weaknesses and strengthening their strength, he instilled in them an undying religious loyalty and national consciousness fit to survive all hostility and persecution.[76]

Almost to the last detail, Moses appears to be in the mainstream of ST spirituality, even ESTJ. Fleming James summarizes the sequence of events that point to Moses' Journey of Works:

[O]nly in the concrete details of the traditions do we find a living Moses. Unless we can have a Moses who smites the Egyptian, succours the daughters of Jethro at the well, argues with God against the commission thrust upon him, strides in before Pharaoh with his demand, speaks assurance to the people at the Red Sea, converses with Jethro, sits all day judging litigants, ascends Sinai to meet God, dashes in pieces the tablets of stone, grinds the golden calf to powder and administers food and water for them, enjoins a perpetual holy war against Amalek, blazes out again and again at rebellion, and the like, we have not after all a Moses of flesh and blood, however nobly and admiringly he may be described.[77]

It is thought only a minority of the eventual twelve tribes of Israel were part of the horde that was the Exodus from Egypt. But the mark left by the leadership of Moses on the population that wandered for forty years east of the Red Sea became the shared story and reality of a whole people and of later Judaism. Dramatic though the escape from Egypt was, the central accomplishment of Moses was the weaving together of the disparate elements of the wanderers into a shared polity under a shared deity. Imagine the first moments of freedom on the east banks of the Red Sea. What now? And very soon, Who are we, that we should stay together and have a common leader? The issue was the shape of the new freedom, how to respond to this new condition — that is, identity, that core consideration in ST spirituality. The leadership task of Moses is summarized by Buber:

A wandering into the unknown had begun under the most difficult external circumstances. Before that wandering could be given a destination it was necessary to shape, no matter in how raw and clumsy a fashion, a folk-character that would have the capacity, as a homogeneous being, to follow a road to a destination. This, in turn, indispensably required the proclamation of a basic constitution founded on the principles of unlimited rule of the one God, equable duration of Israel throughout the changes of years and generations. . . .[78]

At several junctures there were murmurings among the people, leading even to open rebellion such as occurred with the golden calf. Had Moses elevated himself into a position of ultimate dominion, he would not have founded an enduring people. But he always deferred to the authority and power of YHWH and thus elevated the focus of identity to permanent rather than transient authority.

"Hear, O Israel: The Lord our God is one Lord; and you shall love the Lord your God with all your heart, and with all your soul, and with all your might."[79]

These words of Jewish prayer, the Shema, are followed by a clear awareness and exhortation that in theology, cultic practice, and law, this is the central identity of a whole people. Keep telling the story of your liberation and struggles up through to your coherence as a religious people.[80] This imperative survives in the Seder Haggadah ritual: "He brought us out of Egypt, sustained us in the desert for forty years. . . ."[81]

Moses was thus able to give his followers reassurance in a very elementary way, based on his own need for clear authority. According to the Exodus story, in response to the question "Is the Lord among us or not?" Moses went to God himself and came back with the miracle of striking a rock with his rod to produce water to relieve their thirst in the desert. The Moses-God relationship was not vague and abstract, but "face to face." Later, when Moses would enter the "tent of meeting," the people could see the "pillar of cloud" of God's presence.[82] There is always a Sensing presence for authority and a routine Thinking determination to defer to a divine order and power.

> The stern and deep realism of Moses, which could not bear that a sacred symbolism should replace or supplant the factual realization of his faith, determines the type, the order of the power. Power lies in the hands of the "charismatic" leader who is led by God.[83]

Moses' vision was not Intuitive but Sensing. In a famous encounter with Miriam and Aaron, he is contrasted with mere prophets to whom God speaks in dreams and visions. With Moses it is "mouth to mouth."[84]

Moses excelled in defining boundaries, focusing with definition on what is right and what is wrong. In the central story of the accommodation of Aaron and others to the people's need for tangible divinities, and the building of the golden calf, Aaron felt ambiguities in the situation and felt that accommodation to residual popular beliefs was a wise course. Moses was thoroughgoing in his hardheaded determination of what was unacceptable. It came down to, "Who is on the Lord's side?" Three thousand people lost their lives in the retribution that followed, perhaps the dark side of hardheaded decisiveness. Later, in his followers' conquest of peoples in Canaan, Moses warned of accommodating "idolatry" and made it incumbent upon them to smash the idols of the local cultic practice.[85]

The Deuteronomic Code warns of prophets and dreamers who will ask you to "go after other gods." The concept "God is testing you"[86] is proposed as the cosmic context for right or wrong behavior. Buber points out the collective nature of personal ethics: We are not isolated individuals but part of a whole, testing out that integrity in our actions.

> [T]he Bible does not concern itself with character, nor with individuality. . . . The Bible depicts something else, namely, persons in situations. The Bible is not concerned with the difference between these persons; but the difference between the situations in which the person, the creaturely person, the appointed person, stands his test or fails, is all important to it.[87]

The context of behavior as well as identity is the covenant between God and the people. This notion of the covenant has been central in Judaism and in Western history, in such instruments as the Constitution and Bill of Rights of the United States. It may well have been forged near Sinai (or Horeb) in the desert journey with Moses.

> [I]f you will obey my voice and keep my covenant, you shall be my own possession among all peoples; for all the earth is mine, and you shall be to me a kingdom of priests and a holy nation.[88]

The covenant, borne as it were "on eagles' wings," is a larger concept than the law, for example the Ten Commandments, which are revealed to Moses shortly afterward in the Exodus story. The law administers the larger intentions of the covenant. Only God knows "the secret things," the deeper spirit of the covenant, but the people do have "the words of this law."[89]

Moses not only formed a people around this covenant, he also gives us a classic study of ecclesiastical administration. Followers of the Journey of Works are the proprietors of the world's temples. As the center of the life of the Hebrew sojourners coalesced, the stones of the Ten Commandments were placed in a tabernacle, and a tent of meeting was set up in which all disputes and transgressions as well as administrative needs could be adjudicated. Sometimes Moses would be in there alone, communing with God. For example, he showed a great ST evenhandedness in his intercession with God during one of the periods of rebelliousness by the people. He calmed the anger of God with logic based in the solid realities of what neighboring peoples would think of God's reputation.[90]

But the tent of meeting was generally a busy place at the center of the community. Moses faced burnout, for he was the focus for everything. Here his father-in-law, Jethro, the Midianite priest, who may earlier have given him his theological insights, now mentored him in the administration of canon law: "What you are doing is not good. You and the people with you will wear yourselves out, for the thing is too heavy for you; you are not able to perform it alone."[91]

Moses appointed a hierarchy of perhaps seventy judges, who in turn administered the law for subdivisions of the people, and the system built in a continuity of experience and authority that would endure long after their leader's tenure.

When Moses reached the Jordan River after a lifetime of devoted service to his people, he ascended Mount Nebo to talk with YHWH. There Moses learned his own individual fate, that he would not live to enter the promised land of his vision. "I will give it to your descendants. I have let you see it with your eyes, but you shall not go over there."[92]

Nevertheless, Moses felt hope in his heart that his work would come to fruition—not for him, the founder and steward, but for the life that was to follow him. His parting words to his people were central for his lifetime in the Journey of Works:

> I have set before you this day life and good, death and evil. If you obey the commandments of the Lord your God which I command you this day, by loving the Lord your God, by walking in his ways, and by keeping his commandments and his statutes and his ordinances, then you shall live. . . . I have set before you life and death, blessing and curse; therefore choose life, that you and your descendants may live.[93]

Confucius

No ST spiritual tradition has been established longer in one place and for so many people than Confucianism. K'ung Ch'iu (Confucius) lived from 551 to 479 B.C. He was born in the state of Lu in the Chou period. It was a painful time, with frequent wars and intrigues among the states into which China had divided. Local rulers and feudal lords were often brutish, lacking in depth of cultural qualities, exploitive through taxes and conscription, and either oppressive over their people or too timid to initiate reforms.

In a time of trouble, how does one seek to stabilize the world, establish ethics, produce a social milieu that is fair, equitable, and righteous for the well-being of all? What is the right path and how can it be proposed and come to prevail in a chaotic world?

"The Master said, Only when the year grows cold do we see that the pine and cypress are the last to fade."[94] As this proverb implies, while Confucius aspired to a significant ministry in government he never served in more than a minor capacity. He spent a lifetime in the courts of princes, trying to institute his reforms. Several rulers liked him and respected his views but did not dare to implement them. Late in life he left his homeland and wandered from state to state for seventeen years, but no one would appoint him to be his chief adviser.

While outwardly Confucius might be judged a failure, it is in his alternative activities as teacher and scholar that he prevailed. Collecting about seventy disciples around him, he taught his principles. In the course of a lifetime he took the oldest documents of the culture, what came to be known as the Confucian Classics, and recomposed them into a coherent system for the conduct of life. Like reformers everywhere, he knew the strongest appeal in a time of trouble would be to traditional values, as they were chosen and defined for presentation. Through his disciples, his teachings guided society pretty much for the next 2,500 years. His own story gradually assumed legendary and sagelike qualities beyond his own self-image of being a learner, a listener, and seer. He was down-to earth, living in the here-and-now. As one scholar put it, "Confucius' genuineness as a person is a source of inspiration to those who share his humanist wisdom not because of his abstract idealism but because of its concrete practicality."[95]

It is from this orientation that it is thought Confucius invented the term *tao*, the way, to indicate a social path, the right way of life in a cooperative society. In the largest sense, tao represents a cosmic order and power (te) around a society where right behaviors (yi) are normative and fit into their proper places in the whole. Confucius taught his disciples that tao is the right way to go, the ideal way, the only way open if all is going well. If you have wandered from the way, you are lost (yu), falling aside from goodness, human-heartedness (jen).

While little is known of the details of Confucius' life, it is significant that he was born of relatively humble parentage, for it gave rise to his belief that an aristocracy should be natural and not inherited. The other cornerstone of his social ethic, that the well-being and consent of the common people constitute the legitimacy of a government, was reinforced in the people's awareness that he was one of them. You will know that tao is being followed, that government keeps its mandate of heaven, when nature, society, families, and the individual operate cooperatively in their own spheres (yi) and goodness (jen); and right procedure, ritual, or manners (li) prevail.

Reform of society works from the bottom up, in democratic attitudes, looking at all levels of relationships. We should model in our own behavior what we expect of the world. Parents and children, brother and brother, sister and sister, emperor and people, state and nature, all are in relationship, and it is in the interests of all that each will prosper and enjoy happiness. Confucius very carefully defined the qualities of each kind of relationship and provided the tools for decision making in the many kinds of situations in which we might find ourselves. The goal is bringing out the natural human nobility in balanced, well-modulated, appropriate behavior, becoming a gentleman (chün-tzu).

> He said to Tze-Ch'an: there are four components in a proper man's doing: He is reverent in his personal conduct, scrupulously honourable in serving his prince, considerate in provisioning the people, and just in employing them.[96]

How do you know you are behaving ethically? The translator Arthur Waley claimed that in the West we tend to instill ethical principles into young children until they are internalized largely at an unconscious level: This is right; that is wrong. In traditional China, on the other hand, a young child is taught a number of considerations, none of which is absolute. You have to reason out what is appropriate, operable, and right in any specific situation. The ethical process remains conscious. There are gradations of response—from vague and sublime to highly formal and ritualized—and you have to determine what is appropriate.[97] This is what Confucians have long called the rectification of names.

Zilu said: "If the Lord of Wei were waiting for you to run the government, what would you give priority to?" The Master said: "What is necessary is to rectify names. . . ."[98]

Every name implies certain social duties. There should be common understandings to foster trust and predictability in the many levels of social behavior. The ruler should behave in the "way of the ruler," the minister as a minister, father as father.[99]

Herbert Fingarette emphasizes that Confucius differed from Western perspectives in that choice and self-responsibility do not come into play, while self-rededication is seen as the process whereby a person finds himself wanting and seeks to improve. To learn the more appropriate behavior is the task, not to invent a new pathway to travel. The journey of life is not a matter of choosing which way to go but rather is a refining of the life path one is on, that path shared by all others around us in all levels of the society. It is a powerfully Sensing, here-and-now orientation, showing little of the Intui-tive orientation toward future alternatives and possibilities. Fingarette writes:

> Man is not an ultimately autonomous being who has an inner and decisive power, intrinsic to him, a power to select among real alternatives and thereby to shape a life for himself. Instead he is born as "raw material" who must be civilized by education and thus become a truly human man. To do this he must aim at the Way, and the Way must—through its nobility and the nobility of those who pursue it—attract him. This outcome is not conceived as one that enhances a personal power as over against society or the physical environment, but rather as one that sharpens and steadies a person's "aim" or orientation to the point where he can undeviatingly walk the one true Way: he is a civilized human being. Walking the Way incarnates in him the vast spiritual dignity and power that reside in the Way.[100]

A person asks, "Am I worthy of the role I am playing in this situation? Have I prepared myself fully? Am I modeling only excellent behavior as befits me as father or teacher or ruler or business partner? And what about the other person before me? Is he living in keeping with his role or position? What specifically is the substance of his relation to me?" Confucius placed much of his attention on the reciprocity of relationships.

> Jan Jung asked about [ruling by goodness, not by force]. The Master said, Behave when away from home as though you were in the presence of an important guest. Deal with the common people as though you were officiating at an important sacrifice. Do not do to others what you would not like yourself.[101]

This view of reciprocity is often called the negative golden rule, but it is far more sophisticated than not acting. Stated in the positive, the striving for goodness (jen) can be something like this:

> As for Goodness—you yourself desire rank and standing; then help others to get rank and standing. You want to turn your own merits to account; then help others to turn theirs to account—in fact, the ability to take one's own feelings as a guide—that is the sort of thing that lies in the direction of Goodness.[102]

Confucius was no romantic. In his practical ST vision, love does not conquer all, but rather a pattern of years of kindnesses, consideration, helpfulness, honoring the integrity of the other, giving and taking measures of filial piety or neighborliness, carrying your share in a predictable and trustworthy way, settling all accounts with one another every New Year—these sorts of patterns will build relationships, build the family and village, and order the nation and world.

It is thought Confucius began modestly and that his development at some point became collaborative with the disciples who had attached themselves to him. He may well be a case study for good ST type development, for he begins with the most tangible tasks of ritual and music, moves further to elaboration of an ethical system, and finally explores such abstract and hard-to-pin-down concepts as jen, which he never clearly defines but which becomes central to his system. When he moves into the realm of human-heartedness and social harmony, it is clear he has engaged the polarity of NF influences. The range from li to yi to jen is remarkable, and yet it is the gracefulness from mastery of ritual and music that frees him to grow further to complete the loop of balance.

> The Master said, At fifteen I set my heart upon learning. At thirty, I had planted my feet firm upon the ground. At forty, I no longer suffered from perplexities. At fifty, I knew what were the biddings of Heaven. At sixty, I heard them with docile ear. At seventy, I could follow the dictates of my own heart; for what I desired no longer overstepped the boundaries of right.[103]

While at seventy, his behavior was accurate and appropriate, truly jen, Confucius nevertheless never lost track of his Sensing base and his grounding in li.

> There are nine things of which Great Man must be mindful: to see when he looks, to hear when he listens, to have a facial expression of gentleness, to have an attitude of humility, to be loyal in speech, to be respectful in service, to inquire when in doubt, to think of the difficulties when angry, to think of justice when he sees an advantage.[104]

Li as a principle extends back before historical time as traditions of sacred rituals. The famed Shang bronze sacrificial vessels indicate the age of these traditions. The pictograph for li is of a sacrificial vessel.[105] Li extends from sacred origins into the many activities of daily life where ceremonial propriety and rules of conduct may take on a sacred legitimacy far beyond their original intent. To understand the profound ST basis of Confucian spirituality, you must see how Confucius began and based his entire project on li, bringing in this multitude of tangible actions as the foundation for everything else in his vision of humans as ceremonial beings.

Li became the great civilizing force, the expression in any situation of what was fitting, socially acceptable, harmonious, poised, dignified, aesthetically beautiful. Li is the right thing to do, duties, responsibilities, in overt behavior. In li we are able to discipline and express emotion. It consists of communal forms, expressions of the ideal human nature, learned as norms of behavior and perfected into grace and elegance.

> He looks like something cut out, then filed;
> like something carved, then polished.[106]

Li is a road map for the right journey, in a uniquely ST understanding, a series of step-by-step procedures where you journey because this is the way. We come into our humanity in the imagery of li, in community, our contribution animating the ancient traditions.[107] Li is more than the bare acts of propriety; it is the whole bearing of a person: "The Master said, Ritual, ritual! Does it mean no more than presents of jade and silk? Music, music! Does it mean no more than bells and drums?"[108]

Fingarette points out that music is closely analogous to what is meant by li, for there are various perspectives brought to the same acts: the composer's, the context of the performance, the style, and the person's own rendition, inspired or dull and unperceptive. Mastery in a personal way appropriate to the music and context is li.[109] Music and ritual are a continuum at the root of Confucian ethics.

> When he was in Ch'i the Master heard the Succession, and for three months did not know the taste of meat. He said, I did not picture to myself that any music existed which could reach such perfection as this.[110]

In this particular ST perspective, the nature of humanity does not distinguish an individual as independent and against society. The individual is a portion of the whole, more closely attuning his or her participation as a flute player would give a particular and inspired performance as a part of the spiritual whole that is the orchestra. This image of participation is close to what is meant by a second concept, yi, often translated as righteousness, meaning, or the "oughtness" of a situation.[111] For Confucius, it had a more personal and aesthetic connotation:

> The artist does not have a created product in mind, nor is he usually at his creative best when acting in accordance with a plan. What has normative force for the artist is precisely that which achieves articulated presence at the culmination of aesthetic experience.[112]

Thus, Hall and Ames translate yi as signification, working both toward the wider social norms of li and the authoritative personal qualities of jen:

> [H]is personal yi is the capacity to adapt the tradition to his novel circumstances and intentions, and to recover these formal structures as an apparatus for developing and disclosing his own significance.[113]

Well schooled in propriety and tradition, a person can exercise considerable refinement and creative influence on developing tradition as it lives in one's generation.

In a sense, learning li is like a young child learning language. It is highly tangible and specific, and yet the child learns it as a whole in all its integrity and integration (jen), moving from the whole to a perfection of the parts (li). As the young person matures, yi comes into play as the particular stamp of appropriate participation of the person becomes a part of the whole situation of expression.

Only an ST of remarkably integrated type development—a great sage—could have established jen in all its vagueness as the norm of ethics. It is variously translated as human-heartedness, benevolence, altruism, co-humanity, reciprocal good faith, and true knight of the way. Often its component parts are seen as chung and shu. Chung is conscientiousness to others,[114] doing one's best, reverence, having integrity, or giving of oneself fully to the task at hand.[115] It is "to be true to the principles of our nature and the benevolent exercise of them to others."[116] Shu, on the other hand, means altruism, reciprocity, consideration, or evoking analogy within the field of the relationship constituted by self and other.[117]

> The Master said, 'Ts'an! There is one single thread binding my way together.' Tseng Tzu assented. . . . The way of the Master consists in doing one's best and in using oneself as a measure to gauge others. That is all.[118]

This verse includes both words, chung and shu, which Ezra Pound translates in an insightful way: ". . . the big man's way consists in sincerity and sympathy, and that's all."[119]

Jen is integrity, profoundly centered in the person, and radiating with authority in a benevolent sphere in the context of society. When the ruler has jen, others will seek to respond in jen. Jen and li mutually reinforce each other, and an understanding of one is essential to an understanding of the other. Li consists in the qualities of what you do, and jen in the qualities of what you are. "Jen just *is* the perfect giving of oneself to the *human* way."[120]

Herrlee Creel believes that if Confucius had not embarked on his seventeen-year journey, he would have been remembered as China's first teacher, a preacher, but not as a great prophet as well.[121] In typical ST fashion, Confucius was able to feel justified in what he was doing even though it was not universally appreciated:

Tseng Ts'an said, "The gentleman must be brave and courageous, for his burden is heavy and his road long. Manhood-at-its-best is his personal burden, and how heavy it is! After death it is over, but how far off that is!"[122]

On his journey, Confucius appeared before the rulers of the various warring states of the late Chou dynasty, presenting his ideas. The rulers received them politely, but none dared to implement them, even when they secretly admired them. The prince of Confucius' home state of Lu sent his two sons to him to be schooled in the traditions of music and ritual—an example of the wide respect accorded him. There was a tacit understanding, dating from early Chou times and accentuated by Confucius, that the purpose of government and leadership is stewardship, an ST enterprise of trust, with all levels of society and nature in an ecologic collaboration.[123]

Charles Merriam identifies five essential elements of democracy: (1) belief in the dignity of humanity, (2) an inherent drive toward human perfectibility, (3) the sharing and diffusion of material and cultural gains widely and promptly throughout the population, (4) popular decision making for social policy and direction, and (5) confidence in the possibility of conscious social change through a process of consent of the people, not violence.[124] Confucius' proposals embrace all these elements except the fourth; however, his view of rule by a natural, not an inherited, aristocracy, and his invention of the idea of a universal examination system go far toward meeting that goal. Creel attributes the survival of this base of democratic attitudes to Confucian independence towards any "particular metaphysical theories," "lack of absolutism" and closeness "to simple human needs and human sympathies."[125]

Confucius was not deified by his followers for more than 2,500 years. His temple in Ch'u-fu consists of ten buildings set in the landscape of trees and stones where he taught, remarkable for its simplicity and grace blending with the natural elements.[126] At his death he gazed at T'ai Shan mountain and quietly said:

The Sacred Mountain is falling,
The beam is breaking,
The wise man is withering away.[127]

⑥ UNDER STRESS, NEW LEARNINGS

"Life is real! Life is earnest!" is a refrain often heard by STJs; "Get real" by STPs. STs direct clear attention to the task to be done or the problem to be solved and show impatience with extraneous ruminations. While STs will remember hurts and loves that affected their own lives, it is more difficult for them to wait for all the value considerations to percolate up in a situation that demands, for the ST, direct action and completion. At the point of most stress, there is a too-often neglected opportunity to connect with the opposite polarities, Intuition and Feeling.

For some STs, the pull of the NF possibilities and feelings orientation takes on a fearsome fascination, particularly at midlife. There is a general sense that in the thoroughgoing tough-minded realist approach, something of value to others has been missing and that life will not come into balance without it. It is important that STs find techniques for loosening up, backing off, giving space for entering into and nurturing the neglected NF side of their personality. Living with the ensuing clumsiness, and integrating this balance in a congruent way with the native ST orientation, is particularly challenging for many STs.

As STs are often the proprietors of the temple, caring for the institutions of religion, it is important for them to take time to honor the larger purposes and not to micromanage. It is also important to make spaces for the deeper channels of spiritual experience without the press of practical considerations. It is wise at least to help sponsor going beyond definitions and beliefs to mystic visions and inspiration, loving sacrifice and service.

STs need to welcome those moments when stress is high as a time of opportunity, in an otherwise product orientation, to look at ends versus means, at process. For ESTJs: Look at IF. What do you value? For ISTPs: Look at EF, valuing relationships. For ESTPs: Look at IN, your inner possibilities and inspirations. For ISTJs: Look at EN, new options for life, giving up some control to groups and others in your life. Trust the E attitude as you go.

⟳ EDUCATION FOR THIS WAY

A paragraph introducing education in the preceding two chapters bears repeating here. Preparation for all four journeys begins at the earliest age. The most essential elements of spiritual "In Forming" take place before age six or seven, when the functions are relatively undifferentiated. Charles M. Fair calls this "the seeding of young minds . . . to become what we regard as fully human." In his view, it is the function of the neocortex to organize the energies of the more elemental parts of the brain, the emergency and emotional aspects (the id, in Freudian terms) into a rational control. The seminal traditional ideas of the culture must be planted early, to remain beneath the surface of the soil until the sunlight and nurture of various developmental triggers can call them up from memory and enlist them in the formation of character, mind, and spirituality. Fair sees this process as the essential explanation for the rise and fall of cultures. In times of trouble the seeding process has not taken place. The basic ideas of what it is to be human are learned from story, from examples of people around the child, and from sincerely related precept. The child's mind must be impressed by the drama, genuineness, and honesty of input so that the memory remains until it can be utilized developmentally.

In classical ST Confucianism, the process of building on these seeds of the soul is carefully planned in a contextual way:

> The gentleman knows that what lacks completeness and purity does not deserve to be called beautiful. Therefore he reads and listens to explanations in order to penetrate the Way, ponders in order to understand it, associates with men who embody it in order to make it part of himself, and shuns those who impede it in order to sustain and nourish it. He trains his eyes so that they desire only to see what is right, his ears so that they desire to hear only what is right, his mind so that it desires to think only what is right. When he has truly learned to love what is right, his eyes will take greater pleasure in it than in the five colors; his ears will take greater pleasure than in the five sounds; his mouth will take greater pleasure than in the five flavors; and his mind will feel keener delight than in the possession of the world. When he has reached this stage, he cannot be subverted by power or the love of profit; he cannot be swayed by the masses; he cannot be moved by the world. He follows this one thing in life; he follows it in death. This is what is called constancy of virtue.[128]

It is critical that basic guidelines of right and wrong be inculcated in early childhood in a way very similar to what is recommended for SFs: in sayings, proverbs, story, drama, and tangible situations. For STs, stories should have clear heroes and villains, with good triumphing over evil. In the words of one ST, "I am not sentimental. The hero needs to be perfect." The ambiguities of life should be presented after the parameters of right and wrong and the standards of civilized behavior are established.

In the Confucian system, there is a push-pull process in moral education, the push of specific codes of conduct (Yi) and the intrinsic attraction of the power of the Way.[129]

As Thinking, in Newman's model, is located in the left cortex and Sensing is located in the right, the perceiving function is less efficiently regulated by the judging function for STs (and NFs). Sensing needs to be guided by Thinking and, in turn, is grounded in the here-and-now and the practical. A classic anecdote for the importance of developing the ST tie is told of George Washington. Perhaps he chopped down the cherry tree simply because it was there and he happened to have an ax in his hand! But he had learned that you must not tell a lie. Gradually, he also learned to restrain his impulses in favor of appropriate behavior. From such experiences come perspective, responsibility, and prudence—the great strengths of ST character.

It is critical not to allow an ST child to mature without clear moorings in right and wrong, virtue and transgression. Social context is central. For an STJ to be responsible and fair-minded, as she will want to be, she must be connected to expectations of family and community, not adrift on her own. For an STP to learn to serve others, to be a problem solver in behalf of others (not just a streetwise survivor), education needs to take place in a communal context. For all, especially the latter, mentoring relationships can be exceedingly helpful, and apprenticeships can establish economic and social roles for a lifetime and open doors for the spiritual journey.

◁ HOME AND TEMPLE

Often those on the Journey of Works are the proprietors of the temples and caretakers of the institutions of religion. When they are in charge, procedures are well defined, qualifications for membership spelled out, beliefs and requirements are clear and central. Roadside shrines, statues, secluded chapels that are in good repair are probably administered by STs.

By midlife, STs are likely to be going in one of two directions, either becoming more narrowly loyal to and focused on one particular expression of spirituality or able to reach out in an active tolerance and benign encouragement of many alternative expressions. The probably apocryphal story of Washington seeing the Hanukkah candles in one of the soldiers' tents at Valley Forge illustrates the latter. When he saw the candles, he stopped his rounds, entered the tent, and gave the young soldier encouragement. Here the Journey of Works involves a benevolent tolerance, a patriarchal or matriarchal support for others, a care for the world. In contrast, STs who cease to grow in their journey can become entrenched in narrow self-righteousness, worsening in their chosen prejudice or bigotry. The concern for definition and fidelity can cut either way.

◁ GIFT OF THIS JOURNEY FOR OTHERS

STs, because of their realistic and practical bent, are often accused by others, particularly Intuitives, of corrupting the spiritual by bringing antithetical secular values into religion. But STs believe the spiritual is useless unless it lends structure and coherence to life. Unless you can see its effects, it may be draining energies away from what is important, the quality of life, a centering and grounding in everyday issues that matter in the here-and-now.

Intuitive Feeling types tend to blur distinctions and maintain vague boundaries. Sensing Thinkers give religion definition, parameters, plans, and rules. Whereas the Journey of Harmony (NF) tends to look to self-awareness and self-actualization as the spiritual path, the Journey of Works looks to selfless duty, avoiding selfishness and self-centeredness. Often STs are resistant to the psychologizing of religion. Rather than a quest (NF), Sensing Thinkers are often on a mission. This ST–NF polarity contributes helpful distinctions, and the tough-minded and action-oriented ST energy invigorates all journeys.

The theistic ST founders of religions Moses and Zoroaster are recognized by scholars of comparative religion (with their general Intuitive bias), but often another founder, Confucius, is overlooked as a major religious innovator because of the double issue of his ST orientation not being recognized as spiritual and the content of his religious humanism and naturalism. Confucianism is the oldest continuous humanist tradition (with Stoicism, early Buddhism, and the Samkya tradition of Kapila), but many Intuitive writers have difficulty recognizing its spirituality.

Likewise, the attempts by the great Mogul emperor Akbar to create a synthetic religion bonding Moslem, Hindu, Jain, Christian, and Sikh together as one spiritual culture are seldom sufficiently credited, as his profoundly ST approach to this creative task seems clumsy and insensitive. But his was a lifetime of spiritual longing, truly important to investigate as an example of the ST journey. Akbar was a man of action, of profound energy and administrative genius. Beneath was a spiritual-motive force that haunted his empire-building efforts, a motivation to create something enduring and transformative with his life.

HOW STs WILL USE THIS BOOK

STs often prefer to work with a manual to structure their awareness. Any source should be outlined well enough to be a clear step-by-step guide to follow without undue abstraction and leaps of fancy. The major use of direct quotations from the traditions may be helpful. Many STs will skim for the main points to get a grasp of the structure and to see what may have practical application for life in and about the temple.

It is critical for those on the Journey of Works to acknowledge and to honor the reality of the four parallel spiritualities. When an ST pilgrim has a strong sense of being on the right path, it can be hard to grant to others an equal validity and to be open to learning and deepening from the presence of alternative perspectives.

> By meditation some perceive the Self in the self by the self; others by the path of knowledge and still others by the path of works.
>
> Yet others, ignorant of this (these paths of yoga) hearing from others worship; and they too cross beyond death by their devotion to what they have heard.[130]

CHAPTER SEVEN

THE JOURNEY OF HARMONY

LIFE IS PERPETUAL CREATION; IT HAS ITS TRUTH WHEN

IT OUTGROWS ITSELF IN THE INFINITE. BUT WHEN IT

STOPS AND ACCUMULATES AND TURNS BACK TO ITSELF,

WHEN IT HAS LOST ITS OUTLOOK UPON THE BEYOND,

THEN IT MUST DIE.

Rabindranath Tagore, *Personality*

WHILE EACH OF THE Four Spiritualities needs settings that sponsor its unique approach, the Journey of Harmony may be the most adaptable. With imagination, NFs can transform the uses of things with differing interpretations. Open symbols, flexibility, warmth of human presence, and an eclectic reservoir of resources are hallmarks of settings for NF spirituality.

The center for worship and growth invites you to engage the search, utilizing stimulation of different and even competing ideals, always in a quest for hidden harmony or mystic reality beneath all struggles or differences. There is a celebration of life's many wonderful considerations beneficial to such a variety of people. The history of this place provides you with a rich context of metaphor and appreciation of our human emergence. There is much poetry in your worship, and music has many variations, with the rematching or rewriting of new words for new occasions. Your mind soars with the many possibilities for good, and your heart appreciates the many responses you and others are making to evolving ideals.

↶ THE NF PERSONALITY

There are many expressions of this journey around the world, likely to appeal to two Intuitive types with Feeling (INFJ and ENFP) and two Feeling types with Intuition (INFP and ENFJ). Before examining the outlines of this native spirituality, it is useful to have in mind a concept of the NF personality.

As Children and Youth

Some children create whole worlds of people with their imaginations. They don't particularly mimic reality, but invent something new, and the next day something newer still. They will hang on the words of a teacher, parent, or friend, not on the literal words themselves but the intentions, reading between the lines to the real meaning and feeling beneath. Childhood can be for them a wonder world of fairy tale, myth, and symbol. In their own living in every streetscape, in every forest glen, the imagination creates a social heaven or hell of infinite possibilities. Encouraged, this can become the source of great productive creativity, but when put down and discouraged, it becomes an avenue of escape into a dream and fantasy sanctuary.

NF children and youth like to please the adults and peers in their life. They can be easily crushed by disapproval or even indifference. They need frequent strokes from parents, relatives, and teachers if their self-esteem and self-image are not to suffer. Because they can see possibilities in the future (N) and like to gain approval from others, often they will prepare for careers and causes in response to important adult mentors in their lives. They might even enter a family business or a profession other than where their talents and gifts would otherwise point them.

NF youth are exceedingly idealistic, some in a quiet and intense way, others enthusiastic and exuberant. Their idealism is often unpredictable, for NF youth sort for harmony and will often adjust their views to accommodate the visions of their mentors. Young men, in particular, will often overcompensate for their F by expressing their idealism hostilely. They are strongly represented among protesters for social, ecological, and peace issues and may set a course for alternative lifestyles or ideological visions of the good society.

As Adults

If all goes well, NF youth reach adulthood filled with visions of possibilities for people to live in a humane world, to live full lives always growing, always open to enlargement. NF adults are enthusiastic and insightful, recognizing the personal needs of others, the community, and the world; and with a personal warmth and inspiration, they often help others individually and in groups to achieve possibilities for themselves and others. They can keep the good goal, the motivation, and the hope alive. They always see a way to make life better. NFs have an ability to draw people into a discussion and to facilitate consensus-building for social harmony and good. It is the power of positive Intuitive thinking typical of what has been called "the enthusiastic and insightful types."[1] With their warm and friendly manner, and natural sympathy, NFs, who are on a healthy track themselves, will always be drawing people toward their own best selves.

Even from an early age, NFs will often be good communicators, knowing just what is needed for an occasion, bringing creative imagination and the gift of language to their work. This can knit together communities and work teams so that the harmony of relationships increases their effectiveness. NFs will often enter the educational, counseling, sales, and media fields. While NFs account for 12 percent of the population, 44 percent of clergy and a majority of canonized Christian saints are Intuitive Feelers.[2]

NFs are the world's idealists, combining a future orientation with deep feeling for the well-being of others and the world. With N and F linked, values as core convictions combine with global dreams and visions of the good life for all people. The Intuitive proclivity for symbol and metaphor combines with motivations of love for the well-being of the world, making NFs inspired communicators of the ideal. Sometimes taking naive or unconventional forms, and sometimes overzealous or overcommitted, nevertheless NFs anticipate a brighter future for others and themselves and see life moving toward that future.

As an Intuitive, an NF lives life upon a global stage, feeling attuned to the big picture of life in communities, society, or the world. Feeling is focused on possibilities, future benefits for persons, not necessarily on the concrete situation at hand.

Life is always a self-creating process for NFs. Their malleable natures exist to be formed and re-formed in evermore exquisite patterns of self-actualization. The process of becoming can never end. There are always new insights, new aspects of their lives to explore. At some point in the maturing process, the F need to please others will compete with the inner need to be an authentic person. NFs' own expectations will take precedence over others' expectations of them. In situations of adversity, particularly in youth and young adulthood, the NF will feel the need to reject others in order to protect the self. By way of contrast, in situations of support by others young NFs will more likely discover their true self earlier and become able to stand on their own two feet, provided the support is appropriate to their own potentiality. Always NFs must find increasing meaning and spiritual purpose in life.

At times, NFs will take criticism too personally, doing their best work only when appreciated and supported. They will persist when a deep value is at stake, however. They need to trust others if they are to work well with them, and all NFs have had experiences when their credulity and good faith were taken advantage of (i.e., they are not hardheaded Ts or reality-based Ss).

Because they see possibilities, NFs live partly in the future. NFs will be rightly seen at times as fickle—especially NFPs—for a path of action intensely pursued will suddenly be rejected because a new possibility has come into view and they will be off after it with equal enthusiasm. This is especially daunting for STJs, who care for the institutions affected, and to SFs, who have been loyal to the people who may be affected by this change of heart.

NF NATIVE SPIRITUALITY

The native spirituality of the Journey of Harmony concentrates in six manifestations of the genius of the NF personality type: (1) the quest toward authentic, actualized selfhood; (2) mystical harmony; (3) a life attitude of expectancy; (4) the importance of openness to healing and the place of the dream in this process; (5) social idealism; and (6) focus on process in relationships, familial and social.

Quest Toward Selfhood

The Journey of Harmony is first and always a spiritual quest. Life is multilayered, and it is essential to balance each level in turn, and integrate it with the next, until the mystical reality that moves through all existence is revealed. There is a progression of awareness. The search continues through successive transformations. We have many more powers within than we now know, powers of compassion for all beings, of tapping the muse of poetry and art, of intuiting ourselves as partaking of the very nature of spiritual reality, of God.

The American Transcendentalist philosopher Ralph Waldo Emerson grounded his spirituality in nature and in the authority of the individual soul. As he looked at the forms and appearances of the existing landscape, he saw prior forms and potentialities always present:

There is in woods and waters a certain enticement and flattery, together with a failure to yield a present satisfaction. This disappointment is felt in every landscape. I have seen the softness and beauty of the summer clouds floating feathery overhead, enjoying, not so much of the drapery of this place and hour, as forelooking to some pavilions and gardens of festivity beyond. It is an odd jealousy, but the poet finds himself not near enough to his object. The pine-tree, the river, the bank of flowers before him does not seem to be nature. Nature is still elsewhere. . . . It is the same thing among the men and women as among the silent trees; always a referred existence, an absence, never a presence and satisfaction.[3]

His quest is always to understand more and to arrive at an originality of meaning. He describes the endless quest: "There is throughout nature something mocking, something that leads us on and on, but arrives nowhere."[4]

The NF quest cannot ever be satisfied. Something will spark a search for a new aspect of reality thus far not revealed. When begun, the new search gradually dissolves the wholeness of the old into a newer unity. And thus life never becomes content with what it inherited from the past. Emerson wrote:

Life only avails, not the having lived. Power ceases in the instant of repose; it resides in the moment of transition from a past to a new state, in the shooting of the gulf, in the darting to an aim. This one fact the world hates; that the soul *becomes*; for that forever degrades the past, turns all riches to poverty, all reputation to a shame, confounds the saint with the rogue, shoves Jesus and Judas equally aside.[5]

For Emerson, all of nature and all of society rely on the individual, and the individual relies on the original revelation within. Personal discovery and growth are the basis for the continued emergence of the human spirit:

Trust thyself: every heart vibrates to that iron string. Accept the place the divine providence has found for you, the society of your contemporaries, the connection of events. Great men have always done so, and confided themselves child-like to the genius of their age, betraying their perception that the absolutely trustworthy was seated at their heart, working through their hands, predominating in all their being. And we are now men, and must accept in the highest mind the same transcendent destiny; and not minors and invalids in a protected corner, not cowards fleeing before a revolution, but guides, redeemers and benefactors, obeying the Almighty effort and advancing on Chaos and the Dark.[6]

For NFs, the push to self-actualization, to developing their authentic self, is a recommendation to others to enter into their own evolution. Find the meanings yourself and then share with others the results of your experiments. This is how it has always been since the first humans; the spiritual evolution of humanity is the work of individuals upon their own lives, and a publishing of their development to their friends. The Journey of Harmony requires both an open and experimental attitude toward life and a willingness to communicate one's findings to the world.

NFs are often a puzzle to others, particularly to SFs, who share the F concern for the well-being of persons. NFs will focus on a situation of human need, addressing solutions with great idealism, and then be off before the need is met. Such behavior is not usually indifference but a new excitement, a continued quest to make the world better through envisioning how it could come about. The quest itself is the deepest, most intense motivation. Unless chastened by the need to stay connected, the NF will be engaged in the further quest itself. Emerson wrote:

> Life wears to me a visionary face. Hardest, roughest action is visionary also. It is but a choice between soft and turbulent dreams. People disparage knowing and the intellectual life, and urge doing. I am very content with knowing, if only I could know. That is an august entertainment, and would suffice me a great while. To know a little would be worth the expense of this world.[7]

His advice to the seniors of the Harvard Divinity School in 1838 summarizes the importance of the quest as the inspiration of life:

> I look for the new Teacher, that shall follow so far those shining laws, that he shall see them come full circle; shall see their rounding complete grace; shall see the world to be the mirror of the soul; shall see the identity of the law of gravitation with purity of heart; and shall show that the Ought, that Duty, is one thing with Science, with Beauty, and with Joy.[8]

Those on the Journey of Harmony see humanity as an essential part of the flow of a great spiritual stream that runs through all of life and through the fields, forests, sun, and stars. This stream propels us into time and into the emergence of new life in ourselves and in the world, life attuned to the divine in the world. Emerson wrote:

> Place yourself in the middle of the stream of power and wisdom which animates all whom it floats, and you are without effort impelled to truth, to right and a perfect contentment.
>
> The whole course of things goes to teach us faith.[9]

The German poet Rainer Maria Rilke gave the same advice to a young poet friend, that the discipline is an inner voyage of discovery. This is the authentic source.

I can't give you any advice but this: to go into yourself and see how deep the place is from which your life flows; at its source you will find the answer to the question of whether you *must* create. Accept that answer, just as it is given to you, without trying to interpret it. Perhaps you will discover that you are called to be an artist.

. . . out of this immersion in your own world, poems come, then you will not think of asking anyone whether they are good or not.[10]

The NF quest takes place in many aspects of human expression, not only for sages and poets. For the American anthropologist Loren Eiseley (1907–1977), his science was a personal life quest, "an immense journey," and this same science led him to a vision of human emergence realized through the striving of each individual.[11]

But beyond lies the great darkness of the ultimate Dreamer, who dreamed the light and the galaxies. Before act was, or substance existed, imagination grew in the dark. Man partakes of that ultimate wonder and creativeness. As we turn from the galaxies to the swarming cells of our own being, which toil for something, some entity beyond their grasp, let us remember man, the self-fabricator who came across an ice age to look into the mirrors and the magic of science. Surely he did not come to see himself or his wild visage only. He came because he is at heart a listener and a searcher for some transcendent realm beyond himself. This he has worshipped by many names, even in the dismal caves of his beginning. Man, the self-fabricator, is so by reason of gifts he had no part in devising—and so he searches as the single living cell in the beginning must have sought the ghostly creature it was to serve.[12]

Eiseley is remarkably personal in his summary of the importance of his own human quest in the whole range of the evolutionary biological lanscape.

I, the professor, trembling absurdly on the platform with my book and spectacles, am the single philosophical animal. I am the unfolding worm, and mud fish, the weird tree of Igdrasil shaping itself endlessly out of the darkness toward the light.

I have said this is not an illusion. It is when one sees in this manner, or a sense of strangeness halts one on a busy street to verify the appearance of one's fellows, that one knows a terrible new sense has opened a faint crack into the Absolute. It is in this way alone that one comes to grips with a great mystery, that life and time bear some curious relationship to each other that is not shared by inanimate things.

It is in the brain that this world opens. To our descendants it may become a commonplace, but me, and others like me, it has made a castaway. I have no refuge in time, as others do who troop homeward at nightfall. As a result, I am one of those who linger furtively over coffee in the kitchen at bedtime or haunt the all-night restaurants.[13]

Each one of us in our personal ponderings is a part of this "immense journey," which continues to unknown prospects for the future of our human nature.

> Man is partly of the future, and the future he possesses a power to shape. . . . Perhaps there may come to us . . . a ghostly sense that an invisible doorway has been opened—a doorway which, widening out, will take man beyond the nature that he knows.[14]

Mystical Harmony

Often the road to harmony for NFs resolves in mysticism. The quest, after all, must acquiesce to the embrace of something far larger than our own limited perceptions of spiritual reality. The Taoist philosopher Chuang-tzu (fourth century B.C.) gives a classic picture:

> Fishes are born in water
> Man is born in Tao.
> If fishes, born in water,
> Seek the deep shadow
> Of pond and pool,
> All their needs
> Are satisfied.
> If man, born in Tao,
> Sinks into the deep shadow
> Of non-action
> To forget aggression and concern,
> He lacks nothing
> His life is secure.
> Moral: "All the fish needs
> Is to get lost in water.
> All man needs is to get lost
> In Tao."[15]

Water images are a primary way the Taoist and other traditions have conveyed mystical union. Individuals need to bring themselves to the point of immersion in ultimate reality, natural or divine. In the *Tao Te Ching*, there are numerous references:

> Best to be like water,
> Which benefits the ten thousand things
> And does not contend.
> It pools where humans disdain to dwell,
> Close to the TAO.[16]

> Tao's presence in the world
> is like the relation of small river valleys
> to the Yang-tze and the ocean.[17]

Nothing under heaven is softer
And more yielding than water.
Yet when it attacks things hard and resistant,
Receding, returning, again and again,
There is not one of them that can withstand.[18]

A central image is water seeking its own level, the Tao being below and attractive. The valley is the Great Mother:

Be aware of your masculine nature;
But by keeping the feminine way,
You shall be to the world like a canyon,
Where the Virtue eternal abides,
And go back to become as a child.[19]

The *Tao Te Ching* is the only major scripture in the world's spiritual traditions that speaks with a feminine bias. The story of beginnings rests firmly in the mysteries of the Mother:

There is a thing confusedly formed,
Born before heaven and earth.
Silent and void
It stands alone and does not change,
Goes round and does not weary.
It is capable of being the mother of the world.
I know not its name
So I style it "the way."
I give it the makeshift name of "the great."
Being great, it is further described as receding,
Receding, it is described as far away,
Being far away, it is described as turning back.[20]

The spirit of the valley does not die
and is called Mysterious Female.
The door of the Mysterious Female
is called the root of heaven and earth.
It lingers in wisps;
Use it without haste.[21]

For NFs, mysticism is an embracing experience that confirms the harmony of life in the world. We may not understand the mysteries, but the whole of experience coheres. All that we can understand, the authentic quest of life itself, continues in a secure context. It never leaves us. The word the poet William Blake uses for it is *eternity*. In "Auguries of Innocence" (1805) he wrote:

To see a world in a grain of sand
And a heaven in a wild flower,
Hold infinity in the palm of your hand
And eternity in an hour.

How more simply can the goal of life be summarized? Through these little experiences we see the oneness of all life, of the entire cosmos. In a grain of sand, in a tiny, trembling wildflower, we experience God, life, and all time.

But this is not an easy goal. To speak the words hardly summarizes the experience, nor the depth of insight or conviction. How does Blake know this? How does he get to this point? In another poem, "The Little Black Boy" (1789), he speaks through the thoughts of the boy and paints a less-than-ideal picture from the point of view of social equality, for the boy has not reached the point of knowing himself as an equal. So it is through this social and psychological confusion, this absence of the ideal, that we catch a glimpse of the poet's vision of mystic light. He has the boy say:

> Look at the rising sun—there God does live,
> And gives his light, and gives his heat away;
> And flowers and trees and beasts and men receive
> Comfort in morning, joy in the noonday.
>
> And we are put on earth a little space,
> That we may learn to bear the beams of love. . . .

Blake has the little boy seeing the vision of love and peace, through a life of subservience and feelings of inferiority. Here all of us have access to the great unity of life, but we see only partially; we have not put the whole picture together. We have not even experienced the great harmony and bliss we have envisioned. Life is filled with obstacles to our wholeness.

So, likewise, we can only guess that the poet himself was there in "the beams of love," wholly there. It seems from his poetry, his engravings and paintings, that if anyone can, he must have been there. Looking to the east, to the sun, to life freed from gross attachments and preoccupations, he wrote in "Several Questions Answered" (1791):

> He who binds to himself a Joy
> Does the wingèd life destroy;
> But he who kisses the Joy as it flies
> Lives in Eternity's sunrise.

None of us gets a worldview delivered to us at birth. We have to find our way through the maze until life becomes more coherent and our activities more congruent. When do we first get a clue? Childhood? Adolescence? When we get to vote? Middle age?

The Indian poet and philosopher Muhammad Iqbal (1877–1938) believed that the human ego is on a quest for greater freedom and can only realize it as it comes nearest to God, the most complete person, absorbing God into itself. He summarized how his mystic vision reinforces personality:

Personality is a state of tension and can continue only if that state is maintained. . . . That which tends to maintain the state of tension tends to make us immortal. Thus the idea of personality gives us a standard of value: it settles the problem of good and evil. That which fortifies personality is good, that which weakens it is bad. Art, religion, and ethics must be judged from the standpoint of personality.[22]

In what is perhaps considered his greatest poem, "The Secrets of the Self," Iqbal wrote:

Inasmuch as the life of the universe
  comes from the strength of the Self,
Life is in proportion to this strength. . . .
Because the earth is firmly based on
  self-existence,
The captive moon goes round it perpetually.
The being of the sun is stronger than
  that of the earth:
Therefore is the earth bewitched by the
  sun's eye.
The glory of the plane fixes our gaze,
The mountains are enriched by its majesty:
Its raiment is woven of fire,
Its origin is one self-assertive seed.
When Life gathers strength from the Self,
The river of Life expands into an ocean.[23]

Expectancy

Life presents to us incredible complexity. At certain junctures, this complexity becomes overwhelming and the way through the tangle is impossible to discern. Every action leads to new complications. Here NFs are likely to take a somewhat detached attitude of spiritual expectancy, that somehow even though the elements of a future harmony are impossible to sort out now, in the fullness of time they will be revealed.

A classic model of this attitude can be seen in the Joseph story found in the Book of Genesis. In his early childhood, Joseph is extremely spoiled by his father, Jacob, overprotected, favored with his coat of many colors, elite among the twelve brothers. Joseph's relationship with his brothers is symptomatic of the difficulties many Feeling boys, particularly NFs, experience in an ST male context. His sensitivity and the special efforts of his parents to shield him from the harshness of the realities of their condition as nomads incurred the jealousy of his brothers. It came to a head one day far from camp. In the excitement of the moment, his brothers sold him to a caravan going to Egypt, and he became a servant there.

In time, Joseph rose as high as foreign servants could, and the pharaoh heard of his ability to interpret dreams. Joseph predicted a famine, and the pharaoh put him in charge of preparations. He had lived a chaotic life so far. Would he ever be able to see any coherence for his life? In the chaos of his situation would he ever restore his connection with his heritage, restore his familial relationships, be on a more secure footing in Egypt?

Then his brothers appeared. His family were victims of the famine. Without food many would die. His mission in life, the larger picture, became clear. He said to his brothers:

> I am your brother, Joseph, whom you sold into Egypt. And now do not be distressed, or angry with yourselves, because you sold me here; for God sent me before you to preserve life. . . . So it was not you who sent me here, but God.[24]

There was revealed to Joseph the larger pattern; somehow all the events of his fragmented life had come together in a coherent whole. His basic attitude of expectancy in the face of each new opportunity or reversal was now rewarded. His NF centering in relationships was now rounded out as well, and his participation in a larger circle of life reinforced the quality of his most immediate and dearest personal relationships.

The vision of a larger pattern in the world is not usually linked to cause and effect or to action. It is intuited but never proven. Events seem meant to be. A certain wisdom presents itself, even though there are no guidelines for double-checking to be certain of the ground we are standing on. Eventually, life and the world become whole once again.

This is a great theme of the Journey of Harmony: that in the complexity and business of life's problems and tasks, we do not understand, we are not whole, but in our experience we undergo transformation and come into a deeper knowledge or even a special knowledge of the unity of the world. Walt Whitman said in his poem "Song of the Open Road" (1856):

> The earth never tires.
> The earth is rude, silent, incomprehensible at first. Nature
>   is rude and incomprehensible at first.
> Be not discouraged, keep on, there are divine things well
>   envelop'd,
> I swear to you there are divine things more beautiful
>   than words can tell.

Openness to Healing

One of the most restorative places of earth lies in the landscape of Epidaurus on the Peloponnesian peninsula of Greece. It was the home of Asklepios (Asclepius), god of healing. It sits in a modestly wide valley plateau surrounded by hills, twelve miles from the sea. Pilgrims would land and journey up through a zigzag gorge to this peaceful valley with its pine and olive trees. A pilgrim would arrive and enter into "incubation, dreams, communications with the god or the snake, and their healing or recovery."[25] The heart of the healing process took place in the sanctuary of Asklepios and in the Abaton just north of it, where patients would lie in trance and dream attended by white-robed priests. In the courtyard was the Tholos, home of the snakes, for the symbol of Asklepios was a rod entwined with snakes, as seen today in the caduceus of the medical profession or the snakes-with-sun symbol on the scepter of bishops. The serpent is the symbol of regeneration and renewal.

Epidaurus was famous for the healing properties of its spring water and the acoustics of its magnificent theater, where suggestive rites for healing were performed. It was an NF environment—calm and harmonious, caring, unhurried, supportive.

For those on this pathway, "Heal thyself" is always the starting place for spiritual growth, leading them to advocate that society help its members to wholeness and happiness and that individuals heal themselves through healing others. Places like Epidaurus remind us, through changing the pace and focus of our consciousness, that we live in meaning, in a reverential context. The dream brings into this receptiveness the rich depth of wisdom and archetypal imagery of the unconscious, which produces restorative power. The goal at Epidaurus was dream vision, including the serpent and the god. In a sense, what was evoked was the reality lived by the !Kung bushmen, that "there is a dream dreaming us." We seek to return to our own story.[26]

Dreams bring us essential perspective for our lives, allowing us to lighten up on our seriousness with the restorative power of humor. Chuang-tzu wrote:

> Once Chuang Chou dreamt he was a butterfly, a butterfly flitting and fluttering around, happy with himself and doing as he pleased. He didn't know he was Chuang Chou. Suddenly he woke up and there he was, solid and unmistakable Chuang Chou. But he didn't know if he was Chuang Chou who had dreamt he was a butterfly, or a butterfly dreaming he was Chuang Chou. Between Chuang Chou and a butterfly there must be some distinction! This is called the Transformation of Things.[27]

The butterfly, of course, is immortal, containing within itself a perpetual cycle of metamorphosis. The Journey of Harmony always seeks the gnosis, the deeper knowing, wholeness (holiness) and healing, source of joy and wisdom, perhaps whimsical, perhaps mystical. The Indian poet Rabindranath Tagore takes us on a pilgrimage to a mystical landscape that makes even the butterfly transient:

The eternal Dream
>> is borne on the wings of ageless Light
>> that rends the veil of the vague
>>> and goes across Time
>> weaving ceaseless patterns of Being.

The mystery remains dumb,
>> the meaning of this pilgrimage,
>> the endless adventure of existence —
whose rush along the sky
>> flames up into innumerable rings of paths,
till at last knowledge gleams out from the dusk
>>> in the infinity of human spirit,
>>> and in that dim-lighted dawn
>>> she speechlessly gazes through the break in the mist
>>>> at the vision of Life and of Love
>>> emerging from the tumult of profound pain and joy.[28]

Idealism

The Journey of Harmony is enthusiastically idealistic, sometimes to the point of naïveté. For after all, the universe is not a machine with all gears meshing. Disharmony is a given, therefore, and in the flux of change all idealism becomes less the ideal with the passage of time. So the goal of harmony is ever elusive, ever far off, pulling us through the present for another glimpse around the next corner. NFs are dreamers and aspire after a better world for everyone. They can be lucidly insightful, challenging us to grow beyond the good of today to the better goal for tomorrow. Hopes and visions are always tied to deeply held human values, core convictions in the heart.

The eighth-century Chinese poet Li Po wrote:

Why do I live among the green mountains?
I laugh and answer not, my soul is serene:
It dwells in another heaven and earth
  belonging to no man.
The peach trees are in flower,
  and the water flows on. . . .[29]

Li Po has his own interpretation of Chuang-tzu's butterfly dream that paints a picture known today as ecology or, to use a less cold term, Gaia, the organism of earth.

Chuang Chou in dream became a butterfly,
And the butterfly became Chuang Chou
  at waking.
Which was the real—the butterfly or the man?

Who can tell the end of the endless
   changes of things?
The water that flows into the depth
   of the distant sea
Returns anon to the shallows
   of a transparent stream.
The man, raising melons outside the green gate
   of the city,
Was once the Prince of the East Hill.
So must rank and riches vanish.
You know it, still you toil and toil,
   —what for?[30]

What do we aim to create in the context of Gaia, earth? What toil is useless, what occupations build the ideal of supporting all life? The question of the ideal world pulls NFs forward, laden with relationship and intimacy values. Relationship to the integrity of earth, envisioning this (N), and intimate acquaintance with the fortunes of life (F), participation in the "interdependent web of all existence,"[31] pull the Journey of Harmony like a magnet.

Even when the ideal is thwarted or dissolves, NFs work to establish islands of harmony, wilderness areas and reservations, communities within a larger chaos, that create the ideal in microcosm. Chuang-tzu saw his opportunity under a gnarled tree:

> [Hui Tzu] "I have a big tree named ailanthus. Its trunk is too gnarled and bumpy to apply a measuring line to, its branches too bent and twisty to match up to a compass or square. You could stand it by the road and no carpenter would look at it twice. . . ."
>
> [Chuang Tzu] "Now you have this big tree and you're distressed because it's useless. Why don't you plant it in Not-Even-Anything Village, or the field of Broad-and-Boundless, relax and do nothing by its side, or lie down for a free and easy sleep under it? Axes will never shorten its life, nothing can ever harm it. If there's no use for it, how can it come to grief or pain?"[32]

Other NFs can be tough as well as mystical in view of the ideal. Henry David Thoreau wrote:

> Men labor under a mistake. The better part of the man is soon plowed into the soil for compost. By a seeming fate, commonly called necessity, they are employed, as it says in an old book, laying up treasures which moth and rust will corrupt and thieves break through and steal. . . . The mass of men lead lives of quiet desperation. What is called resignation is confirmed desperation.[33]

For Thoreau, the solution was to part company with society and to live in solitude for a time. He was able to minister to the world from his reflections apart, from his "rugged individualism."

Alternatively, and equally attuned to the larger context of nature, Starhawk, prominent in neo-pagan circles today, speaks of an ideal of human well-being that is communal.

> We are all longing to go home to some place we have never been—a place, half-remembered, and half-envisioned we can only catch glimpses of from time to time. Community. Somewhere, there are people to whom we can speak with passion without having the words catch in our throats. Somewhere a circle of hands will open to receive us, eyes will light up as we enter, voices will celebrate with us whenever we come into our own power. Community means strength that joins our strength to do the work that needs to be done. Arms to hold us when we falter. A circle of healing. A circle of friends. Someplace where we can be free.[34]

The Journey of Harmony has long been in conflict over which direction really creates the fullest human nature, the most complete freedom: the lone sage, maverick, recluse or the community member enjoying support and nurturing? Gaia, the Great Mother, OM (woman, womb, home, dome, community, tomb), the continuous organism conflicts with the discontinuous (male) creation, ex nihilo. The ideal flounders here, for the NF cannot choose and must make room for both.

Unlike NTs, however, who aim for synthesis of disparate traditions into a unity, NFs aim for the ideal of peace and harmony, not worrying whether all elements fit as long as participants can be appreciative and supportive of one another. There is a Feeling quality in NF inspiration, as emphasized in this chant from a Starhawk retreat:

> Weave and spin,
>   Weave and spin.
> This is how the work begins.
>
> Mend and heal,
>   Mend and heal.
> Take the dream and make it real.

Not only can NFs suspend conflicting ideals without reconciling them, in the interests of harmony they can also muddy distinctions altogether, as often occurs when the attempt is made to reconcile very different religious traditions. The fifteenth-century Indian poet Kabir, who was born and lived a Moslem, developed the habit of calling God Ram, a Hindu name.[35] Even though Kabir rejected Vedic scriptures and much of the tangible lore of Hinduism, eventually Hindus attempted to claim him as one of them. To many Moslems, Hinduism has an irritating habit of trying to absorb all religious impulses into itself. Mohammed is yet another avatar, and Allah another manifestation of the unity of Brahman.

A remarkable NF effort at religious peace was undertaken by the first Sikh leader, Guru Nanak, in the fifteenth century. The scripture of the new faith, the *Adi Granth*, eventually included 243 verses of Kabir's poetry, along with Sufi and Hindu sources. The *Granth* was a self-conscious attempt at religious tolerance, "intended to be a kind of Peoples' Bible for the Indian humanity."[36] Nanak wrote:

> All who are born are only wayfarers,
> And when the call arrives must depart
>   without delay.
> Only through enlightenment may one
>   realize God;
> For the rest, Hindu or Moslem ritual
>   is of little help.
> All must render their account at God's
>   portal—
> None shall cross over except through
>   good actions.[37]

Elsewhere he adds, "Anyone who has the love of God in his heart and compassion for His creation, is truly religious."[38]

In contrast to the synthetic, blurring-of-distinctions approach, an entirely different premise undergirds the relationship of the religions in Western democracies—the separation of church and state. Here the birthright of freedom is a guarantor of religious practice.[39] Pluralism of forms and beliefs is welcome, with no attempt to blend them in order to harmonize society. Tolerance is a social structure rather than an inner discipline. Thoreau anticipated a future ideal age when this pluralism would be a collection of tongues:

> That age will be rich indeed when those relics which we call Classics, and the still older and more than classic but even less known Scriptures of the nations, shall have still further accumulated, when the Vaticans shall be filled with Vedas and Zendavestas and Bibles, with Homers and Dantes and Shakespeares, and all centuries to come shall have successively deposited their trophies to the forum of the world. By such a pile we may hope to scale heaven at last.[40]

It is hard to imagine a grand harmony that could be fully satisfying. There are flaws, broken places, and sufferings. Sitting before the Maitreya (the Buddha-to-be) is the Great Bodhisattva of Eminent Conduct, who journeys with the vow "However infinite the Buddha-truth is, I vow to attain it."[41] Like his three companions the Bodhisattvas of Steadfast (ST), Pure (SF), and Boundless (NT) Conduct, he will journey toward his ideal until the end of time with the longing for universal attainment.

Process in Relationships

The Journey of Harmony focuses intently on the processes of human relationships, social interaction, and communication. The circle, of course, is the original spiritual form for celebration and social cohesion. It is egalitarian and intimate.

> The circle is cast.
> We are between the worlds,
> Beyond the bounds of time,
> Where night and day,
> Birth and death,
> Joy and sorrow,
> Meet as one.[42]

But the circle works well only for small groups and tribes. The challenge for harmony is to keep the values sponsored by the circle as society enlarges in complexity. Hierarchy, invented to serve complexity, pushes the individual into roles of specialization, and sets in motion along the "chain of command" relationships that can be authoritarian in their impact.

In ancient China the problem of hierarchy was addressed by Taoists with the ideals of nonaction and trust, but the structures of hierarchy were left undisturbed.

> When the Master governs, the people
> are hardly aware that he exists.
> Next best is a leader who is loved.
> Next, one who is feared.
> The worst is one who is despised.
>
> If you don't trust the people,
> you make them untrustworthy.
>
> The Master doesn't talk, he acts.
> When his work is done,
> the people say, "Amazing:
> we did it, all by ourselves!"[43]

In North America the open spaces of the continent widened for the European settlers an experience of the democratic values of cooperation, appreciation, and consideration, expressed with full exuberance by the poet Walt Whitman in "Song of the Open Road":

> From this hour I ordain myself loos'd of limits
>   and imaginary lines,
> Going where I list, my own master total
>   and absolute,

Listening to others, considering well
  what they say,
Pausing, searching, receiving, contemplating,
Gently, but with undeniable will, divesting
  myself of the holds
  that would hold me.

I inhale great draughts of space,
The east and the west are mine, and the north
  and the south are mine.

I am larger, better than I thought,
I did not know I held so much goodness.

And also in "One's Self I Sing":

One's-Self I sing, a simple separate person,
Yet utter the word Democratic,
  the word En-Masse. . . .

Of Life immense in passion, pulse, and power,
Cheerful, for freest action form'd
  under the laws divine,
The Modern Man I sing.

By the twentieth century, however, the great westward spaces had been domesticated, and the democratic process as it matured needed an urgent spiritual sophistication. The Spanish philosopher José Ortega y Gasset wrote before World War II and before the challenges of the electronic media and the postindustrial workplace:

> The political doctrine which has represented the loftiest endeavour towards common life is liberal democracy. It carries to the extreme the determination to have consideration for one's neighbour. . . . Liberalism is the supreme form of generosity; it is the right which the majority concedes to minorities and hence it is the noblest cry that has ever resounded in this planet. It announces the determination to share existence with the enemy; more than that, with an enemy which is weak. It was incredible that the human species should have arrived at so noble an attitude, so paradoxical, so refined, so acrobatic, so anti-natural. Hence, it is not to be wondered at that this same humanity should soon appear anxious to get rid of it. It is a discipline too difficult and complex to take firm root on earth.[44]

The quest of the Journey of Harmony proceeds always sensitive to the quality of the process at all levels of relationship—in families, villages, neighborhoods, states, and the world. The ideal attracts NFs, the well-being of individuals involved moves them, for all processes exist to sponsor the individual person, oneself, and all others equally. "You shall love your neighbor as yourself" is the beginning and the end of the NF quest.

Ꮾ RAJA YOGA

Among the four yogas, raja yoga stands in a special relationship with the other three (jnana: NT; bhakti: SF; karma: ST) because it overlaps each while developing its own unique NF spiritual discipline. Although yoga meditative postures can be seen in the art of the Indus civilization (c. 2700 B.C.),[45] Patanjali is generally credited with writing down in succinct form the essentials of yogic practice. The *Yoga Sutras* of Patanjali were compiled perhaps as early as 400 B.C. Consisting originally of only 83 verses, and now of 195 verses, the work is meant as an outline for teachers who guide their disciples with further details of yogic practice.[46] The different kinds of yoga all defer to or utilize aspects of Patanjali's work.[47]

The *Yoga Sutras* deal with ethical preparations for yogic practice, the regulation of the body and senses, and meditative practices leading to a regulation of the mind. Nearly all yogas employ the ethical preparations (the yama and niyama), and most use variations of the postures (asanas) and the breathing (pranayama) and sensory (pratyahara) regulations. These are known as the five external limbs of raja yoga. Of the remaining three limbs (the inner limbs)—dharana, dhyana, and samadhi—there is wide divergence from the raja school.[48] All yogas begin with purification in various forms, move to a concentration of the physical, emotional, and mental powers, and come at last to a spiritual liberation.

The process and goal of raja yoga are summarized in the Bhagavad Gita:

> To him who has conquered himself by himself,
> his own self is a friend,
> but to him who has not conquered himself,
> his own self is hostile, like an external enemy.

> That in which the mind, restrained
> by the practice of concentration,
> rests quiescent; that in which,
> seeing the Self through the self,
> one rejoices in one's own Self;

> Thus making his self ever steadfast,
> the yoga, freed from sins
> easily enjoys the touch of Brahman,
> which is exceeding bliss.[49]

Raja yoga works primarily with the mind, grounding the process in self-awareness, treating progress along the way as a scientific experiment,[50] trying this, trying that, to see what provokes growth. Raja begins the quest as an adventure, seeking self-actualization, until in the last levels the mind has quieted, the waves on the pond of consciousness are quelled, and the self is in harmony, but without reference to the cosmos one way or the other. En route toward samadhi, the aspirant visits many realms of great psychic possibilities, but if one tarries too long in them they become as much a distraction as social attachments were, or physical and emotional discomforts and blocks, or the overactive intellect. In the advanced stages of the inner limbs, the samyama process, the aspirant keeps moving beyond the fascination with distinctions until the experience of liberation occurs. "When the mind and soul have been equally purified (of each other), isolation is perfect."[51] This destination for raja yoga can be easily misunderstood. The religious scholar Mircea Eliade calls it an initiation into the sacred, and the freedom of yoga is the death prior to rebirth. "Everything depends upon what is meant by freedom."[52]

Why would anyone wish to arduously pursue the eight limbs of raja yoga toward such a goal? Guru Nanak adds to the rationale expressed above in the Bhagavad Gita:

> To live immaculate amidst the impurities
>   of the world—
> This is true Yoga-practice;
> Perfection in Yoga lies not in bragging.
> The true Yogi is one who views in all existence
>   harmony.[53]

Rabindranath Tagore concludes his work *The Religion of Man* with a discussion of the inherent dualism of human life:

> In the Sanskrit language the bird is described as "twice-born"—once in its limited shell and then finally in the freedom of the unbounded sky. Those of our community who believe in the liberation of man's limited self in the freedom of the spirit retain the same epithet for themselves. In all departments of life man shows this dualism—his existence within the range of obvious facts and his transcendence of it in a realm of deeper meaning.[54]

He continues, weaving all four of the yogas into his concluding words:

> It is widely known in India that there are individuals who have the power to attain temporarily the state of Samadhi, the complete merging of the self in the infinite, a state which is indescribable. While accepting their testimony as true, let us at the same time have faith in the testimony of others who have felt a profound love, which is the intense feeling of union, for a Being who comprehends in himself all things that are human in knowledge, will and action. And he is God, who is not merely a sum total of facts, but the goal that lies immensely beyond all that is comprised in the past and the present.[55]

Here Tagore not only validates the reports of those who followed Patanjali's lead in raja yoga all the way to samadhi, but also focuses primarily on the alternative forms of reentry into ongoing life, affirming in quick succession SF, NT, ST, and NF forms.

Another Intuitive Feeling solution to the rigors of raja yoga and the problem of what manner of reentry is required is called "integral yoga" by India's great guru of Ponticherry, Sri Aurobindo. He feels raja yoga puts too much emphasis on progression to the goal, progress through the seven chakras (the nerve centers in the body from which psychic energy flows). This is well and good, but it is important to integrate the lower with the higher, to make the trip back, tying all our work together in an integral spiritual whole.

Integral yoga seeks to combine the goals of each of the four yogas into a transformation Sri Aurobindo calls "the Yoga of spiritual and gnostic self-perfection."[56] His biographer summarizes his contribution, beginning with a key word for each of the traditional yogas: knowledge (NT), bliss (SF), power (ST), and freedom (NF):

> The supramental transformed being, also known as the gnostic being, is characterized by knowledge, bliss, power, freedom; he is beyond conflict, consequently beyond ethical struggle and decision-making. He is the fulfillment of the traditional "spiritual man," differing from this traditional image in that he does not eschew his body but accepts it anew and experiences it as a sign and center of divine presence.
>
> Spiritual freedom, then, is both means and end, both process and purpose. It is a condition for and a characteristic of the evolutionary process in its thrust toward fulfillment; spiritual freedom is also the fullest completion of that process in its transcendent state as cosmic participation and supramental existence.
>
> The recommended means to foster and achieve the full unfolding of the possibilities of spiritual freedom is integral yoga, whereby one enters into the "within" of one's deepest and secret self and there discovers spiritual resources previously untapped. Through yogic concentration and renunciation, the individual disciplines innate desires and intensifies the capacity for self-surrender to the divine, thus entering into full spiritual freedom with its consequent sense of oneness with all beings.[57]

The quest for personal awareness and for mystic harmony can take NFs far from their equally native idealism and passion for humane process in all levels of relationship. This dualism Tagore spoke of, between transcendence and the "range of obvious facts," provides great quantities of energy for harmonizing the whole picture for human well-being. Thus, we see spiritual leaders like Sri Aurobindo and Rabindranath Tagore among the founders of modern India.

ᴄ᷐ MENTORS FOR THIS WAY

While representing approximately 12 percent of humanity, those who follow the Journey of Harmony include many innovators in the history of religion along with inspired poets, mystics, and sages, who might be chosen for mentors. Here we will focus upon one major figure in modern spiritual culture, Rabindranath Tagore, and one of the great founders, Jesus of Nazareth, giving clear indication of the spectrum of diversity within each Journey. Both I believe were Introverted Intuitive Feelers.

Rabindranath Tagore

Tagore was an educator and artist, and believed that all of us have a spiritual longing within us, a "longing to express . . . for the very sake of expression." We need to surpass utility, the "claims of necessity" in our lives, and tap that deep reservoir of personality that is the door to the infinite.[58] When William Butler Yeats first read Tagore's *Gitanjali*, he was so smitten that he carried it around with him and would read the poems on the sly so that others in train stations would not see how moved he was by them. Albert Schweitzer called Tagore the Goethe of India, D. S. Sarma called him "the Leonardo da Vinci of our Renaissance," and Gandhi called Tagore "the Great Sentinel."[59]

Tagore was born in 1861 and died in 1941. His father was leader of the Brahmo Samaj movement in Bengal, a movement of religious renewal that is credited with sparking the renaissance of Hinduism during the past century. As a child, Tagore played with his brothers and sisters and had the run of the household until he was twelve years old. The coming-of-age ceremony at that time for Brahmins involved wearing the sacred thread and learning a mantra called the *Gayatri*, a sacred text from the Vedas. Translated it means:

> Let me contemplate the adorable
> splendor of [the One]
> who created the earth, the air,
> and the starry spheres,
> and sends the power of comprehension
> within our minds.[60]

It suffers in translation, but apparently these words took hold of his mind. It is hard to predict what might change a boy's life at age twelve. He began to see the world with greater depth, drawn into the flow of forces and the wonderful coordination of nature.

At the same time, his formal schooling began, which was for him a negative experience. Learning imposed in school was in profound contrast to the
drama of the world outside. Tagore described the beginnings of poetry for him:

> I came to a rhymed sentence of combined words . . . "It rains, the leaves trem-
> ble." At once I came to a world wherein I recovered my full meaning. My mind
> touched the creative realm of expression, and at that moment I was no longer a
> mere student with his mind muffled by spelling lessons, enclosed by classroom.
> The rhythmic picture of the tremulous leaves beaten by the rain opened before
> my mind the world which does not merely carry information, but a harmony
> with my being. The unmeaning fragments lost their individual isolation and my
> mind reveled in the unity of a vision. In a similar manner, on that morning in
> the village the facts of my life suddenly appeared to me in a luminous unity of
> truth. All things that had seemed like vagrant waves were revealed to my mind
> in relation to a boundless sea. I felt sure that some Being who comprehended
> me and my world was seeking its best expression in all my experiences, uniting
> them into an ever-widening individuality which is a spiritual work of art.[61]

What a wonderful breakthrough so early in life! His mantra, the *Gayatri*, was
sparking his awareness of the mystic harmony of the world and the way poetry can resonate with this oneness.

Several years later, Tagore emerged as a creator of religious poetry.

> When I was eighteen, a sudden spring breeze of religious experience for the first
> time came to my life and passed away leaving in my memory a direct message
> of spiritual reality. One day while I stood watching at early dawn the sun send-
> ing out its rays from behind the trees, I suddenly felt as if some ancient mist had
> in a moment lifted from my sight, and the morning light on the face of the
> world revealed an inner radiance of joy. The invisible screen of the common-
> place was removed from all things and all [persons] and their ultimate signifi-
> cance was intensified in my mind. . . . That which was memorable in this
> experience was its human message, the sudden expansion of my consciousness
> in the super-personal world of [humanity]. The poem I wrote on the first day of
> my surprise was named "The Awakening of the Waterfall." The waterfall, whose
> spirit lay dormant in its ice-bound isolation, was touched by the sun and, burst-
> ing in a cataract of freedom, it found its finality in an unending sacrifice, in a
> continual union with the sea. After four days the vision passed away, and the lid
> hung down upon my inner sight. In the dark, the world once again put on its
> disguise of the obscurity of an ordinary fact.[62]

Again, he calls this experience "the first day of my surprise" and contrasts it
with the "disguise of the obscurity of an ordinary fact." There is a whole
worldview in this contrast. The world is one, but we don't ordinarily see its
deeper reality. How do we gain access? How can we truly see, and hear and
touch this reality? There is no ready answer. Even if you are on a quest, you
must be awakened in a surprise. It is almost as if we trick ourselves to enter
the realm of inmost awareness. The cadence of a poem, the message of a

dream, the tragedy or passion or joy can suddenly surprise us into an aware-ness we had no warning was there. To see the world shimmering in oneness, to see all elements flowing in a sublime symphony, requires an access into ourselves, for it is the inmost self that sees the inmost world.

Tagore defines God as an inner–inter relationship. The world is God. We are God. But we do not know this. Our spirituality comes into being when we begin to be conscious of this inner–inter relationship, when it breaks into our experience. And once our spiritual identity is experienced, our religion is an effort to be true to what we know. There are many who pro-pose strategies of renunciation and asceticism, life denial, in order to dis-cover spiritual reality. Tagore powerfully argues for the polar opposite, life affirmation, experiencing the world with full joy and love, completely giving of oneself and experiencing the wellspring of renewal coming in from the deep places of the soul. He exhorts us to "do your work," but not to "let your work cling to you." Work that clings will "kill [your] soul."[63] He advocates self-realization. Keep in creative motion, he advises. God will fill your soul from within. Each of us has great offerings for the world, spiritual gifts we long to express.

Tagore's spiritual vision is revealed in *Gitanjali*:

> The same stream of life that runs through my veins
> night and day runs through the world and dances in
> rhythmic measures.
> It is the same life that shoots in joy through the dust
> of the earth in numberless blades of grass and breaks
> into tumultuous waves of leaves and flowers.
> It is the same life that is rocked in the ocean-cradle
> of birth and death, in ebb and in flow.
> I feel my limbs are made glorious by the touch of this
> world of life. And my pride is from the life-throb of
> ages dancing in my blood this moment.
> Is it beyond thee to be glad with the gladness of this
> rhythm? to be tossed and lost and broken in the
> whirl of this fearful joy?
> All things rush on, they stop not, they look not behind,
> no power can hold them back, they rush on.
> Keeping step with that restless, rapid music, seasons
> come dancing and pass away—Colors, tunes, and
> perfumes pour in endless cascades in the abounding
> joy that scatters and gives up and dies every moment.[64]

This is a poem of deep connection to the world. It is passionately life-affirm-ing, and yet it includes death as a part of life. Tagore experienced a great deal of tragedy in his life. In a period of only five years in his forties, his wife died, followed by his daughter, his best friend, his father, and his son.

After his wife died, his daughter, Renuka, became extremely ill. He took her to a retreat in the hills in hopes of saving her, but she died anyway, six months after her mother. It was at this retreat that Tagore wrote *The Crescent Moon*, his wonderful collection of child poems—for example, "The Beginning":

> "Where have I come from, where did you pick
> me up?" the baby asked its mother.
> She answered half crying, half laughing, and
> clasping the baby to her breast—
> "You were hidden in my heart as its desire,
> my darling.
> You were in the dolls of my childhood's games;
> and when with clay I made the image of my
> god every morning, I made and unmade you then.
> You were enshrined with our household deity,
> in its worship I worshipped you.
> In all my hopes and my loves, in my life, in the
> life of my mother you have lived.
> In the lap of the deathless Spirit who rules our
> home you have been nursed for ages.
> When in girlhood my heart was opening its petals,
> you hovered as a fragrance about it.
> Your tender softness bloomed in my youthful limbs,
> like a glow in the sky before the sunrise.
> Heaven's first darling, twin-born with the morning
> light, you have floated down the stream of the
> world's life, and at last you have stranded on my
> heart.
> As I gaze on your face, mystery overwhelms me;
> you who belong to all have become mine.
> For fear of losing you I hold you tight to my breast.
> What magic has snared the world's treasure in
> these slender arms of mine?"[65]

We see clearly here Tagore's sense of the inner–inter relationship that is the inmost self and God, or what Hindus call Brahman-Atman. And it has a feminine quality, of the grandmother, mother, daughter continuity. "You have floated down the stream of the world's life" carries the same theme as the poem from *Gitanjali*, "the same stream of life that runs through my veins night and day runs through the world," dancing in grass, leaves, flowers, music.

Another poem was written just before his son contracted cholera and died:

> Bless this little heart, this white soul that has won
> the kiss of heaven for our earth.

He loves the light of the sun, he loves the sight of
his mother's face.
He has not learned to despise the dust, and to
hanker after gold.
Clasp him to your heart and bless him.
He has come into this land of an hundred
cross-roads.
I know not how he chose you from the crowd,
came to your door, and grasped your hand to
ask his way.
He will follow you, laughing and talking, and not
a doubt in his heart.
Keep his trust, lead him straight and bless him.
Lay your hand on his head, and pray that though
the waves underneath grow threatening, yet the
breath from above may come and fill his sails
and waft him to the haven of peace.
Forget him not in your hurry, let him come to
your heart and bless him.[66]

Tagore's poem carries a great depth of NF healing, for as he focuses on the immediate relationship of parents and child, he brings in the larger "kiss of heaven," the "light of the sun." In his discussion of immediate trust and love, he is always oriented in the inner–inter relationship of nature, the trust and love that saturate his vision of the cosmos. There is always an embracing, life-affirming joy. "Life is immense!" he says, in knowledge, love, service, and realization.[67]

Tagore wrote over a hundred books of poetry and nearly as many volumes of drama, short stories, novels, political and religious prose. He composed thousands of songs, anthems, and operas. He painted. He was one of the leaders of the Indian nationalist movement and was the first to anoint Gandhi "Mahatma."[68] But with the great idealism characteristic of the Journey of Harmony, he was most devoted to the establishment and well-being of his school at Shantiniketan. He remembered not so fondly his own formal schooling: "My studies in the school I neglected, because they rudely dismembered me from the context of my world and I felt miserable, like a caged rabbit in a biological institute."[69]

So he was determined to create an alternative, a school held outdoors under magnificent trees, one that began education in the heart of the student, not an imposed curriculum, one that operated democratically and poetically. He founded his school on inspiration. In his words: "Our soul becomes stunted when we have no object of profound interest, no prospect of heightened life, demanding clarity of mind and heroic attention to maintain and mature it."[70]

Like his school, his spirituality was based on inspiration. "The progress of our soul is like a perfect poem," he wrote.[71] "My religion is a poet's religion."[72] Tagore's spirituality was lived without ecclesiastical rules and dogma, without an ascetic, otherworldly denial, or even a perfected systematic theology. He affirmed the center of the world at the center of life, a life-affirming spirituality.

> Deliverance is not for me in renunciation. I feel the embrace of freedom in a thousand bonds of delight. Thou ever pourest for me the fresh draught of thy wine of various colours and fragrance, filling this earthen vessel to the brim.
>
> My world will light its hundred different lamps with thy flame and place them before the altar of thy temple.
>
> No, I will never shut the doors of my senses. The delights of sight and hearing and touch will bear thy delight.
>
> Yes, all my illusions will burn into illumination of joy, and all my desires ripen into fruits of love.[73]

Jesus of Nazareth

The great turning point in the ministry of Jesus came when he asked one of his closest disciples, Peter, "Who do the people say that I am?" The disciples answered variously and then he asked a second question, "But who do you say that I am?" At this point, Peter gave the answer, "the Christ of God" (meaning "anointed of God" or prophet in Greek).[74] These questions are central in the Journey of Harmony. NFs are always asking what others think, generally and with their closest associates. It is the confirmation of the journey, for to the extent that others notice one's struggles and progress, grasping the deeper meanings is one's own quest leavening and transforming society.

It was particularly heartening for Jesus to hear the deeper perceptions from Peter, his polar nemesis, an ST. Shortly afterward, three of the disciples witnessed marvelous premonitions from another realm, the transfiguration scene on a mountaintop. It was as if Moses and Elijah were speaking with their leader. At this point Jesus "set his face to go to Jerusalem,"[75] a resolution based in his self-awareness and the ideal he had set before himself.

Jesus' early life is nearly as mysterious. When he was twelve, his parents journeyed with him to Jerusalem to present him at the temple. A day's distance on the way home, his parents discovered he was not in the caravan. They returned and searched the city for him, and when they found him with the elders in the temple he said in rather adolescent tones, "How is it that you sought me? Did you not know that I must be in my Father's house?"[76]

We have no glimpse of him again for about seventeen years. Scholars doubt that he was an apprentice in his father's carpenter shop; more likely he was secluded with the Essenes or listening to the scriptures and pondering the dynamics of justice for a subjugated society. We next meet him in the wilderness, encountering the temptations of selfishness, fanaticism, and power. Introverted religious leaders always burst into history from spiritual experience in seclusion. Perhaps he had resonated with the message of John the Baptist, when he appeared as a candidate for baptism: "I am the voice of one crying in the wilderness."[77]

At the beginning of his public ministry came a well-prepared summary of his teachings for living, known as the Beatitudes:

> Blessed are the poor in spirit, for theirs is the kingdom of heaven.
>
> Blessed are those who mourn, for they shall be comforted.
>
> Blessed are the meek, for they shall inherit the earth.
>
> Blessed are those who hunger and thirst for righteousness, for they shall be satisfied.
>
> Blessed are the merciful, for they shall obtain mercy.
>
> Blessed are the pure in heart, for they shall see God.
>
> Blessed are the peacemakers, for they shall be called sons of God.
>
> Blessed are those who are persecuted for righteousness' sake, for theirs is the kingdom of heaven.
>
> Blessed are you when men revile you and persecute you and utter all kinds of evil against you falsely on my account. Rejoice and be glad, for your reward is great in heaven, for so men persecuted the prophets who were before you.[78]

Rather than a list of sayings about virtue, this is a social program for living in an alternative spiritual kingdom of God. According to biblical scholar John Dominic Crossan, all of the sayings of Jesus were at once individual and social, political and religious. Jesus was engaged in a revolutionary social movement of empowerment that was radically egalitarian, opposing colonial Rome, the Herodian urbanization impoverishing the peasantry of Galilee.[79] Jesus focused his ministry on the poorest level of society in healing, shared eating, and teaching. It was an uncompromising NF idealism.

In Luke's version of the Beatitudes, they are immediately followed by woe statements:

> But woe to you that are rich, for you have received your consolation;
>
> Woe to you that are full now, for you shall hunger.
>
> Woe to you, when all men speak well of you, for so their fathers did to the false prophets.[80]

A continuing debate among scholars involves the eschatology of Jesus, whether the kingdom of heaven was about to come or whether it was already in their midst. As the blessings and woes just quoted indicate, the sayings are in both present and future tenses. John the Baptist had preached what Crossan calls an "Apocalyptic eschatology," imminent and cataclysmic divine intervention to restore peace and justice to a disordered world.[81] Morton Scott Enslin believes Jesus continued this same vision:

> He had become convinced that the long-expected fulfillment of God's promise of old was immediately to be realized; and he had also become convinced that he, Jesus, had been selected by God as his prophet to announce this fact.[82]

In Mark's gospel this became the first announcement in the ministry of Jesus: "The time is fulfilled, and the kingdom of God is at hand; repent, and believe in the gospel."[83] But an alternative interpretation of this and other passages has Jesus locate the kingdom of God in the present in what Crossan calls a "Sapiential eschatology," meaning the wisdom "of knowing how to live here and now today so that God's present power is forcibly evident to all."[84] For example, in the Gospel of Thomas:

> His disciples said to him, "When will the kingdom come?"
>
> "It will not come by looking for it. Nor will it do to say, 'Behold over here!' or 'Behold, over there!' Rather, the kingdom of the Father is spread out on the earth, but people do not see it."[85]

The same saying is utilized by the author of Luke: "The kingdom of God is not coming with signs to be observed; nor will they say, 'Lo, here it is!' or 'There!' for behold, the kingdom of God is in the midst of you."[86]

If this interpretation takes precedence, a number of events and sayings assume an added poignancy—for example, the feeding of the 5,000, reported by all four canonical gospels. Jesus had been teaching and healing on a remote hillside when it came to be lunchtime for the huge crowd. All the disciples had was five loaves of bread and two fish. Jesus not only had the powerful ideal of the kingdom of God in view but also an NF concern for process, how to reveal it. He asked all to sit on the grass in compatible groups of perhaps fifty each, took the loaves and fishes, blessed them, and divided them into twelve baskets for all to share. It was not long before the miracle was revealed: human generosity. Rarely, of course, do people set out for a day trip on foot without bringing food and drink along. But the poor would have carefully secured and hidden it all. As soon as the people genuinely met each other, face to face, the sharing began and the kingdom was in their midst.[87]

If the kingdom of God was seen as Apocalyptic, as the imminent end of history and the start of a new age, then the ethics taught by Jesus might be seen as an "interim ethic," or what Enslin calls the "kingdom ethic."[88] But if the kingdom was already present to be discovered, then it would be expected to be the norm for an ongoing intergenerational movement. Either way, it is remarkably thoroughgoing.

> Love your enemies, do good to those who hate you, bless those who curse you, pray for those who abuse you. To him who strikes you on the cheek, offer the other also; and from him who takes away your cloak do not withhold your coat as well. Give to every one who begs from you;
>
> Love your enemies, and do good, and lend, expecting nothing in return. . . .[89]

This was an ethic addressed to those who had little or nothing to lose. Jesus was asked by a rich man what he needed to do to enter the kingdom:

> And a ruler asked him, "Good Teacher, what shall I do to inherit eternal life?" And Jesus said to him, "Why do you call me good? No one is good but God alone. You know the commandments: 'Do not commit adultery, Do not kill, Do not steal, Do not bear false witness, Honor your father and mother.' " And he said, "All these I have observed from my youth." And when Jesus heard it, he said to him, "One thing you still lack. Sell all that you have and distribute to the poor, and you will have treasure in heaven; and come, follow me." But when he heard this he became sad, for he was very rich. Jesus looking at him said, "How hard it is for those who have riches to enter the kingdom of God! For it is easier for a camel to go through the eye of a needle than for a rich man to enter the kingdom of God."[90]

This incident is a succinct summary of both the social program and the ethic that accompanied the kingdom ideal of Jesus. In addition, the author of Luke shows how for Jesus it is the kingdom that is the focus, not any of several speculations about his human or divine status. In the words of Kirsopp and Silva Lake:

> All interpreters agree on one point—in Galilee Jesus did not announce himself to the people as Messiah or as Son of Man. To the Galileans he was the herald of the Kingdom, the preacher of repentance, a great exorcist and a great healer.[91]

It is possible that Jesus, like Mohammed, was illiterate and that most of his early followers were illiterate as well as poor. His teaching was primarily in the form of sayings and parables that could be grasped aurally, often containing a dilemma or controversy that would engage his listeners in discussion and debate. As an NF, Jesus had a remarkable ability to enlist his tertiary Sensing in his speech. For example, he spoke of the mustard seed, a pesky tiny seed which if it gets into a grain field proliferates so as to choke out the crops being cultivated. Speaking to the oppressed and indebted of Galilee, in a revolutionary setting, was he identifying his hearers with the crops or with the mustard seed? "The kingdom of heaven is like a grain of mustard seed. . . ."[92] And he likened signs of the presence of the kingdom to a fig tree in spring: "From the fig tree learn its lesson: as soon as its branch becomes tender and puts forth its leaves, you know that summer is near."[93]

His examples were drawn from everyday life: absentee landlords, stewards, servants, day laborers, Pharisees, scribes, publicans, little children, a woman accused of adultery, a burglar, a bridegroom, a prodigal son, a wedding feast, lilies, swallows, a log and mote, a door, fish and bread, wine, leaven, a lamp, serpent and dove, sowing seed, a pearl, coin, seine net, a lost sheep.

Jesus entered into the life of his people as a wanderer: "Foxes have holes, and birds of the air have nests; but the Son of man has nowhere to lay his head."[94] It was an integral part of his program as announcer for the kingdom of God. Midway through his ministry in Galilee, he sent his followers out in twos to heal, teach, and bring people into the kingdom of God. The strategy was to be completely vulnerable, to be at least as lowly as those with whom they would associate:

> "And preach as you go, saying, 'The kingdom of heaven is at hand.' Heal the sick, raise the dead, cleanse lepers, cast out demons. You received without pay, give without pay. Take no gold, nor silver, nor copper in your belts, no bag for your journey, nor two tunics, nor sandals, nor a staff; for the laborer deserves his food."[95]

Later in Jerusalem at the Passover/Last Supper, Jesus asked his disciples whether, looking back at their experiences in Galilee, they still felt this had been an important foundation for their ministry: " 'When I sent you out with no purse or bag or sandals, did you lack anything?' They said, 'Nothing.' "[96]

Jesus himself had always behaved in the same pattern. One of his closest friends was Lazarus, whom he is credited with raising from the dead. When his sister, Martha, told Jesus of the tragedy, he wept. But in some way he commanded Lazarus to come out of his tomb. They soon after had supper together, Jesus, Martha, Mary, and Lazarus.[97] Another time when the Pharisees saw Jesus eating with "tax collectors and sinners," they asked him why. He answered, "Those who are well have no need of a physician, but those who are sick; I have not come to call the righteous, but sinners to repentance."[98]

More often than not, his time with people combined healing, teaching, and eating. There was an interdependence of healer and healed, teacher and responder, that was mutually empowering. Jesus, in the company of his humble disciples and friends, was always on a Journey of Harmony. The kingdom of God was relationship-centered.

There is a mystical side of Jesus, seen in his retreats to mountains or in Gethsemane. At the transfiguration he had three disciples with him, but they witnessed only in a very fuzzy way what for him was a turning point in his destiny.[99] Likewise, in the Gospel of John, his followers often sense only dimly what is powerful for him. Nicodemus, an SF, does not appreciate the NF mysticism of Jesus:

> "You must be born anew. The wind blows where it wills, and you hear the sound of it, but you do not know whence it comes or whither it goes; so it is with every one who is born of the Spirit." Nicodemus said to him, "How can this be?" Jesus answered him, "Are you a teacher of Israel, and yet you do not understand this? Truly, truly, I say to you, we speak of what we know, and bear witness to what we have seen; but you do not receive our testimony."[100]

Here the Intuitive mystic does not understand the literal orientation of the Sensor. It is Nicodemus, however, who will care for Jesus' body at his death. Jesus had more immediate success with the woman at the well in Samaria, again employing tangible objects as metaphors for spiritual realities:

> Every one who drinks of this water will thirst again, but whoever drinks of the water that I shall give him will never thirst; the water that I shall give him will become in him a spring of water welling up to eternal life.[101]

Jesus of Nazareth, on the Journey of Harmony, was born and died in his native Judaism. In the centuries following his death, many variations of practices based on his teachings emerged and came to be known as "Christian." Common themes among them all were baptism, teaching, healing, and the eating together of sardines, bread, and wine.[102] The kingdom of God continued a tenuous quest for Christian aspirants, now hidden, now revealed. A saying preserved in a dry desert is attributed to Jesus near the close of his life:

> Do not let the kingdom of heaven waste away. For it is like a palm shoot that dropped its dates all around. It produced buds, and after they had grown, the stalk dried up. This is what happened with the fruit that came from this single root. After it was harvested, more dates were produced by many new shoots. It certainly would be good if this new growth could be produced now, so that you might find the kingdom.[103]

⟲ UNDER STRESS, NEW LEARNINGS

When NFs are overwhelmed in situations of stress, their inferior functions, S or T, temporarily come into play. They can become quickly myopic in vision or critical in their acceptance of self and others, for in the inferior, NFs do not operate with the positive facility of natives in those functions. But if they are able to learn from these experiences, NFs will be more accepting of realistic bounds for their expectations and more accepting of their own limitations. Nobody is perfect. For NFs to assume from their inferior function experiences that they are unworthy or unspiritual is simply wrong. And to derive from these experiences energy for believing that NF is somehow more spiritual than ST is simply to eliminate whole realms from which new insights could be learned and balancing strengths developed. NFs need to concentrate on positive energies for engaging in spiritual disciplines.

Sometimes reactivity to ST is based on learnings from early childhood, when an ST milieu somehow blocked NFs from their native inclinations, tying them in knots of feeling inadequate and critical. These knots need to be untied so that NFs can creatively benefit from the polarity of NF with ST. Much writing on spirituality has a bias of spiritual progression, from ST to NF, from ST tangibilities to NF mysticism, often from ST to introverted forms of NF. These assumptions ultimately will not be helpful either to spiritual progress or to the need for appreciation of others.

When NFs are stressed by the world as it is, some will push their idealism into forms of utopianism, which can easily be seen as a way of avoiding or not dealing with reality as it is. Perfection is not a realistic expectation of ourselves or others. The universe cannot be perfect, for if it were, there would be complete stasis, or a state where struggle, suffering, creativity, or choice would be in abeyance. The quest for harmony must always be in touch with the realities.

⟲ EDUCATION FOR THIS WAY

In the preceding three chapters we have repeated a description of the views of Charles Fair, which bears repeating here. Preparation for all four journeys begins at the earliest age. The most essential elements of spiritual "In Forming" take place before age six or seven, when the functions are relatively undifferentiated. Fair calls this "the seeding of young minds . . . to become what we regard as fully human." In his view, it is the function of the neocortex to organize the energies of the more elemental parts of the brain, the emergency and emotional aspects (the id, in Freudian terms) into a rational control. The seminal traditional ideas of the culture must be planted early, to remain beneath the surface of the soil until the sunlight and nurture of various developmental triggers can call them up from memory and enlist them in the formation of character, mind, and spirituality. Fair sees this process as the essential explanation for the rise and fall of cultures. In times of trouble the seeding process has not taken place. The basic ideas of what it is to be human are learned from story, from examples of people around the child, and from sincerely related precept. The child's mind must be impressed by the drama, genuineness and honesty of input so that the memory remains until it can be utilized developmentally.

NFs place a high value on relationships with the people who will influence their educational development. They will need patience with their global ruminations and support for their idealism and humane responses. Those on the Journey of Harmony tend to have great difficulty with authoritarianism. They want to know why it is important to undertake a particular educational venture, and while they differ from one another on the amount of structure they prefer to work in, they do value their independence as learners. Many ENFs will be drawn to group experiences, and INFs will prefer a best friend or independent study. The seeds of their humanity that Charles Fair speaks of, planted in early childhood, will need to be nurtured in the context of NF values later in youth and young adulthood. Elements of these learnings can find expression in inspiring prophetic or poetic forms.

Because relationships are essential in the educational process, often NFs will suppress their dominant N or F to respond to S or T personal influences in their environment. Particularly during college years, their NT mentors can woo them to suspend their native strengths. Much of later adulthood for NFs can involve sorting through various influences and returning to themselves. These coming-home experiences can be very powerful.

Because, as we pointed out for STs, in Newman's model the perceiving function, N, and the judging function, F, are in different hemispheres, it is harder for the judging function to ride herd on NF Intuition than for types having cognitive functions in the same hemisphere (NT and SF). INFJs and ENFPs have the purest form of Intuition, relatively unregulated and dominant. For this reason, NFs from childhood on need to develop ways of harnessing their Intuition for sustained projects of creativity if they are to make enduring contributions benefiting the world and their own growth.

The Journey of Harmony generally requires a rather structured discipline for advanced progress on the way. Keeping a journal, practicing raja or integral yoga, tai chi, even Sufi dancing can help NFs to define boundaries, affirm distinctions, set out on a particular course. The Robert Frost poem "The Road Not Taken" must have been written for NFs and should be taken to heart.

⸙ HOME AND TEMPLE

The Journey of Harmony as expressed in home and temple can be chameleonlike, first one spiritual adventure, then another, trying new things, later dropping them for new excitements. NFs cross traditional boundaries easily, appropriating for their own growth elements of religions not their own via an inclusive process, easily blurring distinctions and ignoring claims to exclusive truth that would be very important to other types. Religious artifacts, symbols, and practices are likely to be eclectically assembled. Often NFs will add originality and poetic expression, taking liberties with inherited traditions.

In group life and in the governance of the temple, good process is a high priority, both in importance and time. NFs tend to avoid conflict whenever possible, putting harmony in relationships above differences.

ᖆ GIFT OF THIS JOURNEY FOR OTHERS

Natives on the Journey of Harmony are the great carriers of traditions from one branch of culture to another. They would seem to predominate in the neo-pagan movement, in some forms of Hinduism in North America, and in revival of Native American spirituality. While this is exceedingly important in cultural history, NFs' efforts can be distressing to those who practice such spiritualities who are the guardians of the integrity and purity of their traditions. In recent decades, for example, NFs have discovered St. Francis as the "ecological saint." When they learn more of his life story (as an SF), their enthusiasm may recede. Indeed, the tenure of NFs' borrowings tends to be transient and fickle, as they move on to new enthusiasms.

Those on the Journey of Harmony seldom claim that their way is superior, higher, or more advanced than the other journeys. However, NFs have a tendency to claim to combine all traditions. For example, many who are oriented toward raja yoga may claim that they tend to absorb all yogas in their practice. They tend not to think hierarchically, but through their Intuition will often amalgamate, absorbing disparate elements together, where the discrete elements left separate would be of more use and support real differences.

NFs are the peacemakers and carry the banner of tolerance among traditions. In India the technique tends to be through absorption. All pathways lead to the same goal, Brahman-Atman. In the West, on the other hand, the approach has been pluralism, through the idea of the social contract. We are born with the right to develop our personal religious faith and practice it without hindrance by others. In this latter case, NF idealism and emphasis on process make common cause with the NT emphasis on principles and the ST emphasis on the social contract.

ᖆ HOW NFs WILL USE THIS BOOK

Many on the Journey of Harmony will eagerly try to appreciate their way inside each spirituality they encounter on these pages. They will try each and attempt to make as much as possible fit their own practice. They will enjoy rummaging and incorporating. They will want to be informed so that they can facilitate the Four Spiritualities for others. Many NFs will wonder why they cannot be all types, and some ENFPs will believe that they are all types! Perhaps these verses from the Bhagavad Gita can be a helpful curb on Intuitive Feeling excesses.

> By meditation, in the self see
> some the self by the self;
> Others by discipline of reason,
> And others by discipline of action.

> But others, not having this knowledge,
> Hearing it from others, revere it;
> Even they also, nevertheless, cross over
> Death, devoted to the holy revelation which
> they hear.[104]

III.

CONTINUING

CHAPTER EIGHT

DEEPENINGS

OUR LIFE IS AN APPRENTICESHIP TO THE TRUTH
THAT AROUND EVERY CIRCLE ANOTHER CAN BE
DRAWN; THAT THERE IS NO END IN NATURE, BUT
EVERY END IS A BEGINNING; THAT THERE IS
ALWAYS ANOTHER DAWN RISEN ON MID-NOON,
AND UNDER EVERY DEEP A LOWER DEEP OPENS.

Ralph Waldo Emerson, "Essay on Circles"

THE DISCOVERY OF ONE'S NATIVE spirituality empowers and energizes. When the journey is undertaken where the particular spiritual orientation and practices dovetail seamlessly with one's own personality type, the individual can evolve considerable spiritual poise. From this center, enriching can take place from a creative understanding of the other three spiritualities. This chapter will explore ways to conceptualize and deepen your spiritual journey already under way, showing the mandala of relationships in its fullness, illuminating the personal, communal, and cosmic spiritual unity.

Individually we can always be enriched by alternatives. Communally an active tolerance based on mutual appreciation is essential for individual and planetary peace and survival. Cosmically the mandala of spiritual types ties in with the compass points and the world axis at the hub of the wheel. It is the sum total of our connection with all of humanity, Gaia, the collective unconscious of being. Consider the figures and discussions that follow to be opportunities both to understand others in an active tolerance as a basis for all levels of human relationships and to learn from all in a deepening of self. Both will be essential as we explore in chapter 9 the process of reentry from the concentrated journey into the routines of everyday life.

⟳ FOUR SPIRITUALITIES MANDALA

The circle is the oldest form for both communal and personal spirituality. For spiritual communities it is the gathering form that most knits individuals together in celebration and communication. It is the participatory and egalitarian form. And as we saw in chapter 5, in its archaic origins the intensity of the circle was so concentrated it was capable of uniting body and soul in one communal moment of transcendent oneness.

For the individual, the circle can be a mandala for the concentration of meditation, with associations that suggest avenues for spiritual growth. The circle integrates the world, bringing in essential elements from the four directions of the cosmos for our assimilation and reflection. The circle provides a most efficient assistance in the process of mindfulness of the world while concentrating inner reflections for personal enlightenment.

As we saw in chapter 1 and figure 2, when the four functions are arranged in a circle, each taking a quarter of the space, with the perceptive functions opposite each other, and the judging functions opposite each other, we gain a sense of opposition of dominant and inferior, auxiliary and tertiary. These polarities are creative. Likewise, with the many influences upon us from earliest childhood, we can be in degrees influenced or not by adjacent parts of the circle, a perceiving function by two judging functions, a judging function by two perceiving functions. The wheel of the circle can rock or spin with these influences always in play.

When we add the Four Spiritualities at the cardinal points of this mandala circle, as shown in figure 4, we create a powerful synergy between adjacent functions and energize even further the polarities present across the circle. In one step we may arrive at the Four Spiritualities Mandala, displayed in figure 5, where the powerful relationships between adjacent spiritualities and the polarities come into their completeness. It is as if the eye approaches a diamond door to the infinite, a star gate, in which all humanity must be in coordination for the door to open. A mandala is for contemplation as gradually the parts form one whole and integrity in the reflective consciousness.

Figure 5 provides an alternative to the chart that is usually employed in MBTI contexts to graphically illustrate the relationships among the sixteen types.[1] The Four Spiritualities Mandala gives entry into the dynamic qualities of typology often not obvious in the usual rectangular form. A rectangle can have a static and passive effect, whereas the circle always implies motion, energy generated among the elements of the whole.

This figure honors the lead of Isabel Briggs Myers in placing types of like dominant in the same attitude adjacent to each other, for example, INTJ beside INFJ or ESTJ beside ENTJ. Extraverts rim the outside of the circle, Introverts the interior hub. Single functions each have a triangle

FIGURE 4   Elements for Four Spiritualities Mandala

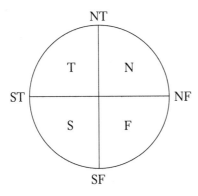

concentrating that function at the interface of the spiritualities, whereas at the cardinal points of the spiritualities there is the equal combination of the two functions that compose that spirituality. Thus, for example, at the SF pole are dominant Extraverted Sensors and Feelers side by side. The overall effect of this mandala of the Four Spiritualities is to show the sixteen types in their relation to one another with introspection at the hub, outreach at the rim.

The most prominent feature is placement of the Four Spiritualities at the cardinal points with a polarity of opposites. NT (the Journey of Unity) is opposite SF (the Journey of Devotion), and ST (the Journey of Works) is opposite NF (the Journey of Harmony). In each quadrant, the four types that compose each spirituality are arranged along the axis across from the opposite spirituality. For example, INFJ is opposite ESTP, and ISTJ is opposite ENFP. In this arrangement you will find other types in your spirituality next to you and opposites visibly opposite, making this figure useful as a tool for reflection in comparison and contrast.

A second feature is the polarity of dominant and inferior functions (and a polarity of your auxiliary and tertiary functions). When you find your dominant, the four types that share that dominant function are all adjacent. Thus, those who share your dominant or inferior, or auxiliary, and so on, can all be seen in relation to your type and to their native spirituality. How close is your partner, spiritual guide, or soul mate? Closeness may signal one kind of sharing, whereas opposition may reveal an equally significant and stimulating form of spiritual assistance.

All is not equilibrium in the Jungian typological universe. There are inequities that keep the wheel spinning. The rational judging functions oppose each other, each with its four types, representing about 25 percent of the population. The irrational perceiving functions[2] also oppose each other,

FIGURE 5 Four Spiritualities Mandala

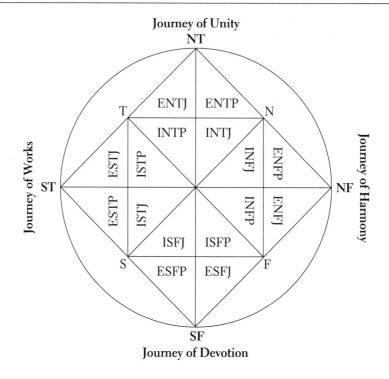

each with its four types, but the Intuitive types represent about 12 percent of the population and the Sensing types 38 percent. "Gravity" then pulls the Sensing side of the circle toward the center of the earth, which is just as it should be, for Sensing grounds us all.

In addition, there is a compensation built into the mosaic, for the rational Introverts are also adaptables (P) and the irrational Introverts are also decisives (J), balancing the whole around the center, whereas the Extraverts at the polarities are one of each, one adaptable (P) on the irrational side and one decisive (J) on the rational side at each pole. While the social significance of this may be quite subtle (the overall weighing of the whole chart toward the southwest and the decisive irrational pole of the Sensing preference), the aesthetic symmetry of it is enjoyable. We have, therefore, not a stasis but a dynamic wheel that turns. Since the rational judging functions act upon the world and the irrational perceiving functions take in from the world in a more passive mode, a kind of rocking dynamic is in play, with the Intuitives (12%) up and the Sensors (38%) down, compensated by the decisive perceptives at the center. But, again, balance in Jungian typology never means stasis.

↶ LEFT BRAIN-RIGHT BRAIN

Those who have followed the left brain–right brain pop literature know there is a good deal of glib talk about the virtues of learning to use our right brain more to counter the dominance of the left in language, science, business, politics, warfare, or whatever is considered to be in excess. We know that many of these generalizations are oversimplified, particularly if we follow cognitive psychologist James Newman in his mapping of a Jungian model of the cognitive functions onto the hemispheres.[3] The polarities of the Four Spiritualities Mandala reflect immediately his left brain (NT)–right brain (SF) model. He places Intuition in the posterior left and Sensing in the posterior right, Thinking in the anterior left and Feeling in the anterior right.

According to Newman, the judging functions regulate the perceiving functions with varying degrees of facility: most efficiently if the judging function is dominant and on the same side of the brain; less efficiently if the perceiving function is dominant; less efficiently still if the dominant judging function is on the other side of the brain; and least efficiently if the perceiving function is dominant with the judging function on the other side. For example, N is purest and least regulated by the judging function in INFJs and ENFPs. S is purest in ISTJs and ESTPs. N is most efficiently enlisted by the judging function for INTPs and ENTJs. S is most efficiently enlisted for ISFPs and ESFJs. There are subtle balances, then, of great importance in understanding our home-base spirituality.[4]

↶ TOOLS FOR REFLECTION

Figures 6 through 8 allow your mind to ruminate until you feel you have a good grasp and appreciation of all Four Spiritualities. Imagine yourself as each one, how you would work, play, and journey spiritually. Imagine, too, all Four Spiritualities sharing equally in creating, monitoring, and benefiting from a spiritual community. What will each contribute? How will each accommodate the others? What will each receive from the other three participants that they will cherish and that will bond all four together as one? Use all three figures together in your reflections.

"Eight Qualities," as shown in figure 6, gives four qualities at the cardinal points for the Four Spiritualities and four more between them at the single function points. To the MBTI qualities for the cognitive function pairs, identifications of a more spiritual focus are indicated. The MBTI *Manual* identifies NTs as "the logical and ingenious types," and George R. Frisbie refers to them as "theoretical visionaries." I have singled out the quest for *clarity* as a most exquisite mark of NT spirituality, flanked by *justice* and *wisdom*. The MBTI *Manual* identifies SFs as "the sympathetic and friendly

FIGURE 6 Eight Qualities

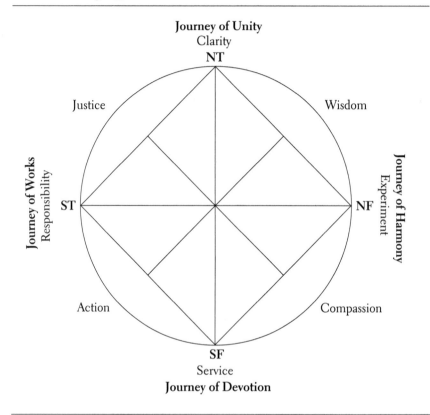

types"; Frisbie calls them "social cooperators." For the Journey of Devotion I have chosen *service* as a most exquisite mark, flanked by *action* and *compassion*. The MBTI *Manual* identifies STs as "the practical and matter-of-fact types"; Frisbie's term for ST is "practical stabilizer." I have chosen *responsibility* as the sterling mark of ST spirituality, flanked by *action* and *justice*. The MBTI *Manual* identifies NFs as "the enthusiastic and insightful types," to which Frisbie adds "idealistic catalysts."[5] I have chosen *experiment* as the spiritual characteristic for those who journey as NFs, flanked by *wisdom* and *compassion*, for there is no final destination in the quest for the well-being of self and humanity.

One word each, however, cannot summarize a journey. Figures 7 and 8 extend this exercise in comparison and contrast in more explicitly religious ways. Our spirituality can be at its most vulnerable and sensitive when the dominant function relaxes so that the other three, particularly the inferior, come into play spontaneously, assuming a prominence in our balance of

FIGURE 7 Which Is Primary?

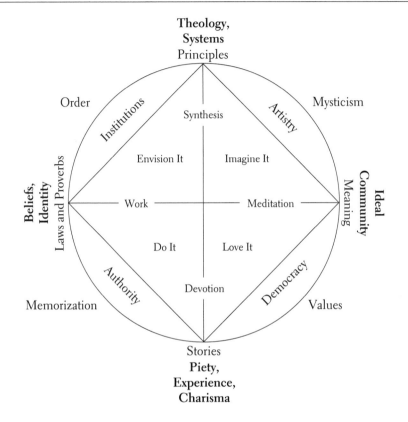

awareness. Such moments do not last very long because they can be scary, chaotic, and overwhelming. The very vulnerability and sensitivity that are the genius of spirituality will help us to learn from these experiences rather than dismissing or repressing them. This learning helps us to integrate our tertiary and particularly our inferior functions into a balanced type development, where we use each function as appropriate in our daily lives. Spiritual experience from moments of learning recedes into a more continuous reality we call religious. Between our moments of most exquisite spirituality come what we hope is a well-type-developed religious sensibility.

In figure 7, "Which Is Primary?", each of the four journeys tends to accentuate the kinds of activities it can handle with the greatest facility. Listed are twenty-four categories that tend to be the province either of the Four Spiritualities or the territories between them. Everyone does all twenty-four and more with good type development. But each of the four journeys

FIGURE 8 When the Center Holds

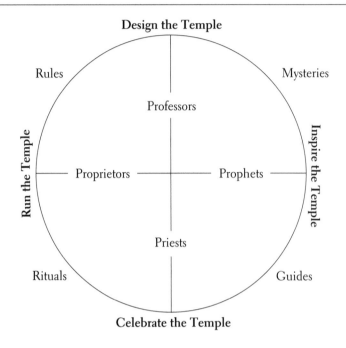

Celebrate the Temple

tends to concentrate some aspects of the religious life to itself and to do them well. Often the activity is demanding and consuming, so much so that we begin to lose perspective and appreciation for others. Doesn't, shouldn't everyone do religion, experience spirituality, as we do? Which is primary, then? We could not have balanced religions serving the many elements of society without all four. To regain our equilibrium, we must return to the active tolerance sponsored by appreciation of the Four Spiritualities.

Figure 8, "When the Center Holds," charts our common pilgrimage in the Four Spiritualities, most tangibly illustrated by the image of the temple (mosque, synagogue, church, pagoda, shrine, meetinghouse, grove, mountain, altar, etc.). Without all four journeys tangibly living at the religious center, and sublimely living in spiritual awareness and practice, the temple falls, the center of society—indeed, the center of the world—languishes. At this point, return to figures 6 and 7 until it all fits or until you have reworked the material in your reflections to your satisfaction.

Worldviews

As early as 1957 the literary critic Northrop Frye identified four distinctly different genres of literature, which he called Ironic, Romantic, Tragic, and

FIGURE 9 Northrop Frye's Worldviews

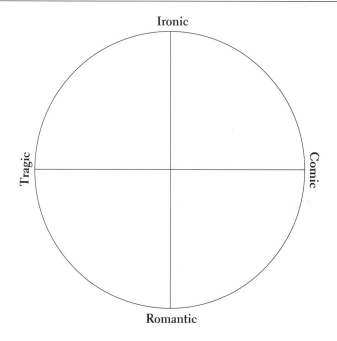

Comic, as shown in figure 9.[6] An Episcopal priest, James Hopewell, translated Frye's four genres into Christian orientations, substituting the terms
Empiric, Charismatic, Canonic, and Gnostic, respectively.[7] In Hopewell's
view, one of these will characterize a whole congregation. A town with four
Protestant churches, for instance, might have one of each. The
Tragic–Canonic and Comic–Gnostic orientations translate quite readily
into ST (the Journey of Works) and NF (the Journey of Harmony), respectively. The Romantic–Charismatic enlivens the SF pole (the Journey of
Devotion), giving it an SP action cast. Qualities of the Romantic can be
found in NT and NF as well. The Ironic is often found as a quality of NT
thought (the Journey of Unity), but Hopewell's designation, "Empiric," is
terribly unfortunate, bringing to it an overwhelmingly S and realistic definition not required by Frye's original meaning.[8] With these preliminary revi-
sions, then, the following definitions will add further insights and depth for
consideration with the Four Spiritualities.

In the Ironic view (North), the world has syntropy, balance; life has love,
support, mutuality. We should live the good life, work for justice, equity, and
plenitude for all, and not expect any supernatural rescue from the fortunes
and misfortunes of life. The full life is to live well, love our neighbors, exercise a healthy skepticism and doubt, and sponsor growth and well-being in

ourselves and in others. (Absent in this definition is Hopewell's designation, "Empiric," with its dependence on the five senses. Empiric science would work for many NTs but not all.) A motto might be, "Have you hugged your kid today?"[9]

At the opposite pole (South) is the Romantic or Charismatic orientation. Picture setting out on an adventure to wrestle with the forces of good and evil. You must leave the familiar and routine, risk catastrophe, relate personality to a transcendent God or source of miracles, and prevail. The spiritual adventure through a paradoxical world ends in personal exaltation. Mottoes for this journey could be "Miracles can happen" or "Let go, let God."

The Tragic or Canonic view (West) acknowledges that the world is entropic, life ends in death, the sun sets but we can live in covenant, submitting ourselves to what is right and true until the sunset comes upon us. The world has its cycles, life has its posterity if we do our best. Submerge the self in order to help life. A motto might be, "Pride goeth before a fall."

The fourth genre (East) is the Comic or Gnostic, beginning with the premise that there is an underlying harmony in the world that flows through us, but illusion and powers of usurpation or our own confusion and problems keep us from seeing and living in this harmony. Deepening of consciousness brings us to unity, happiness, the divine. A Comic motto might be, "All's well that ends well."

The most insightful part of Hopewell's descriptions for me was his personal story of what turned out to be his terminal bout with cancer. It was the four sharply distinct patterns of pastoral communications received then that sparked his own work to define worldviews.[10] These, it seems to me, translate directly into the Four Spiritualities.

When visited by Ironic–Empirics (NT), he would hear: "If you sense death approaching, do it well, embrace your loved ones, settle the affairs of your life, and depart in the full dignity of your humanity."

The Romantic–Charismatics (SF) would say: "Place your faith in God, intensify your trust, and your perseverance will be rewarded."

His Tragic–Canonic (ST) visitors would advise: "Accept your fate. Live well in the interim, and the life you live in the time remaining will justify you then."

And finally the Comic–Gnostics (NF) would testify: "Get with your illness. Be one with it, for it is part of the whole picture. When you accept it, the best outcome will come forth for you." Although they are not a perfect fit, a consideration of worldviews can enrich the journey in each of the Four Spiritualities.

FIGURE 10   Qualities of the Four Directions

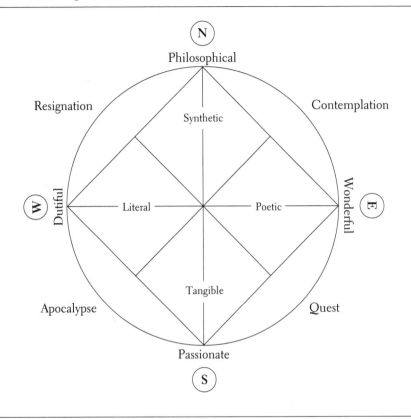

The Compass

Figure 10, "Qualities of the Four Directions," shows how each of the Four Spiritualities might be assigned one of the cardinal directions to add further nuance to each. The idealism and hope of NF spirituality suggest the dawn, whereas the steadfast and dutiful bearing (tinged with a tragic sense) of ST suggests dusk. The Ironic and reflective qualities of NT suggest north and night, while the tangibly warm qualities of SF spirituality suggest noon and south.

In the pagan perspective, however, the elements and colors associated with the four directions may need to be modified a bit. In the Celtic world, the sea was always in the west and the element, water, and color blue, therefore were associated with the west. On the east coast of North America, for example, this does not work as well. East is traditionally associated with air, but NF values seem quite watery to me. Air should be placed in the north, and earth ("dust to dust") in the west. Fire still belongs in the south. The neo-Pagan tradition, like all others, is in flux over time and may eventually accommodate these modifications.

One of the attractions of the pagan revival is a felt need for reattunement to the cycles and qualities of the natural environment. How many know whether the moon is waxing or waning? Imagine a time when whole societies gathered on hillsides at the full moon rituals, no streetlights, no flashlights, no droning of engines. So, too, the marking of the solstices, equinoxes, and the cross-quarter passages of seasons holds intrinsic value, suggesting new qualities and tasks for our interdependent relationship to earth. The qualities in the cycles of nature are reflected by inward qualities, inward seasons of spring (NF), summer (SF), autumn (ST), and winter (NT).

It is here that I recomend using figure 5 and the five following figures in this chapter as mandalas for exploring these inward qualities in a process of meditation. You will find that some qualities lie outside the quadrant of your native spirituality in a neighboring or opposite spirituality. Try to tie this awareness of qualities in with the narrative of your personal story, which we mentioned in chapter 3. What is your vocation, your wisdom, for this world? What experiences, turning points, powerful core awarenesses mark out new segments for the journey ahead? And how will you mark this reflection: with a diary entry, a special sharing with friend or mentor, a ritual of oneness in nature, a poem that captures a quality or moment of deepest mindfulness?

↺ POLAR INFLUENCES

There are two kinds of polar influences shown in figure 5, the opposition of S and N, T and F, and the opposition of NT and SF, ST and NF. We have referred to the large volume of literature dealing with the former, particularly the role of the inferior function. Here it is important to emphasize how completely opposite are NT and SF, ST and NF. Both functions in one are superior to both functions represented in the other and vice versa. If you are an NT, for example, SF will be your inferior and tertiary functions. Such extreme opposition generates energy in the relationship. Energy moves and motivates and gives cause to pay attention to the differences. Differences sharpen and illuminate what we must do on our native journey. Spiritual growth is furthered as much by the stimulation as the appreciation of our polar opposition.

While the opposite pole is quite alien to your home base, it also exerts something of a magnetic attraction as well, a fascination with difference, even a numinous quality. In that attraction is our hope that we can learn from our differences rather than live as strangers or adversaries. Much of what we project as the danger, stupidity, or shallowness of the spirituality of others at our polar opposite has to do with our uneasiness and fears over our own inferior functions. We must first overcome any projections from the weaker side of our own personality; then the appreciation and learning may begin.

Central is an active tolerance, encouraged when differences can be clearly seen in their integrity. Review of the chapter describing your polar opposite will be helpful in this process. The temptation to gloss over distinctions in a false tolerance, with comments about how practices of religion are much the same in their goals and intentions, must be removed. We cannot learn from our polar opposition when in denial of our differences. Spiritual growth through active tolerance and dialogue is an adventure challenging our capacities to listen, to experience, and to understand from deep within.

ᠻᠤ DEASIL INFLUENCES

Deasil in Celtic traditions simply means to spin the wheel sunwise or clockwise (NT to NF, NF to SF, SF to ST, ST to NT). For the eight types in table 2, this means encountering the adjacent journey which shares your dominant function. This is called a *primary deasil influence*. Since your dominant and tertiary may share the same attitude, you may be able to absorb some of the genius of the adjacent journey without much of the turmoil often associated with use of the inferior function. Since the tertiary resides partly in the conscious and partly in the unconscious, it is subject to the action of the conscious will and with careful attention may open up avenues of learning and experience valuable in your spiritual journey. For example, as an INFP I have derived great satisfaction from absorbing experience through my Sensing, in photography when stopping to see what is there in all its detail, in writing poetry to dwell on textures, smells, and sounds, to let them resonate in memory as well, until the experience reaches epiphanic moments for me. The experience overlaps with SF spirituality in my state of being at the time, enough so that I can appreciate the inner side of SF devotion, even while my experience ventures out, still in an NF context of personality. See whether your type is in the list of primary deasil influences in table 2 and reflect in what ways you may overlap with the genius of the spiritual journey adjacent to your own.

The eight pairs found in table 3 represent functions that operate in your least-preferred attitude. If you are an Introvert, then the auxiliary and inferior will be Extraverted. When the inferior is considered alone, it can be a powerful force for both chaos and a threat to the conscious ego and/or a messenger with spiritual meanings that come out of the unconscious part of the self. At other times, however, as it shares the same attitude with our auxiliary function, it can be enlisted in manageable doses to enrich the role of the

TABLE 2 Primary Deasil Influences

Type	Deasil Influence	Functions
ENTP	NF Extraverted	dominant and tertiary
INTJ	NF Introverted	dominant and tertiary
ENFJ	SF Extraverted	tertiary and dominant
INFP	SF Introverted	tertiary and dominant
ESFP	ST Extraverted	dominant and tertiary
ISFJ	ST Introverted	dominant and tertiary
ESTJ	NT Extraverted	tertiary and dominant
ISTP	NT Introverted	tertiary and dominant

TABLE 3 Secondary Deasil Influences

Type	Deasil Influence	Functions
INFJ	SF Extraverted	inferior and auxiliary
ENFP	SF Introverted	inferior and auxiliary
ISFP	ST Extraverted	auxiliary and inferior
ESFJ	ST Introverted	auxiliary and inferior
ISTJ	NT Extraverted	inferior and auxiliary
ESTP	NT Introverted	inferior and auxiliary
INTP	NF Extraverted	auxiliary and inferior
ENTJ	NF Introverted	auxiliary and inferior

auxiliary in our lives, either in its extraverting or in its introverting. Reflect upon times when you have related to one of the four spiritual journeys as indicated with the attitude (E or I) of your auxiliary. What did you learn to appreciate in that journey and what were you able to incorporate as an influence in your own journey?

ᕦ WIDDERSHINS INFLUENCES

If your type was not in table 2, it will be found in table 4. Widdershins in Celtic usage means to spin the wheel counterclockwise (NT to ST, ST to SF, SF to NF, NF to NT), with the same benefits for the eight types listed

TABLE 4 Primary Widdershins Influences

Type	Widdershins Influence	Functions
INFJ	NT Introverted	dominant and tertiary
ENFP	NT Extraverted	dominant and tertiary
ISFP	NF Introverted	tertiary and dominant
ESFJ	NF Extraverted	tertiary and dominant
ISTJ	SF Introverted	dominant and tertiary
ESTP	SF Extraverted	dominant and tertiary
INTP	ST Introverted	tertiary and dominant
ENTJ	ST Extraverted	tertiary and dominant

TABLE 5 Secondary Widdershins Influences

Type	Widdershins Influence	Functions
ENTP	ST Introverted	inferior and auxiliary
INTJ	ST Extraverted	inferior and auxiliary
ENFJ	NT Introverted	auxiliary and inferior
INFP	NT Extraverted	auxiliary and inferior
ESFP	NF Introverted	inferior and auxiliary
ISFJ	NF Extraverted	inferior and auxiliary
ESTJ	SF Introverted	auxiliary and inferior
ISTP	SF Extraverted	auxiliary and inferior

here as for the eight listed for primary deasil influences. Read the discussion that applies to these eight types as well.

If your type was not in table 3, it will be found in table 5. All that is mentioned in introducing that list holds for the eight types listed in table 5. As an INFP, I have found the enlisting of my inferior T by my auxiliary N extremely valuable in relating to the outside world. Often it is hard to tell them apart, perhaps because they are both left-brained as well and enjoy a manner of structural connection in what Newman calls the "intellectual or mental sphere."[11] Whether the secondary deasil or widdershins influences work equally well for Extraverts in their introverting as for Introverts in their extraverting is an open question.

ᐤ THE SACRED MOUNTAIN, THE WORLD TREE

When we spin the wheel deasil and widdershins, and explore the polarities north and south, east and west, we have set the world of personality into a position of constant motion, influence, and challenge. Our circle of personality types has taken on the quality of a wheel with an axis.

In numerous mythologies, the center of the spiritual world is represented by a sacred mountain or a tree of life. The Buddha achieved enlightenment under the bodhi tree. In Western mythology the tree of life was in the center of the Garden of Eden and later was the instrument of the death and resurrection of the savior god. The cross is an ancient symbol of the world axis, the intersection of the polarities of the four cardinal directions. All elements of the world of life meet at this place. In the Taoism of Chuang-tzu, the image is of a gnarled tree around which life has swirled for countless generations.[12] It can be by a roadside or on a remote mountainside, its roots intertwined in ledges and cliffs. The sun and moon, in turn, can be seen through its branches, rising over the peak of the mountain. Mount Olympus, Sinai, Hira (Jabal Nur), and Sumeru are classic images of the world axis. In flat or desert areas, ziggurats, pyramids, and temples were often erected to serve as the focal point. The spire of the village meetinghouse served as a center reference for the New England Puritan commonwealth. In pagan circles the Maypole at Beltane gives the circle a focus usually occupied by the god or goddess at the full-moon rituals. In Native American cultures both the sacred mountain and the image of the tree at the center of the medicine wheel or hoop are found.[13]

There is a universal need to place the whole diversity of life, personality, and spiritual expression around a unifying symbol (NT), ideal or harmonious center (NF), focus for devotion and service (SF), and steadfast pillar of identity (ST). There is a need to invoke qualities of the north, east, south, and west (deasil), bringing them together for a time as one, as a concentration of the best energies of all, spiraling into a synergy of power, and then to disperse back to our own home base at the cardinal point (widdershins) enriched in our native journey.

A story of great pathos is told by Laurens van der Post, South African author and close friend of Carl Jung, of the last traces of the oldest continuous spiritual culture remaining on earth in Southwest Africa. He had a profound childhood memory of someone in his grandparents' generation reporting seeing one of the last of the !Kung bushmen cave painters shot to death, with a dozen zebra horns strapped around his middle filled with paints. Post himself made a pilgrimage to the Tsodilo Hills, which had once been a gathering place for the many bushmen clans.[14] He found exquisite paintings there and encountered at the deep levels of his spiritual awareness "the Spirits of the Slippery Hills."

Every life needs a sacred pilgrimage place to which you may return, if not physically then in your memory. This place will be with you always. It can be a glorious cathedral, a gnarled tree in the deep forest, or a ledge by the sea. It is a place where the themes of your life can come together for review and assimilation. It is a place that evokes deepest feelings of sadness, joy, and awe by simply being there when you must return to its embrace. For you it is at the center of the wheel of life.

CHAPTER NINE

DESTINATION

WE POUR INTO THE VESSEL OF SELF THE ACCUMULATED EXPERIENCE,

VISION, AND INTERPRETATION FROM THE CULTURAL VESSELS OF

TIME, THE TRADITIONS AND LORE AND SCIENCE OF HUMANITY. . . .

UNTIL A RELIGION FOR ONE WORLD DISCOVERS ITS INDIGENOUS

FORMS IT WILL BE HANDICAPPED.

Kenneth L. Patton, *A Religion for One World*

ᗌ A COSMIC VIEW

WE ARE BORN FROM OUR mothers in a continuity stretching back to the first mother and to Mother Earth itself. The air we breathe and the sun that warms us are in a sense our father. The moon reassures us in the night in its waxing and waning. The stars in the night sky remind us of a vast cosmic context in which we will find the meaning of our lives. In chapter 8 we explored an equally remarkable inner balancing of elements to that of sun (F, SF) and sky (T, NT), earth (S, ST) and moon (N, NF).[1] We examined the four directions, north (NT), south (SF), west (ST), and east (NF), all associated in one unity of the tree of life and viewed in clarity and warmth, integrity and harmony, from the sacred mountain of human spirituality.

We discovered in our "Deepenings" that a natural cosmology emerges from our human nature itself. As I mentioned at the beginning, I see the Four Spiritualities as a Rosetta stone for our spiritual life, gaining us entrance from our own experience into every branch of human religious culture. As citizens of the planet, we have access into the spiritual foundations of our life together wherever we may be, whatever insights and practices it is time to avail ourselves of. Heart and mind, body and soul, are as accessible in myriad expressions as earth and sky, sun and moon.

From the simple confluence of human and natural forces in the boughs of one tree, the branches of the spiritual tradition have improvised innumerable variations in the Four Spiritualities. Each unique person in pilgrimage elaborates elements even further, leaving a legacy of experience for those who follow. Thus, one of our hopes as we anticipate elderhood is that something of the lessons of our journey will remain for others.

For some, the journey to greater spiritual depth was fraught with struggle, crisis of identity, a deep night of the soul. They will never be the same as before. Relationships, vocation, demeanor have changed, sometimes in a complete break with the past. For many, the journey has been experienced at least as drastically life-altering and set apart from the mainstream of their life commitments. In descending from the mountain of pilgrimage, there is the crisis of return, the reintegration of deeper spiritual experience and awareness into the ongoing focus of life as a householder, worker, citizen, and participant in religion. The traveler returns deepened, matured, spiritualized. In this chapter we trace some of the arenas in which individuals transformed by their journey may participate as elders, teachers, guides, servants, or trustees within their social environment.

⟨ THE TEMPLE

Originally all human culture was focused in the temple: the arts; science; medicine; the hunt, field, pasture, and forest vocations; music; dance; and governance. The priest or priestess and council of elders presided over the whole, the holy unity that was society. Society entered the temple, which in turn existed as a reflection of the sacred cosmos that sustains and embraces all of life.

Even hermits have a religious community for reference, support, and memory. We are social beings. In our social nature our spirituality will emerge. No endeavor is more important for the religious community than the spiritual growth of its members. We need community to actualize in microcosm the practice and fulfillment of the vision we have for the well-being of the world. The temple is the crossroads and celebration of that vision. The congregation is its embodiment. Priests, prophets, professors, proprietors are its agents. All together carry on its ministry to life.

The goal of the temple must be to nurture the Four Spiritualities in its constituency. Beginning with themes portrayed in stone and wood, tapestries, mosaics, paintings, and implements that compose its forms and usage, the silent messages need to portray the aspirations of all in their respective journeys, like a magnet drawing us forward. This is the beginning of education, before we can read and before we begin the more intentional later spiritual journeys of our lives. Therefore, it is important that those experienced in journeying in one of the Four Spiritualities and in integrating the lessons all four have to give each other be involved centrally in the councils of the temple. The central messages must be clearly present to be absorbed from our earliest years forward.

FINDING A COMMUNITY

In the interfaith world we are rapidly entering, as often as not a child's parents will be of very different religious backgrounds. Jewish–Christian, Hindu–Moslem, pagan–Buddhist couples may have accommodated the marriage by suspending their own religious development.[2] Then come the crises and passages of their lives, and the issue of intentional spiritual growth arises. The Four Spiritualities may serve as a means to transcend the reluctance to face the need to journey that results from the fear of resparking differences with the partner's religion of origin. Now each of the Four Spiritualities can be identified in the religions of both partners. The dialogue can be between spiritualities and bypass or place into perspective the irreconcilable differences between traditional religions. The Four Spiritualities are found in all branches of human religious culture, nurtured in some places more effectively than in others, but practiced universally. Likewise, children can be introduced to the spiritual tradition of humankind via the Four Spiritualities without threatening the religious standing of their parents with each other.

Casting the issue of life in an interfaith world into its most positive arrangement, it is important to find a religious community that can be an extended family for the participation of all members of your household. At the same time, it needs to be supportive of whatever you require for participation beyond the community's immediate circle of influence to sustain your progress in your own spiritual pilgrimage. Too often, religious communities are so competitive or even antagonistic toward one another that they cannot wholesomely support the needs of individuals in their own constituency to reach beyond for a part of their spiritual stimulation or nurturance. While rare, communities do exist that intentionally encourage their members to engage whatever elements of the spiritual tradition of humankind that can minister to their needs.

Community helps in two ways, which I believe are not mutually exclusive. Similar personality types will be drawn into small groups within the larger community for mutual support and understanding. But the larger religious community needs to exist for all types, not for similar types only. We need a place where we can work together to build in microcosm a support system for human spirituality that we recommend for the larger macrocosm of humanity. What we accomplish will encourage other communities around the world. We must have a place where we all work together, learning the complementarity of types in a context of mutual appreciation and support.

⤶ EDUCATIONAL IMPERATIVES

Education must take place in the context of community: community values and principles, community caring and justice, communal commitment to each other. The institutionalization of education and the credentialing and licensing of teachers have done much to sterilize and isolate learning, oppress and imprison the learner, and separate him or her from the reality and immediacy of human support in community. Education must be a living process. The disparities between how education is practiced and how it might be transformed in a holistic model will be evident to the spiritual initiate during the process of reintegration.

Too much of the discussion in MBTI literature about education addresses the nature of adaptation to schooling as it is. It largely serves as a consultant to the present system rather than showing appropriate alternative ways of encouraging learning for children and adults. A typical school classroom with a teacher and thirty students may not be a place for optimum employment of MBTI insights. In this postindustrial age of computers and mediated communications, small religious communities may well be an appropriate socialization context for education that can be largely learner-driven.

Thus, one approach, which is outlined below, would be a model in which Four Spiritualities is the context for learning. In a learner-centered education, the environment of community and temple must be attractive to the inner inquisitiveness of learners, provide access to educational resources the learners believe they need, and a spiritual context whereby via any (and to some extent all) of the Four Spiritualities the learners will be able to integrate the learning adventure in a spiritual context.

Chapters 4 through 7 described in some detail the educational emphases needed for each of the Four Spiritualities. Here we look at general curriculum concerns within which learners must gradually take charge of their own education, as developmentally they come on board to operate from their home base—NT, SF, ST, or NF. Our spirituality is the frame by which we interpret the whole and which mediates meanings of the journey as we travel. What could be more important at the center of any curriculum?

Most curriculum possibilities that are worth teaching are usable from the earliest ages forward, in a spiral approach to content and based on developmental abilities. The task of educators and the community is to hold the world open for the learner. Content must be attractive to learners out of their own spiritual center and desire to know and to understand their lives, relationships, and world. No required curriculum would be needed, only offerings in place with the power to attract, as a magnet attracts iron.

Curriculum begins with the body. Most physical education today is useless long before a person reaches middle age. Aside from aerobic running and chopping wood, yoga, tai chi, and other centering and prana (breathing) exercises would be available at the beginning and at the end of each day. In addition, rituals would focus the attention within the context of meaning, rituals for honoring earth, for gazing at stars, for observing consideration of our neighbors, and for learning appreciation of our world cultural and religious inheritance. Music would be taught primarily in the context of the worship life of the community and rituals that would open and close each day. To learn in a context of worship grounds for SFs, gives a context of credible belief for STs, evokes a sense of the unity that learning elucidates for NTs, and enlarges the human context with meanings and wonder for NFs.

The study of literature would begin at a very early age, with the great epics, fables, moral stories, and fairy tales. Deriving from this context would be the arts of poetry, drama, storytelling, rhetoric, and reading. The world's scriptures would be recited aloud (which is how many of them were originally meant to be transmitted), and important passages would be memorized, particularly passages offering moral wisdom or solace or exaltation. Not in vogue in this century, the memory has fallen into disuse (a particularly tragic loss for S types).

For the sciences, I would begin with synergetic geometry, what Fuller calls "nature's own coordinates," to replace the obsolete Euclidean geometry and algebra of "imaginary numbers" that are taught in most schools today. This can be modeled and therefore introduced at the beginning rather than the end of one's learning adventure. From it will flow arithmetic, astronomy, physics, and chemistry. In addition, I would expose children to basic mechanical machines, such as a pendulum clock, and to house-building sites to illustrate basic principles. It is critical to show the unity of the world by placing the sciences and mathematics together, not in separate "departments" of schooling. Likewise, evolution, biology, nutrition, cooking, gardening (herbs, vegetables), animal husbandry, and physical education are one study.

If the universe is one, so is Gaia, the earth, one living system. Geology is an evolution with biology, geography consists in branches of one whole, history is the story of how humans have adapted to system earth and the meanings we have discerned for earth as home base. Civics, concepts of liberty and democracy, the nature of the human commonwealth, economics as a study of the whole support system for the good life—all should be integrated. Maps are tools for thought and should not give a distorted or parochial view as the Mercator form does (I recommend Fuller's "dymaxion map," which does neither). Religious festivals, the world around, should be integrated in one calendar for humankind to show patterns of observance and to make practices accessible to the learner.

Language, communication, and aesthetics are essential and form a continuum. Key word and concept derivations are rooted in earliest language families: Polynesian, Sanskrit, Chinese, Greek, Hebrew, hieroglyphics. It is desirable that learners employ more than one presently spoken language. Museums must be enlisted to bring to the learner their world inheritance in the arts, as well as a critical appreciation for history, geography, and religion. Calligraphy needs to be taught to show the continuity of art and language (particularly important for Sensors). Composition of the written word needs to be taught beside composition and art in the electronic media. The Confucian "rectification of names" is an important consideration, along with the study of the nature of propaganda and how it can be discerned in written as well as electronic forms. The electronic media, particularly radio, video, and the computer, are critical parts of the environment in which we live today as well as tools for communication and learning. Still photography, graphics, desktop publishing, and the production of plays, dance, and film all relate to the world of communication and aesthetics and, in a larger sense, the continuing emergence of human culture on earth. Much of today's mass education brings students to a point of enough literacy so that they can be easily manipulated as citizens and consumers. Critical thinking beyond mere literacy and basic marketable skills must be a goal of education that prepares students for their world in which the spiritual journey will open for them as a prospect for life.

Social service is an important component of learning, for in service we enter into relationships we help create, and thereby it is an opportunity for learning initiative, discerning need and solutions for it, and for learning empowering approaches for helping others. It is a way for moving one's moral values, principles, and sense of justice from theory into action. And it is an opportunity for intergenerational collaboration, with the dialogue and planning that precedes it.

All of the above will be considered as they manifest the Four Spiritualities. At no time will students wander so far that they will not know how to coordinate what they learn with the spiritual center of their own lives. Integrity awareness as found in each age of development will tie all together as a whole within each person.

A vision for education centered in spirituality would encompass all levels equivalent to preschool through graduate school. Learning is a lifelong

process. And in the context of religious communities, rather than gradua-
tions there would be rites of passage into youth, adulthood, and elderhood.
The most difficult obstacle for implementation would be the inertia of the
schooled mind. It is hard, even for Intuitives, to imagine a complete alternative to mass education for learning.

In America and other pluralistic societies where separation of church
and state is a central principle, this model of education would need to be
sponsored and initiated entirely by the religious communities. It is important to honor the conventions for protection of the rights of minorities. A
model of education in the context of spiritual practice in community would
flounder if it were imposed by the general society upon its members. It must
grow independently from the people engaged in learning through their
voluntary associations.

Many religious communities neglect all but the prevailing spiritualities
in their own constituencies. Children who might be attracted to one of the
four, recognizing it as their own, find little for their nurture and begin dropping out by the time of the puberty rites. Tragically, many conclude that
there is nothing in religion for them. It is essential that children discover the
plurality of spiritualities young so that they may carry this knowledge with
them until the time is right in their lives to accelerate the journey. This problem is absorbed when the whole learning environment is holistic, with spirituality at the center.

⟳ PLURALISM

While when seen through the lenses of the Four Spiritualities the world's
religions have a great deal in common, referenced through the Jungian cognitive functions of our personalities, they differ widely in their content.
Aspirants may prefer to enter into the journey of their native spirituality
through intensification of their participation within one tradition, or they
may journey more eclectically, drawing on sources from many traditions,
preferring the perspective of participation in their global spiritual inheritance.

In the reintegration process, travelers will encounter alternative interpretations of the importance of their learnings, identified by comparative
religious scholar Diana Eck as exclusivism, inclusivism, and pluralism.[3]
Exclusivism in all likelihood will appeal to only a few, as it posits that one
tradition holds "the one and only truth."[4] The inclusivist alternative is attractive to some as it attempts to include the energies and insights of other traditions as subordinate to or serving prior or universalized impulses of one's
own tradition.

Pluralism moves beyond exclusivism and inclusivism in either of two ways. One form of pluralism begins in commitment to one tradition, entering into dialogue with others. This form, favored by Eck, seeks to understand differences and assumes that the challenge of alternatives will sharpen and deepen one's own journey. There is no attempt to synthesize the many religions into one, or to leave the field open as in relativism, without commitment to one's own religion among the many.

A second variety of pluralism begins with commitment to one world of human spirituality, finding the whole to be a dramatic story and synergy itself in relation to its parts. Here variations in the branches of human religious culture are honored as practiced with integrity by the custodians of their traditions. Dialogue remains essential to further understanding and working relationships within the planetary mosaic. Appreciation of the many variations of religious practice is furthered greatly through the agency of the Four Spiritualities. And individuals are encouraged to incorporate elements of the traditions into the matrix of their own journey.

A major issue of reintegration is the finding of appropriate forms of participation in religious community. Exclusivist, inclusivist, and the first variety of pluralist travelers have their communal forms, temples, and educational institutions already in place. The second form of pluralism, however, is in its infancy, presenting few already existing contexts in which to work. This is particularly unfortunate for interfaith families, which need communities that will intentionally support spiritual growth within multiple traditions and often in more than one of the Four Spiritualities. Such fledgling communities seek appropriate forms for their temples in order to support globally oriented worship, education, and service.

Participation in supportive religious communities is influenced by the surrounding norms of societies. In many social contexts, some exclusivist religious movements and even inclusivist perspectives (which may take on imperialist qualities) have been known to oppose pluralism in both its forms either by bullying tactics if they are minorities or through tyranny if they are majorities. But there is a long tradition of religious freedom to permit pluralism, from Emperor Asoka's edicts in the third century B.C., to the proclamation at the Diet of Torda in 1568 that "no one shall compel them,"[5] to Jefferson's "wall of separation between Church and State."[6] A person who has journeyed in one spirituality, appreciative and responsive toward the other three, will be a champion of freedom, for open dialogue, and mutual understanding.

⟨⟨ FAITH DEVELOPMENT

To prepare for and to undertake the journey is itself an act of faith. A sense of trust and deeper confidence continues, leaving us open to further experiences and challenges that provoke spiritual growth. A reopening of doubts and misgivings, or a sense of letdown from the previous exhilaration and concentration of the journey, will also stimulate opportunities for further development. It is important to respond to challenges and not allow depreciation of the central importance of the spiritual journey and its continuing impact for spiritual growth. There is a continuing need to refresh the mediating role of the MBTI, to interpret the nature and steps of the journey itself, and to monitor the relationship of the spiritual and ethical dimensions as they continue to guide your life.

There is a danger in the use of the MBTI that one will routinize its interpretation, robbing newcomers of the excitement in its dynamics. For example, this may be the source of John Akerman's finding in his use of the MBTI in his congregation that it describes only "the horizontal," its tendency to explain phenomenon but not to incite change. In his words, "The MBTI as it is usually taught gives no clues for growth. It seems to identify a point of view that justifies our remaining one-sided."

Akerman then puts forward a *vertical* model that seems to be completely independent and unconnected. He postulates five relationship-based *stages of psychological growth*, which are really elucidations of the life cycle: (1) child–dependent, (2) rebel–counterdependent, (3) young adult–mutually dependent, (4) adult–confident, and (5) wise adult–interdependent.[7] However, it is hard to see how the vertical integrates with the horizontal. Developmental theories such as those put forward by Grant, Duniho, and others discussed in chapter 2 work better with the MBTI.

An important vertical model is put forward by Dorothy Berkley Phillips as a six-step process: (1) choice, (2) purgation, (3) self-knowledge, (4) self-acceptance, (5) devotion to the good, and (6) rebirth.[8] Not wedded to theories of the life cycle, these steps could be followed in the context of any of the Four Spiritualities at any point in the life cycle that a person reaches spiritual crisis. This progression is not too far removed from Joseph Campbell's journey of the hero: (1) separation or departure, (2) trials and victories of initiation, and (3) return and reintegration with society. He agrees with Phillips that birth (or rebirth) is the only way to spiritual transformation. You cannot patch up the old or hold the present; something new must come into the world.[9] Elsewhere he says you must first decide what is important (choice) and "follow your bliss."[10]

Are these beyond good type development and a balancing of the self put forward in Jungian circles? I believe there is ample flexibility in the Jungian model to accommodate a full choice, purgation, initiation, and rebirth. Here each of the Four Spiritualities contains traditions of the journey and spiritual transformation. And there are influences among the spiritualities that stimulate the journey. While we discussed the hero's journey in the context of the Journey of Devotion, the romantic SF, the gnostic NF Journey of

Harmony can be influenced widdershins; the tragic ST Journey of Works can be influenced deasil; and even the ironic NT Journey of Unity is attracted by the north-south polarity. There is plenty of creative tension and energy within and among the spiritualities for journeys of transformation.

I believe there is a strength and advantage to being able to begin the journey in a search for and affirmation of one's native spirituality. After all, the horizontal dimension is real, and it would be detrimental to one's integrity and center to abandon it for the journey. There is plenty of depth and height to be discovered right there, even in the midst of spiritual crisis and despair. Every journey must have a return, and a foundation for integration to follow. Good type development need not sound sterile when a person has access to the rich human traditions to be found in each of the Four Spiritualities.

Some distinguish spirituality from ethics, seeing spirituality as a progression beyond ethics. As noted in chapter 3, all traditions see ethics as a prerequisite and platform on which spiritual growth can be sustained. I have not come across a model in which one's ethical orientation continues to evolve along with the spiritual journey. In the Four Spiritualities, however, you can discern ethical growth as integral in the spiritual journey. If you weigh the key elements of each of the Four Spiritualities, giving each a valence either toward the ethical or toward the spiritual, you will readily see their interdependence. Thus, in the Journey of Unity (NT), clarity has a spiritual valence and justice an ethical valence; in the Journey of Devotion (SF), devotion has a spiritual valence and service an ethical one; in the Journey of Works (ST), covenant weighs towards the spiritual and stewardship toward the ethical; and in the Journey of Harmony (NF), harmony has a spiritual valence and the quest for the ideal an ethical one. Another way of juxtaposing the spiritual and the ethical valences is to see the spiritual as a being mode and the ethical as a doing mode. Thus, the spiritual journey is by no means an escape from the world. Being and doing are one journey. Spirituality and ethics are interdependent and synergistic.

It is essential in the context of the return of the journey from the sacred mountain to the valley of social life and well-being that one enter into this life body, mind, and heart, for it is a reconnecting with the "spiritual solidarity of humankind" (as noted in the Introduction). Whereas the journey was the great opening of awareness of our vision and reality of the whole, the return is the enacting of our participation, whatever will be our gift to humanity here and now, our legacy for the onward motion of the most sacred reality. The ethical and the spiritual move as one life.

⟆ SERVING SOCIETY

The efficacy of the spiritual journey always includes connecting with human purpose, in which the general well-being of society is enhanced because the journey continues. The bodhisattva ideal, St. Bernadette's devotion to healing care after the visions subsided, Gandhi's walk to the sea in nonattachment, the returning process of integral yoga—all point to the need for elements of closure as the journey continues, for grounding the search in the web of existence. Even extended meditation in cloistered isolation requires a returning. The return involves four ways of benefiting society with the hard-gained depth of the journey, based in justice (NT), service (SF), stewardship (ST), and pursuit of the ideal (NF). At the center of the circle of spirituality, the world tree of spiritual life bears fruit for the society that gives it birth and nurture.

As the pilgrim descends from the sacred mountain and enters the valley of communal life, lives reborn work their transformations in society. The pilgrim holds the possibility of spiritual journey and the Four Spiritualities open for others who otherwise may be lost or adrift from their native spiritualities. Part of returning is one's heightened sensitivity to others who are just becoming ready to embark.

We have mentioned in this chapter the importance of the temple and its religious community. We need to stress the institution of the temple as in itself the servant of society. The institution as it becomes a center of support, right and whole (holy) relationship, and center of beauty for life, in executive and Quaker lay leader Robert Greenleaf's words, is itself "a powerful serving force."[11]

It is extremely difficult to serve a postindustrial society today without working through institutions, and we would do well to restore the temple to the center. Particularly in a postmodern and even postapocalyptic age, there is a great need to intensify efforts for new cultural meanings and forms in religious communities.[12] In every age of overwhelming and wrenching change, it is the monasteries and religious communities that are able to intensify and develop apart, that bring to the world a new cultural reformation that can grow into a new support for social life.

ᚲ A RITE OF PASSAGE FOR MIDLIFE

Along with special exigencies to be addressed by religious communities in our age, there are perennial passages in the life cycle to be marked and perhaps new ceremonies of passage that need to be brought forward. Universally there are ceremonies for welcoming infants, initiating youth at puberty, marriage for life partners, and rites of remembrance for the dead. To these four are often added membership in a community and ordination of clergy. There are suprisingly few rites for midlife passage, perhaps because patterns for the rites of passage were established long before the dramatic lengthening of the life span in this century. For many Moslems, the hajj, pilgrimage to Mecca, has served as this passage. In Hinduism, entry into the vanaprastha or sannyasin stages of life constitutes a rite of passage at midlife. In Wicca there is the elevation of the wise woman at age fifty-six.

Many do not experience a profound shift in their lives from previous patterns of living to a new life built on an alternative platform. Spiritual growth is gradual and nontraumatic. But there are exceptions. At midlife, Abraham left Ur and never returned. The disciples of Jesus pulled up stakes and left their former lives behind. The great Indian emperor Chandragupta left his empire to join the Jain community, Sravanabelgola. Something common to all of us is the realization at midlife that according to the actuarial tables our lives are half over. A ceremony would portray that the glass is half full, not half empty, that spiritual beginnings lie ahead, that the benefits of this life for the world have reached a great potential and that the heart that resides within is a generous and compassionate heart.

With the commitment required to identify and take up one of the Four Spiritualities, to follow this native journey in the mutually appreciative company of the other three, as outlined in this book, you are already on your way. A ceremony created in the life of your religious community will help you sustain this new level of intensity in pursuing your pilgrimage. It will set in motion a social context for spiritual growth, showing its importance leading up to that spiritual and ethical integration that is the accomplishment for the final transition of our lives to elderhood.

On the other hand, by midlife the journey of sorting and developing your native spirituality may have matured and you may have journeyed through the shadow regions of deepening with the inferior function and be ready to distill the wisdom of the journey and become a caretaker and mentor for others at midlife. The ceremony would instead take on these qualities or merge entirely with an entrance into communal elderhood.

⟳ ELDERHOOD

There is considerable lament in Western culture that elders are not accorded the respect they deserve by virtue of their age. I suspect, however, that respect does not follow automatically even in traditional societies. Respect for elders derives from their spiritual accomplishment, from memory of the traditions and their preserving, acts of benevolence or service, prophetic insight and powers, wisdom from the journey, poetic or artistic spirituality. And this respect is in response to the visible integration of spirituality and the ethical dimension that is the basis for personal authority among our peers in the community. It is either visibly evident out in the larger society that a person has devoted the remainder of his or her life to spiritual pursuits or known in the religious community in which he or she participates. Religious authority in a local setting is earned, not awarded according to one's age or position.

ᠥ THE GOAL OF LIFE

There can be no final destination. Neither time nor space ends. But life always moves toward its goals, not as a perfection but as the attraction of an ideal. The goals of our Four Spiritualities complement one another, for spirituality is perceived through four lenses we can call the absorption ideal (NT), the compassion ideal (SF), the stewardship ideal (ST), and the fulfillment ideal (NF). To know the One (NT), to be devoted to Oneness in others (SF), to guard and guide the integrity of Oneness in the world (ST), to explore potentials for realization of the One (NF)—all form for us an intimate acquaintance with spiritual reality, the goal of life. Possibilities (N) and particulars (S), love (F) and comprehension (T), become as One. Our native journeys, fully explored, bring us all together in fullest human integrity and kinship. When you hear the call deep in your spirit, follow, deepen, return, for in your life you may become one in eternity.

INTRODUCTION

1. Jacquetta Hawkes and Sir Leonard Woolley, *Prehistory and the Beginnings of Civilization*, Vol. 1, *UNESCO History of Mankind* (New York: Harper & Row, 1963), p. 7.

2. Ibid., p. xiii.

3. John Warrington, trans., *Julius Caesar: The Gallic Wars* (New York: Heritage Press), Book Six.

CHAPTER ONE

1. The best introductory works presenting the MBTI in far more detail than is possible here include Isabel Briggs Myers' classic *Gifts Differing* (Palo Alto: CPP, 1980, 1993), and her short *Introduction to Type* (Palo Alto: CPP, 1962), revised by Linda K. Kirby and Katharine D. Myers in a fifth edition, 1993; Otto Kroeger and Janet M. Thuesen, *Type Talk* (New York: Delacorte Press, 1988); Sandra Hirsh and Jean Kummerow, *Life Types* (New York: Warner Books, 1989); Alan Brownsword, *It Takes All Types* (San Anslemo, CA: HRM Press, 1987); and David Keirsey and Marilyn Bates, *Please Understand Me* (Del Mar, CA: Prometheus Nemesis Books, 1978).

2. Myers, *Gifts Differing*, p. 53.Z

3. Statistics are taken from Keirsey and Bates, *Please Understand Me*, pp. 14–25 unless otherwise noted. They in turn rely upon Katherine Bradway's article in *The Journal of Analytical Psychology*, Jung's Psychological Types," 1964. While Keirsey and Bates appear to give rounded off numbers the general picture has remained even though more narrowly focused studies have differed in details.

4. James Newman, *A Cognitive Perspective on Jungian Typology* (Gainsville, FL: Center for Applications of Psychological Type, 1990), p. 16.

5. Terence Duniho, *Wholeness Lies Within* (Gladwyne, PA: Type & Temperament, 1980), pp. 12–21.

6. Arthur Waley, trans., *The Way and Its Power: A Study of the Tao Te Ching* (London: George Allen & Unwin, 1934), p. 174. xxv.

7. *Matthew* 11:15. All biblical references are to the Revised Standard Version.

8. Newman, *Cognitive Perspective on Jungian Typology*, p. 5.

9. Ibid., pp. 20, 23.

10. Duniho, *Wholeness Lies Within*, pp. 19–20.

11. Loren Pedersen, *Sixteen Men: Understanding Masculine Personality Types* (Boston: Shambhala Publications, 1993), p. 28.

12. Ibid., p. 41.

13. Roy Oswald and Otto Kroeger, *Personality Type and Religious Leadership* (Washington, D.C., Alban Institute, 1988), p. 40.

14. See Myers, *Gifts Differing*, pp. 83–116; Keirsey and Bates, *Please Understand Me*, pp. 167–206; Hirsh and Kummerow, *Life Types*, pp. 71–270; and Kroeger and Thuesen, *Type Talk*, pp. 214–80.

15. Compiled from Keirsey and Bates, p. 167–206.

16. Ibid.

17. Myers, *Gifts Differing*, p. 10.

18. Isabel B. Myers and Mary McCaulley, *Manual: A Guide to the Development and Use of the Myers-Briggs Type Indicator* (1985), p. 36.

19. A definitive work on the place of the inferior function is Naomi Quenk, *Beside Ourselves* (Palo Alto, CA: Davies-Black Publishing, 1993).

20. It is not uncommon to come across discussions of spirituality in terms of the single cognitive functions as represented in figure 2. (For example, Earle C. Page, "Finding Your Spiritual Path? Following Your Spiritual Path." Workshop handout. Gainseville, FL: Center for Applications of Psychological Type, 1982). Usually, these discussions contrast the four function, seeing spiritual growth as the fulfillment of the dominant functions, or by matching a function with itsopposite to stimulate spiritual growth. Combining the cognitive function pairs, however, allows for the full influence of the attitudes and brings to bear upon spiritual growth both the type dynamics discussed in this chapter and chapter 2, and type development, which is outlined in chapter 2. For a fine general treatment of type dynamics and development, beyond the scope of this chapter, see Katharine D. Myers and Linda K. Kirby, *Introduction to Type Dynamics and Development* (Palo Alto, CA: Consulting Psychologists Press, Inc., 1994). In chapter 8, further discussion of the cognitive function pairs brings the circle motif in figure 2 forward into the full Four Spirituality mandala (see figures 4 and 5).

21. Genesis 5:1.

22. Lin Wu-chi, *A Short History of Confucian Philosophy* (Baltimore: Penguin, 1955), p. 25.

CHAPTER TWO

1. A similar model can be found in Eleanor S. Corlett & Nancy B. Millner, *Navigating Midlife* (Palo Alto, CA: Davies-Black Publishing, 1993). p. 51.

2. Mentioned in chapter 1 (note 19), Naomi Quenk's book on the inferior function takes, for each of the sixteen types, three ways the inferior function erupts, giving numerous examples. She contrasts the expression of the function as an inferior "in the grip" with the way that same function is expressed for those types who have it as their dominant.

3. W. Harold Grant, Magdala Thompson, and Thomas E. Clarke, *From Image to Likeness* (New York: Paulist Press, 1983), p. 186.

4. Ibid., p. 20.

5. Ibid., p. 23–24.

6. Terence Duniho, *Wholeness Lies Within* (Gladwyne, PA: Type & Temperament, 1980), pp. 69–78.

7. Robert and Carol A. Faucett, *Personality and Spiritual Freedom* (New York: Image Books, 1987), pp. 87–88.

8. Pedersen, *Sixteen Men*, p. 29.

9. Ibid., p. 26.

CHAPTER THREE

1. Luke 18:18.
   A word of caution: When I quote scripture I will hope you will have your own translations ready at your side. I urge the collecting of multiple translations for such essential works as the *Tao Te Ching*; the Koran; the *Dhammapada*; the Jewish–Christian *Bible*; the *Analects of Confucius*; the *Meng-k'o*; the *Hsuan-tzu*; the *Chuang-tzu*; the *Upanishads*; the Bhagavad Gita; Patanjali's *Yoga Sutras*; and the world's great stories and poetry.

2. Matthew 8:22.

3. Amos 7:14.

4. Quoted in Christmas Humphreys, ed., *The Wisdom of Buddhism* (New York: Random House, 1960), p. 87.

5. B. K. S. Iyengar, trans., *Light On the Yoga Sutras of Patanjali* (London: Aquarian/Thorsons, 1993), p. 135. Charles Johnston, trans., *The Yoga Sutras of Patanjali* (New York: Quarterly Book Department, 1912), p. 66.

6. Alain Danielou, *Yoga: Mastering the Secrets of Matter and the Universe* (Rochester, VT: Inner Traditions International, 1991), p. 39.

7. S. V. Ganapati, trans. *Patanjali's Yoga Sutras* (Madras: Hindi Pracher Press, 1962) p. 7.

8. The leading description of the neo-pagan movement only a short time ago mentions the word *ethics* just once, fourth from the end on a list of "What are the most important issues facing Pagans today." Margot Adler, *Drawing Down the Moon* (Boston: Beacon Press, 1986), pp. 414–15.

9. Joseph Politella, *Taoism and Confucianism* (Iowa City: Crucible, 1967), p. 1.

10. Jared Sparks, *The Life of Benjamin Franklin Containing the Autobiography, with Notes and a Continuation* (Boston: Tappan, Whittemore, and Mason, 1848), pp. 105–7.

11. Albert Schweitzer, *Indian Thought and Its Development* (Boston: Beacon Press, 1936), pp. 23, 196–265. See also D. S. Sarma, *Hinduism Through the Ages* (Bombay: Bharatiya Vidya Bhavan, 1967), pp. 254–57.

12. Matthew 7:1–5.

13. R. Buckminster Fuller, *Synergetics* (New York: Macmillan, 1975), p. 15. Generalized design-science exploration is concerned with discovery and use by human mind of complex aggregates of generalized principles in specific-longevity, special-case innovations designed to induce humanity's consciously competent participation in local evolutionary transformation events invoking the conscious comprehension by ever-increasing proportions of humanity of the cosmically unique functioning of humans in the generalized design scheme of Universe. This conscious comprehension must in turn realize ever-improving implementations of the unique human functioning as well as an ever-increasingly effective concern for the relevant ecological intercomplementation involved in local Universe support of humanity's functioning as subjective discoverer of local order and thereafter as objective design-science inventor of local Universe solutions of otherwise unsolvable problems, design-science solutions of which will provide special-case, local-Universe supports of eternally regenerative generalized Universe.

14. Lawrence W. Jaffe, *Liberating the Heart* (Toronto: Inner City Books, 1990), pp. 163–64.

15. Jane Goodall, *In the Shadow of Man* (Boston: Houghton Mifflin, 1971), pp. 52–53. See also Dudley Young, *Origins of the Sacred* (New York: St. Martin's Press, 1991), pp. 47, 91, 95–97.

16. Loren Eiseley, *The Firmament of Time* (New York: Atheneum, 1960), pp. 112–13.

17. Heinrich Zimmer, *The Art of Indian Asia* (New York: Bolligen, 1955), vol. 2, plate 1b. See also P. Thomas, *Hindu Religion, Customs and Manners* (Bombay: D. B. Taraporevala Sons), p. 3.

CHAPTER FOUR

1. Albert Schweitzer, *Out of My Life and Thought* (New York: New American Library,) p. 124.

2. William E. Channing, "Likeness to God," 1828, in *The Works of William E. Channing, D.D.* (Boston: James Munroe, 1843), pp. 233–34. (Channing is difficult to pin down typologically beyond IN, perhaps INTJ or INFJ.)

3. Albert Camus, Stuart Gilbert, trans., *The Stranger* (New York: Vintage Books, 1959), p. 154.

4. W. H. D. Rouse, trans., *Great Dialogues of Plato* (New York: New American Library, 1956), p. 121.

5. Perry Miller, ed., *Margaret Fuller* (Garden City, N.Y.: Doubleday, 1963), p. ix.

6. Quoted in ibid., p. 27.

7. Julian Huxley, *Religion Without Revelation* (New York: New American Library, 1957), p. 46.

8. Michael Polanyi, *The Tacit Dimension* (Garden City, N.Y.: Doubleday, 1967), p. 91.

9. Martin E. Marty, *A Cry of Absence* (San Francisco: Harper & Row, 1983), p. 66.

10. Ibid., p. 102.

11. *Theodore Parker's Experience as a Minister* (Boston: Rufus Leighton, 1859), p. 117.

12. Amos 7:8.

13. Amos 5:21–24.

14. Amos 4:1.

15. "Hymns to the One God," in Lewis Browne, ed., *The World's Great Scriptures* (New York: Macmillan, 1946), p. 39.

16. Rolfe Gerhardt, "Unitarian Universalists and Other Personality Types," in *Selected Essays* (Boston: U.U.M.A., 1987), pp. 117–18.

17. Timothy Richard, trans., *Ashvagosha: The Awakening of Faith* (New Hyde Park, N.Y.: University Books, 1960), p. 58.

18. Edward Conze, ed., *Buddhist Texts* (New York: Philosophical Library, 1954), p. 70.

19. Claud Field, trans., *The Confessions of Al Ghazzali* (Lahore: Sh. Muhammad Ashraf) pp. 57–59). Al-Ghazali's arranging of the four functions into a hierarchy of "stages of perception" served to provide the Sufi movement in Islam with a systematic rationale better connected to the mainstream Sunni traditions.

20. Horace Mann, *Twelve Sermons: Delivered at Antioch College* (Boston: Ticknor and Fields, 1861), p. 76.

21. Nikkyo Niwano, *Buddhism for Today: A Modern Interpretation of the Threefold Lotus Sutra* (Tokyo: Kosai), p. 180.

22. Thomas Merton, *The Seven Storey Mountain* (New York: New American Library, 1948), p. 314.

23. Ibid., p. 325.

24. Ibid., p. 327.

25. Ibid., p. 345.

26. Ibid., p. 411.

27. Ibid., p. 365.

28. A good brief description of Thomistic prayer can be found in Chester P. Michael and Marie C. Norrisey, *Prayer and Temperament: Different Prayer Forms for Different Personality Types* (Charlottesville, VA: Open Door, 1991), pp. 79–85.

29. Bertrand Russell, *Mysticism and Logic* (Garden City, N.Y.: Doubleday Anchor Books, 1957), p. 52–53.

30. Christmas Humphreys, ed., *The Wisdom of Buddhism* (New York: Random House, 1960), p. 45.

31. Ibid.

32. Martin Buber, *I and Thou*, Ronald G. Smith, trans. (New York: Scribner, 1958), pp. 11–12.

33. Georg Feuerstein, *Sacred Paths* (Ithaca, N.Y.: Larson Publications, 1991), p. 69.

34. "Brihadaranyaka-Upanishad," in Shree Purohit Swami and W. B. Yeats, *The Ten Principal Upanishads* (London: Faber and Faber, 1937), p. 132.

35. Winthrop Sargeant, trans., *The Bhagavad-Gita* (Albany: State University of New York Press, 1984), pp. 258–59. 5:16–17.

36. Alain Danielou, *Yoga: Mastering the Secrets of Matter and the Universe* (Rochester, VT: Inner Traditions, 1991), pp. 118–20.

37. Swami Vivekananda, *Jnana Yoga* (Calcutta: Advaita Ashrama, 1992), p. 398; p. 77.

38. Walpola Sri Rahula, *What the Buddha Taught* (New York: Grove Weidenfeld, 1974), pp. 18–19.

39. Eugene W. Burlingame, *Buddhist Parables* (New Haven, CT: Yale University Press, 1922), pp. 92–94.

40. Humphreys, *Wisdoms of Buddhism*, pp. 36–37.

41. Ibid., pp. 80–81.

42. Ibid., pp. 85–86.

43. Bhikkhu Khemo, *What Is Buddhism?* (Bangkok: Prachandra Press, 1957), p. 55.

44. P. Lal, trans., *Dhammapada* (New York: Farrar, Straus & Giroux, 1967), p. 45.

45. The host of bodhisattvas were led by "the four outstanding bodhisattvas," boundless conduct (NT), pure conduct (SF), steadfast conduct (ST), and eminent conduct (NF) (parenthetic types mine). Nikkyo Niwano, *A Guide to the Threefold Lotus Sutra* (Tokyo: Kosei, 1981), pp. 104–9.

46. Edward Conze, *Buddhism: Its Essence and Development* (New York: Harper & Row, 1959), p. 23.

47. Frederick J. Streng, trans., *Vigrahavyavartani: Averting the Arguments*, in *Emptiness: A Study in Religious Meaning* (Nashville: Abingdon Press, 1967), p. 227.

48. Rune E. A. Johansson, *The Psychology of Nirvana* (New York: Anchor Books, 1969), pp. 109–10.

49. Lal, *Dhammapada*, pp. 32–33.

50. Quoted in R. Buckminster Fuller, *Ideas and Integrities* (New York: Collier, 1963), p. 70.

51. E. J. Applewhite, *Cosmic Fishing* (New York: Macmillan, 1977), p. 150.

52. Quoted in ibid., p. 146.

53. Fuller, *Ideas and Integrities*, p. 45.

54. R. Buckminster Fuller, *No More Secondhand God* (Carbondale: Southern Illinois University Press, 1963), p. 141.

55. R. Buckminster Fuller, *Education Automation* (Carbondale: Southern Illinois University Press, 1962), p. 35.

56. Fuller, *No More Secondhand God.* p. 128.

57. Sidney Rosen, *Wizard of the Dome* (Boston: Little, Brown, 1969), p. 5.

58. R. Buckminster Fuller, *Nine Chains to the Moon*, (Carbondale: Southern Illinois University Press, 1963), pp. 18–19.

59. Ibid., p. 99.

60. Ibid., p. 350.

61. R. Buckminster Fuller, *Earth, Inc.* (Garden City, N.Y.: Doubleday [Anchor Books] 1973), p. vii.

62. R. Buckminster Fuller, *Utopia or Oblivion* (New York: Bantam Books, 1969), p. 123.

63. For example, see R. Buckminster Fuller, *Critical Path* (New York: St. Martin's Press, 1981), p. 203; or his last book, *Grunch of Giants* (New York: St. Martin's Press, 1983), p. 54.

64. R. Buckminster Fuller, *And It Came to Pass—Not to Stay* (New York: Macmillan, 1976), pp. 94–97.

65. Applewhite, *Cosmic Fishing*, p. 29.

66. Fuller, *No More Secondhand God*, p. 165.

67. Ibid., p. 28.

68. For details, consult his two-volume *Synergetics*, or the delightful *Tetrascroll, Goldilocks and the Three Bears: A Cosmic Fairy Tale* (New York: St. Martin's Press, 1982).

69. Applewhite, *Cosmic Fishing*, p. 154.

70. Ibid., pp. 152–54.

71. Alan W. Watts, *The Way of Zen* (New York: New American Library, 1957), p. 152.

72. Daisetz T. Suzuki, *Manual of Zen Buddhism* (New York: Grove Press, 1960), pp. 33, 184.

73. Conze, *Buddhism*, p. 202.

74. Paul Reps, ed., *Zen Flesh, Zen Bones* (Garden City, N.Y.: Doubleday, 1961), p. 32.

75. Suzuki, *Manual of Zen Buddhism*, p. 74.

76. Ibid., pp. 127–44; p. 128, plate 11.

77. Charles M. Fair, *The Dying Self* (Middletown, CT: Wesleyan University Press, 1969), pp. 84, 82.

78. Joseph Campbell, with Bill Moyers, *The Power of Myth* (New York: Doubleday, 1988), p. 92.

79. Henry David Thoreau, *Walden* (1854; reprint, New York: New American Library, 1957), p. 97.

80. Acts 9:1–9; Romans 1:16–17, 20; Galatians 5:13–14; I Corinthians 12:4–26.

81. N. A. Nikam and Richard McKeon, trans., *The Edicts of Asoka* (Chicago: Phoenix Books, 1959) p. 36.

82. Hans Küng, *Global Responsibility* (New York: Continuum, 1993), p. 69; pp. 127–28.

83. Ibid., pp. 126, 128, 132.

84. Best known of these "perennial philosophers" might be Aldous Huxley, whose *Perennial Philosophy* (1944) includes a chapter, "Religion and Temperament," which uses three of the yogas found in the Bhagavad Gita (karma, jnana, bhakti), along with insights of Jung and American psychologist, William Sheldon's body types. Unfortunately, Huxley worked before the advent of the MBTI instrument and did not utilize Jung's cognitive functions, only his early work on Extraversion and Introversion. See *The Perennial Philosophy* (New York: World Publishing, 1962), pp. 146–61.

85. Küng, *Global Responsibility*, p. 104.

86. Adeltaa Siitaa Devii, trans., *Giitaa: A Samskirt-English Bridge* (Madras: The Theological Publishing House, 1955), pp. 261–62. 13:24–25.

CHAPTER FIVE

1. Kroeger and Thuesen, *Type Talk*, p. 247.

2. D. H. Trump, *Malta: An Archaeological Guide* (Valetta, Malta: Progress Press, 1990), p. 28.

3. Marija Gimbutas, *The Civilization of the Goddess* (San Francisco: Harper, 1991), p. 176.

4. Matthew 2:13–21.

5. André Ravier, *Bernadette: The Saint of Poverty and of Light* (Paris: Nouvelle Librairie de France, 1974), pp. 9–10.

6. Daniel 3:12; 1:8; 3:19–30.

7. Muhammad Asad, *The Road to Mecca* (New York: Simon & Schuster, 1954), pp. 294–95.

8. Robert Graves, trans., *The Golden Ass* (New York: Pocket, 1954), pp. 230–53.

9. Ibid., pp. 237–38.

10. William Irwin Thompson, *The Time Falling Bodies Take to Light* (New York: St. Martin's Press, 1981), pp. 150, 153.

11. Throughout Greece, near or on every archaeological site of any consequence stands a Byzantine church, usually constructed of materials from the rubble of the ruins. In Rome most of the major churches have Egyptian obelisks in front of them. Major churches founded on the ruins of older religions include the Pantheon, Church of Santa Maria sopra Minerva, Basilica Aemilia, Church of Santa Francesca Romana, Church of Santo Stefano Rotondo, Church of Santa Maria degli Angeli (in the baths of Diocletian!), Church of San Bartolomeo, and others.

12. Swami Nikhilananda, trans., *The Gospel of Sri Ramakrishna* (New York: Ramakrishna-Vivekananda Center, 1942), p. 565.

13. Ibid., p. 150.

14. *The Ramakrishna Movement* (Calcutta: Ramakrishna Mission Institute of Culture, 1991), p. 3.

15. Nikhilananda, trans., *Gospel of Sri Ramakrishna*, p. 115.

16. Ibid., Introduction by Swami Nikhilananda, pp. 12–13.

17. The Brahmo Samaj was founded by Rammohun Roy in 1828 and carried on by capable leaders such as Debendranath Tagore and Keshub Chunder Sen. See P. C. Mozoomdar, *The Faith and Progress of the Brahmo Somaj* (Calcutta: Calcutta Central Press, 1882); D. S. Sarma, *Hinduism Through the Ages* (Bombay: Bharatiya Vidya Bhavan, 1967) pp. 63-81; Spencer Lavan, *Unitarians and India: A Study in Encounter and Response* (Boston: Skinner House, 1977).

18. Ramakrishna, quoted in Solange LeMaitre, *Ramakrishna and the Vitality of Hinduism* (New York: Funk and Wagnalls, 1969), p. 166.

19. Key proponents of temperament theory for our purposes here are Keirsey and Bates, *Please Understand Me*; Louise Giovannoni, Linda Berens, and Sue Cooper, *Introduction to Temperament* (Huntington Beach, CA: Telos Publications, 1986); Oswald and Kroeger, *Personality Type and Religious Leadership*; and Michael and Norrisey, *Prayer and Temperament*. See also chapter 1, p. 12.

20. John 3:1–12.

21. John 19:38–42.

22. See ch. 5, "On the Dancing Ground," on the origins of religion, in Dudley Young, *Origins of the Sacred* (New York: St. Martin's Press, 1991), pp. 93–123.

23. Campbell, *Power of Myth*, p. 5.

24. Arthur Waley, trans., *The Nine Songs* (San Francisco: City Lights Books, 1973), p. 27.

25. Luke 10:38–42. See also John 12:1–8.

26. Arthur Waley, trans., *The Book of Songs* (New York: Grove Press, 1960), p. 175.

27. Burton Watson, trans., *Mo Tzu* (New York: Columbia University Press, 1963), pp. 88, 108–9.

28. Michael H. Kohn, trans., *The Shambhala Dictionary of Buddhism and Zen* (Boston: Shambhala, 1991), pp. 119–20.

29. Richard Carlyon, *A Guide to the Gods* (New York: Quill, 1982), p. 83.

30. Rene Grousset, *Chinese Art and Culture* (New York: Grove Press), p. 268.

31. C. A. S. Williams, *Encyclopedia of Chinese Symbolism and Art Motives* (New York: Julian Press, 1960), p. 239.

32. Niwano, *Buddhism for Today*, p. 180.

33. Mother Teresa quoted in Rev. Mark Bellentini, et. al., eds., *Singing the Living Tradition* (Boston: Beacon Press, 1993), #562.

34. Henry Van Dyke, *The Story of the Other Wise Man* (New York: Harper, 1901), pp. 48, 60, 82.

35. Matthew 2:1–12.

36. Huston Smith, *The Religions of Man* (New York: Harper & Row, 1958), p. 52.

37. Swami Atmananda, *The Four Yogas* (Bombay: Bharatiya Vidya Bhavan, 1991), p. 67.F

38. Feuerstein, *Sacred Paths*, pp. 83–84.

39. Swami Vivekananda, *Bhakti Yoga* (Calcutta: Advaita Ashrama, 1991), p. 111.

40. Swami Tyagisananda, trans., *Narada Bhakti Sutras* (Mylapore: Sri Ramakrishna Math, 1967), Sutra 82, p. 25.

41. In his commentary on Sutra 82, Tyagisananda (ibid., p. 275) provides a list:

    Narada and Vyasa are always found delighting themselves in singing the glories of the Lord, helping to convert others to a life of spirituality and love. The Gopis of Brindavan were naturally attracted by Krsna's enchanting beauty, and they revelled in it. Ambarisa spent his whole life in worship, Prahlada in remembrance, Hanuman in service. Uddhava and Arjuna had the attitudeof friendship, Rukmini and Satyabhama loved Him as a husband, and Kausalya and Devaki as their son. Bali and Vibhisana are supreme examples of complete self-surrender to the Lord; and the great Rsis like Sanatkumara and Yajnavalkya immersed themselves in His bliss.

42. S. P. Bahadur, trans., *Ramayana of Goswami Tulsidas* (Bombay: Jaico Publishing House, 1972), p. 200.

43. W. G. Archer, *The Loves of Krishna* (New York: Grove Press, 1961), p. 75.

44. Richard Schiffman, *Sri Ramakrishna: A Prophet for the New Age* (New York: Paragon House, 1989), p. 54.

45. Ibid.

46. James Hewitt, *The Complete Yoga Book* (New York: Schocken Books, 1977), pp. 473–74.

47. Sri Aurobindo, trans., Bhagavad Gita, 9:26–27, p. 132.

48. Sadananda Chakrabarti, *Our Master Sri Sri Sitaramdas Onkarnath* (Calcutta, 1957), pp. 151–52.

49. Tyagisananda, trans., *Narada Bhakti Sutras*, pp. 11–12.

50. James McCartney, *The Philosophy and Practice of Yoga* (Romford, Essex: L. N. Fowler, 1978), p. 64.

51. Tyagisananda, trans., *Narada Bhakti Sutras*, p. 8.

52. Joseph Politella, *Hinduism* (Iowa City: Sernoll, 1966), pp. 70–71.

53. Abdullah Yusuf Ali, trans., *The Holy Qur-an* (Lahore: Sh. Muhammad Ashraf, 1969), XCIII:6–8. p. 1752.

54. Arthur J. Arberry, trans., *The Koran Interpreted* (New York: Macmillan, 1955) LIII:19, p. 244.

55. Tor Andrae, *Mohammed: The Man and His Faith* (New York: Harper, 1960), p. 43.

56. Günter Lanczkowski, *Sacred Writings* (New York: Harper & Row, 1956), p. 71.

57. Andrae, *Mohammed*, p. 44.

58. Emile Dermenghem, *Muhammad and the Islamic Tradition* (London: Longmans, Green, 1958), p. 18.

59. Sayyid Abul A'la Maududi, *Towards Understanding Islam* (Delhi: Markazi Maktaba Islami, 1993), p. 17.

60. Yusuf Ali, trans., *The Holy Our-an*, XIX:93–95. p. 786.

61. There are many sources that describe the Five Pillars of Islam: for example, Thomas W. Lippman, *Understanding Islam* (New York: New American Library, 1982), pp. 6–30; Smith, *Religions of Man*, pp. 319–29.

62. Allama Sir Abdullah Al-Mamun Al-Suhrawardy, trans., *The Sayings of Muhammad* (New York: Citadel Press, 1990), p. 53.

63. Andrae, *Mohammed*, p. 75.

64. Suhrawardy, trans., *Sayings of Muhammad*, pp. 60–61.

65. H. A. R. Gibb, *Mohammedanism* (New York: New American Library, 1955), p. 33.

66. Andrae, *Mohammed*, p. 185.

67. Arberry, trans., *Koran Interpreted*, III:97 p. 87; II:257. p. 65; CIX:5, p. 352.

68. Ezzeddin Ibrahim and Denys Johnson-Davis, *Forty Hadith Qudsi* (Beirut: Dar Al-Koran Al-Kareem, 1980), p. 100.

69. Asad, *Road to Mecca*, pp. 143–44.

70. Valentino Turetta, *Saint Francis of Assisi* (Perugia: Santuario Porziuncola, 1977), p. 15.

71. Leo Sherley-Price, trans., *The Little Flowers of Saint Francis* (Baltimore: Penguin Books, 1959), p. 195.

72. ESFP is the considered opinion of Michael and Norrisey, *Prayer and Temperament*, p. 138, as well.

73. Sandro Chierichetti, *Assisi* (Milan: Industrie Grafiche Nicola Moneta, circa 1990), p. 75.

74. Turetta, *Saint Francis*, p. 21.

75. Chierichetti, p. 75.

76. Sherley-Price, *Little Flowers*, p. 18.

77. Turetta, *Saint Francis*, p. 35.

78. Bertrand Russell, *A History of Western Philosophy* (New York: Simon & Schuster, 1945), p. 449.

79. Ignatius Brady, trans., *The Writings of Saint Francis of Assisi* (Assisi: Casa Editrice Francescana, circa 1990), p. 172.

80. Sherley-Price, *Little Flowers*, p. 195.

81. Turetta, *Saint Francis*, p. 55.

82. Ibid., p. 57.

83. Brady, trans., *Writings of Saint Francis*, p. 182.

84. Turetta, *Saint Francis*, p. 47.

85. Sherley-Price, *Little Flowers*, p. 199.

86. James Dalton Morrison, ed., *Masterpieces of Religious Verse* (New York: Harper, 1948), p. 130.

87. Fuller, *Utopia or Oblivion*, p. 114.

88. R. Buckminster Fuller, *Operating Manual for Spaceship Earth* (Carbondale: Southern Illinois University Press, 1969), p. 120.

89. Juan Mascaro, trans., *The Bhagavad Gita* (Baltimore: Penguin Books, 1962), 13: 24–25, p. 101.

CHAPTER SIX

1. Robert William Rogers, *Cuneiform Parallels to the Old Testament* (New York: Abingdon Press, 1926), p. 402.

2. Rustom Masani, *Zoroastrianism: The Religion of the Good Life* (New York: Collier Books, 1962), p. 90.

3. Sarvepalli Radhakrishnan and Charles A. Moore, eds., *A Source Book In Indian Philosophy* (Princeton, N.J.: Princeton University Press, 1957), p. 174.

4. Ibid.

5. Deuteronomy 4:40.

6. Lin Yutang, *The Importance of Living* (New York: Reynal & Hitchcock, 1937), p. 408.

7. Waley, trans., *Book of Songs*, pp. 260–61.

8. Edward E. Hale, *Sermons of the Winter* (Boston: J. Stilman Smith, 1893), pp. 141–42.

9. Edward E. Hale, Jr., ed., *The Life and Letters of Edward Everett Hale* (Boston: Little, Brown, 1917), p. 122.

10. Edward E. Hale, *Ten Times One Is Ten* (Boston: Roberts Brothers, 1891), p. 256.

11. Matthew 7:12.

12. Ibid., 22:38.

13. Ibid., 6:12.

14. M. K. Gandhi, *Hind Swaraj* (Ahmedabad: Navjivan Publishing House, 1938), p. 61.

15. Tiruvalluvar, *The Kural*, trans. P. S. Sundaram (New York: Penguin Books, 1990), p. 31.

16. *The Book of Common Prayer and Administration of the Sacraments and Other Rites and Ceremonies of the Church According to the Use of the Episcopal Church* (New York: Church Hymnal Corporation and the Seabury Press, 1977), p. 321.

17. Edward Everett Hale, *The Man Without a Country* (Boston: Ticknor and Fields, 1863), p. 7.

18. Romans 14:7.

19. Edward Everett Hale, "The Life in Common," in *From Fast to Christmas: Sixteen Sermons* (Boston: George H. Ellis, 1880), p. 3.

20. Hale, Jr., ed., *Life and Letters of Edward Everett Hale*, p. 39.

21. Ch. 2:31–36, 47. An excellent discussion of ch. 2 of the *Bhagavad Gita* is found in A. L. Herman, *A Brief Introduction to Hinduism* (Boulder: Westview Press, 1991), pp. 91–101.

22. M. K. Gandhi, *The Bhagavadgita* (New Delhi: Orient Paperbacks, 1980), 2:31, 34, p. 36.

23. Swami Chinmayananda, trans., *The Holy Greeta* (Bombay: Central. Chinmaya Mission Trust, 1992), 2:37, p. 97.

24. Ibid., 2:47, p. 114.

25. Arthur Waley, *Translations from the Chinese* (New York: Knopf, 1964), pp. 228–29.

26. James R. Ware, trans., *The Sayings of Mencius* (New York: New American Library, 1960), 4A:5; 4A:4, p. 100.

27. D. C. Lau, trans., *Mencius* (New York: Penguin Books, 1970), 1A:6, pp. 66–67.

28. Niwano, *Buddhism for Today*, p. 180.

29. Conversation, Cairo, Egypt, January 1991.

30. Henry Bettenson, *Documents of the Christian Church* (London: Oxford University Press, 1963), p. 284.

31. Roland H. Bainton, *Here I Stand: A Life of Martin Luther* (New York: New American Library, 1950) p. 144.

32. *Hymns of the Spirit* (Boston: Beacon Press, 1937), #567.

33. These words forming the conclusion of some versions of the Lord's Prayer are not part of the original text as found in Matthew and Luke.

34. Burton Watson, trans., *Hsün Tzu* (New York: Columbia University Press, 1963), p. 29.

35. Reported by Parker T. Pearson, grandfather of the author.

36. The efficiency of the regulating function of the frontal lobes where, in his model, James Newman locates the judging functions, is greatest when the judging and perceiving functions are in the same sphere, NT to the left, SF to the right. For STs, there is continued regulation of N by T but little regulation of S. For NFs, there is continued regulation of S by F but little regulation of N. See Newman's tape *The Human Brain: A Frontier of Psychological Type* (Gainesville, FL: Center for Applications of Psychological Type).

37. *The Practice of the Presence of God: Being Conversations and Letters of Brother Lawrence* (London: A. R. Mowbray, 1961), p. 10.

38. Ibid., p. 23.

39. Ibid., p. 18.

40. Lin Yutang, *My Country and My People* (New York: Reynal & Hitchcock, 1935), pp. 53, 43.

41. Lui Tsun-Yuen, *Exotic Music of Ancient China* (New York: Lyrichord, LL122).

42. Waley, trans., *Book of Songs.*

43. Ibid., p. 336.

44. Watson, trans., *Hsün tzu*, p. 147.

45. Quoted in Campbell, *Power of Myth*, p. 34.

46. Ibid.

47. George Washington, Farewell Address, quoted in Peter T. Richardson, *The Spiritual Founders of Our Constitution* (Kennebunk, ME: privately printed, 1987), p. 39.

48. Judges 8:27.

49. Robert Moore and Douglas Gillette, *King Warrior Magician Lover* (San Francisco: HarperCollins, 1990), p. 52.

50. Robert Bly, *Iron John* (Reading, MA: Addison-Wesley, 1990), pp. 106, 110.

51. Ware, trans., *Sayings of Mencius*, p. 108.

52. Ibid.

53. Moses Hadas, ed., *Essential Works of Stoicism* (New York: Bantam Books, 1961), p. 197.

54. Ibid., p. 152.

55. Vincent B. Silliman, ed., *A Selection of Services for Special Occasions* (Boston: Unitarian Universalist Ministers Association, 1981), p. 51.

56. Job 1:21.

57. Job 14:1–2, 7, 10, 18–19.

58. Job 31:5–8.

59. Job 42:10. It is generally agreed the true Book of Job ends with ch. 42, verse 6.

60. Peter A. Botsis, *What Is Orthodoxy?* (Athens: circa 1990), p. 7.

61. Isaiah 53:5.

62. Ibid., 42:3, 6–7.

63. Hadas, ed., *Essential Works of Stoicism*, p. 127.

64. Lin Yutang, *My Country and My People*, pp. 347–48.

65. Edward J. Thomas, trans., *The Song of the Lord: Bhagavadgita* (London: John Murray, 1931), 3:5, p. 42.

66. McCartney, *Philosophy and Practice of Yoga*, p. 49.

67. W. Douglas P. Hill, trans., *The Bhagavad-gita* (London: Oxford University Press, 1953), 3:35, p. 100.

68. Gandhi, *Bhagavadgita*, p. 86; p. 81.

69. M. K. Gandhi, *An Autobiography, or The Story of My Experiments with Truth* (Ahmedabad: Navajivan Publishing House, 1958), p. 195.

70. Acharya Vinoba Bhave, *Talks on the Gita* (New York: Macmillan, 1960), p. 33.

71. Ramanand Prasad, *The Bhagavadgita* (Fremont, CA: Gita Press West, 1988), 3:24.

72. Ibid., 3:21.

73. Gandhi, *Bhagavadgita*, p. 78.

74. A. Powell Davies, *The Ten Commandments* (New York: New American Library, 1956), p. 55.

75. Exodus 2:10–12.

76. Robert H. Pfeiffer, *Religion in the Old Testament* (New York: Harper, 1961), pp. 47–48.

77. Fleming James, *Personalities of the Old Testament* (New York: Scribner's, 1954), pp. 2–3.

78. Martin Buber, *On the Bible* (New York: Schocken Books, 1968), p. 111.

79. Deuteronomy 6:4–5.

80. Ibid. 6–15; 20–23; 4:9–14.

81. Central Conference of American Rabbis, *The Union Haggadah* (New York: Bloch, 1908), p. 23.

82. Exodus 17:4: 1–7; 33:11; 33:10.

83. Martin Buber, *Moses* (Oxford: East & West Library, 1946), p. 87.

84. Numbers 12:8.

85. Exodus 32: 26; 34:11–16.

86. Deuteronomy 13:1–3.

87. Buber, *On the Bible*, p. 137.

88. Exodus 19:4–6.

89. Deuteronomy 29:29.

90. Numbers 14:13–19.

91. Exodus 18:17–18.

92. Deuteronomy 34:4.

93. Ibid. 30:15–19.

94. Waley, trans., *Analects of Confucius*, 9:27, p. 144.

95. Tu Wei-Ming, *Confucian Thought: Selfhood as Creative Transformation* (Albany: State University of New York Press, 1985), pp. 59–60.

96. Ezra Pound, trans., *Confucian Analects* (New York: Hudson Review, 1950), 5:15, p. 21.X

97. Waley, trans., *Analects of Confucius*, p. 57.

98. Raymond Dawson, trans., *The Analects* (Oxford: Oxford University Press, 1993), 13:3, p. 49.

99. Fung Yu-Lan, *A Short History of Chinese Philosophy* (New York: Macmillan, 1960), pp. 41–42.

100. Herbert Fingarette, *Confucius: The Secular as Sacred* (New York: Harper & Row, 1972), pp. 34–35.

101. Waley, trans., *Analects of Confucius*, 12:2, p. 162.

102. Ibid., 6:28, p. 122.

103. Ibid., 2:4, p. 88.

104. James R. Ware, trans., *The Sayings of Confucius* (New York: New American Library, 1955), 16:10, p. 107.

105. Herrlee G. Creel, *Confucius and the Chinese Way* (New York: Harper, 1949), p. 82.

106. Quotation from the *Odes* in Ware, *Sayings of Confucius*, 1:15, p. 23.

107. Fingarette, *Confucius*, pp. 68–69.

108. Waley, trans., *Analects of Confucius*, 17:11, p. 212.

109. Fingarette, *Confucius*, p. 53.

110. Waley, *Analects of Confucius*, 7:13, p. 125.

111. Fung Yu-Lan, *Short History of Chinese Philosophy*, p. 42.

112. David L. Hall and Roger T. Ames, *Thinking Through Confucius* (Albany: State University of New York Press, 1987), p. 105.

113. Ibid., pp. 83–84.

114. Fung Yu-Lan, *Short History of Chinese Philosophy*, p. 43.

115. Hall and Ames, *Thinking Through Confucius*, p. 285.

116. James Legge, quoted in Lionel Giles, trans., *The Sayings of Confucius* (New York: Grove Press, 1961), p. 100.

117. Hall and Ames, *Thinking Through Confucsius*, pp. 285–286.

118. D. C. Lau, *The Analects* (New York: Dorset Press, 1979), 4:15, p. 74.

119. Pound, trans., *Confucian Analects*, 4:15, p. 17.

120. Fingarette, *Confucius*, p. 56.

121. Creel, *Confucius and the Chinese Way*, p. 52.

122. Ware, *Sayings of Confucius*, 8:7, p. 56.

123. Creel, *Confucius and the Chinese Way*, pp. 147–48.

124. Merriam quoted in ibid., pp. 164–65.

125. Ibid., pp. 165, 169–70.

126. W. and B. Forman, *The Face of Ancient China* (London: Spring Books, 1960), pp. 104–28.

127. Karl Ludvig Reichelt, *Meditation and Piety in the Far East* (New York: Harper, 1954), p. 130.

128. Watson, trans., *Hsün Tzu*, pp. 22–23.

129. Fingarette, *Confucius*, p. 27.

130. S. Radhakrishnan, trans., *The Bhagavadgita* (New York: Harper, 1948), XIII:24–25, p. 310.

CHAPTER SEVEN

1. Myers and McCaulley, *Manual*, p. 35.

2. Oswald and Kroeger, *Personality Type and Religious Leadership*, p. 90.

3. Ralph Waldo Emerson, "Nature" (1836), in *The Essays of Ralph Waldo Emerson* (New York: Heritage Press, 1934), pp. 224–25.

4. Ibid., p. 223.

5. Ralph Waldo Emerson, "Self-Reliance" (1841), ibid., p. 29.

6. Ibid., p. 19.

7. Ralph Waldo Emerson, "Character" (1844), ibid., pp. 182–83.

8. Ralph Waldo Emerson, "The Divinity School Address," in Conrad Wright, ed., *Three Prophets of Religious Liberalism: Channing, Emerson, Parker* (Boston: Beacon Press., 1961), p. 112.

9. Ralph Waldo Emerson, "Spiritual Laws" (1841) in *Essays*, p. 56.

10. Rainer Maria Rilke, *Letters to a Young Poet* Stephen Mitchell, trans., (1903–1908; reprint, New York: Vintage Books, 1986), pp. 8–9.

11. Loren Eiseley, *The Immense Journey* (New York: Vintage Books, 1957), pp. 125–26.

12. Loren Eiseley, *The Unexpected Universe* (New York: Harcourt, Brace & World, 1969), p. 55.

13. Loren Eiseley, *The Firmament of Time* (New York: Atheneum,1960), pp. 168–69.

14. Ibid., pp. 180–181.

15. Thomas Merton, trans., *The Way of Chuang Tzu* (New York: New Directions, 1965), p. 65.

16. Steven Addis and Stanley Lombardo, trans., *Tao Te Ching* (Indianapolis: Hackett Publishing, 1993), p. 8.

17. Michael LaFargue, trans., *The Tao of the Tao Te Ching* (Albany: State University of New York Press, 1962), 32 (63), p. 136.

18. Jacob Trap, *Tao Te Ching: The Wisdom of the Lao Tzu* (Santa Fe, N.M.: Yucca Printing), 78.

19. R. B. Blakney, trans., *The Way of Life: Lao Tzu* (New York: New American Library, 1955), #28, p. 80.

20. D. C. Lau, trans., *Lao Tzu: Tao Te Ching* (Baltimore: Penguin Books, 1963), #XXV, p. 82.

21. Tam C. Gibbs, trans., *Lao-Tzu: My Words Are Very Easy to Understand* (Berkeley, CA: North Atlantic Books: 1981), 6, p. 39.

22. Muhammad Iqbal, *The Secrets of the Self* (London: Macmillan, 1920), pp. xix–xxii.

23. Ibid., pp. 20, 21–22.

24. Genesis 45:4–8.

25. Reinhard Struckmann, "Asklepios in Epidauros," in *Important Medical Centres in Antiquity: Epidaurus and Corinth* (Athens: Editions Kasas, 1990), p. 29.

26. Laurens van der Post, *The Heart of the Hunter* (New York: Morrow, 1961), p. 152; p. 172.

27. Burton Watson, trans., *Chuang Tzu: Basic Writings* (New York: Columbia University Press, 1964), p. 45.

28. Rabindranath Tagore, "The Eternal Dream," in *The Religion of Man* (Boston: Beacon Press, 1961), p. 11.

29. Shigeyoshi Obata, *The Works of Li Po* (New York: Dutton, 1922), p. 71.

30. Ibid., p. 106.

31. Part of Principle 7, Article II, Bylaws, Unitarian Universalist Association, Boston. Principle 7 reads in full: "Respect for the interdependent web of all existence of which we are a part."

32. Watson, trans., *Chuang Tzu: Basic Writings.* pp. 29–30.

33. Thoreau, *Walden*, pp. 8, 10.

34. Starhawk (Miriam Simos), *Dreaming the Dark* (Boston: Beacon Press, 1982), p. 92.

35. Charlotte Vaudeville, *A Weaver Named Kabir* (Delhi: Oxford University Press, 1993), p. 57.

36. Gurbachan Singh Talib, ed., *Selections from the Holy Granth* (New Delhi: Guru Nanak Foundation, 1982), p. 4.

37. Ibid., p. 82.

38. Balwant Singh Anand, *Guru Nanak: His Life Was His Message* (New Delhi: Guru Nanak Foundation, 1983), p. 64.

39. For further development, see Richardson, *Spiritual Founders of Our Constitution.*

40. Thoreau, *Walden*, p. 74.

41. Niwano, *Buddhism For Today*, p. 180.

42. Starhawk (Miriam Semos), *The Spiral Dance* (San Francisco: Harper & Row, 1979), p. 57.

43. Stephen Mitchell, trans., *Tao Te Ching* (New York: Harper & Row, 1988), #17.

44. José Ortega y Gasset, *The Revolt of the Masses*, trans. (New York: Norton, 1932, 1957), p. 76.

45. Zimmer, *Art of Indian Asia*, vol. 1, p. 26: vol. 2, plate 1b.

46. Phulgenda Sinha, *The Gita As It Was: Rediscovering the Original Bhagavadgita* (La Salle, IL: Open Court, 1986), pp. 48–49, 122–23.

47. While a number of authors describe only three principle yogas—jnana, bhakti, and karma—seeing Patanjali's work as the classic of all yogas, an important group of authors concur with my judgment that the raja yoga has distinguishing characteristics (which I identify as NF spirituality) that make it a distinctive pathway parallel with the other three, true whether or not the others draw elements from Patanjali's classic raja, *Yoga Sutras*. Key authors in this group are Swami Atmananda, *The Four Yogas* (Bombay: Bharatiya Vidya Bhavan, 1991); Sri Aurobindo, *The Mind of Light* (New York: Dutton, 1971); Archie J. Bahm, trans., *Yoga, Union with the Ultimate (Yoga Sutras)* (New York: Ungar, 1961); the *Bhagavad Gita* itself; Alain Danielou, *Yoga.* (Rochester, VT: Inner Traditions International, 1991); James Hewitt, *The Complete Yoga Book* (New York: Schocken Books, 1977); James McCartney, *Philosophy and Practice of Yoga* (Romford Essex, England: L. N. Fowler, 1978); Peter Occhiogrosso, *The Joy of Sects* (New York: Doubleday, 1994); Joseph Politella, *Hinduism* (Iowa City: Sernoll, 1966); Huston Smith, *The Religions of Man* (New York: Harper & Row, 1958); Rabindranath Tagore, *Sadhana* (New York: Macmillan, 1913); Swami Vivekananda, *Raja Yoga*, in a series of four volumes—one for each of yoga) (Calcutta: Advaita Ashrama, 1990).

48. The reader is advised to review the three yogas discussed in chapters 4 through 6. It can be easily seen that the jnana focus on analysis and discrimination, the bhakti on joyful invocations of personal deities, and the karma on action without attachment diverge primarily in the inner limbs and by degrees embrace more fully the practices in the five external limbs.

49. Swami Nikhilananda, trans., *The Bhagavad Gita* (New York: Ramakrishna-Vivekananda Center, 1952): 6:6, 20, 28, pp. 163, 167, 170.

50. Smith, *Religions of Man*, pp. 67–68.

51. Bahm, trans., *Yoga*, III:55, p. 144.

52. Mircea Eliade, *Yoga: Immortality and Freedom* (New York: Pantheon Books, 1958), p. 364.

53. Talib, ed., *Selections from the Holy Granth*, p. 69.

54. Tagore, *Religion of Man*, p. 204.

55. Ibid., p. 206.

56. Sri Aurobindo, *The Mind of Light* (New York: Dutton, 1971), p. 18.

57. June O'Connor, *The Quest for Political and Spiritual Liberation* (Cranbury, N.J.: Associated University Press, 1977), p. 101.

58. Rabindranath Tagore, *Personality* (New York: Macmillan, 1917), p. 27.

59. William Butler Yeats, Introduction, to Rabindranath Tagore, *Gitanjali* (New York: Macmillan, 1916), p. xiii; Albert Schweitzer, *Indian Thought and Its Development* (Boston: Beacon Press, 1936), p. 249; D. S. Sarma, *Hinduism Through the Ages* (Bombay: Bharatiya Vidya Bhavan, 1967), p. 162; Marjorie Sykes, *Rabindranath Tagore* (London: Longmans, Green, 1947), p. 86.

60. Tagore, *Religion of Man*, p. 93.

61. Ibid., pp. 95–96.

62. Ibid., pp. 93–94.

63. Tagore, *Personality*, (New York: Macmillan, 1916) p. 85.

64. Tagore, *Gitanjali*, pp. 69–70.

65. Rabindranath Tagore, "The Beginning," in *The Crescent Moon* (New York: Macmillan, 1917), pp. 15–16.

66. Ibid., "Benediction," pp. 74–75.

67. Rabindranath Tagore, *Sadhana* (New York: Macmillan, 1913), p. 22.

68. Stephen N. Hay, *Asian Ideas of East and West: Tagore and His Critics in Japan, China, and India* (Cambridge, MA: Harvard University Press, 1970), p. 282.

69. Tagore, *Religion of Man*, p. 99.

70. Ibid., p. 121.

71. Tagore, *Sadhana*, p. 157.

72. Tagore, *Religion of Man*, p. 92.

73. Tagore, *Gitanjali*, p. 68.

74. Luke 9:18, 20.

75. Luke 9:51.

76. Luke 2:49.

77. John 1:23.

78. Matthew 5:3–12.

79. John Dominic Crossan, *The Essential Jesus* (New York: Harper San Francisco, 1989), p. 23; p. 12.

80. Luke 6:24–26.

81. Crossan, p. 8.

82. Morton Scott Enslin, *The Prophet from Nazareth* (New York: McGraw-Hill, 1961), p. 45.

83. Mark 1:15.

84. Crossan, p. 8.

85. Thomas, Saying 112, in Marvin W. Meyer, trans., *The Secret Teachings of Jesus: Four Gnostic Gospels* (New York: Random House, 1984), p. 51.

86. Luke 17:21.

87. This story is found in Mark 6:30–56, Matthew 14:13–36, Luke 9:10–17, and John 6:1–15. In all of these stories he carefully plans an escape from the crowds so that he could be alone, typically for him, to recharge his energy, in keeping with his Introversion. Jesus was likely an INFP, perhaps an INFJ.

88. Enslin, p. 125.

89. Luke 6:27–30, 35.

90. Luke 18:18–25.

91. Kirsopp and Silva Lake, *An Introduction to the New Testament* (New York: Harper, 1937), p. 233.

92. Matthew 13:31.

93. Mark 13:28.

94. Matthew 8:20.

95. Matthew 10:7–10.

96. Luke 22:35.

97. John 11:1–12.

98. Luke 5:31.

99. Mark 9:2–13.

100. John 3:7–11.

101. John 4:13–14.

102. Crossan, p. 14, lists the most popular themes in Christian art in the first three centuries: eating, healing, teaching, and baptizing.

103. *The Secret Book of James*, 4:0–12, in Meyer, trans., *Secret Teachings of Jesus*, pp. 7–8.

104. Franklin Edgerton, trans., *Bhagavad Gita* (New York: Harper & Row, 1944), XIII:24-25, p. 67.

CHAPTER EIGHT

1. The usual MBTI chart (see figure 1) is useful for pairing first-cousin types (which share a common dominant and attitude) for purposes of description. But for that reason it leaves one with a static bias. I therefore add this figure with a mandala shape to encourage a dynamic bias, to bring alive the polarities as well as the adjacent influences of the sixteen types.

2. Jung called the perceptive types "irrational" because the information gathered by perception is before reason. For further definition of rational and irrational consult Daryl Sharp, *Jung Lexicon* (Toronto: Inner City Books. 1991), pp. 78–80, 112. Isabel B. Myers in her invention of the life-orienting scale (J and P), softened the need to distinguish between similar types in this way (for example, to distinguish the difference between the two Introverted Intuitive Feeling types). See Myers, *Gifts Differing*, pp. 22–25.

3. James Newman, *A Cognitive Perspective on Jungian Typology* (Gainesville, FL: Center for Applications of Psychological Type, 1990), and three audiotapes, *Cognition and Consciousness: A Jungian Perspective on Mind and Brain* (Gainesville: CAPT).

4. To engage in some speculation: Newman mentions the likelihood (in the tapes cited in note 3) that the cognitive functions came on board in the history of humankind in the following order: first S, then SF, then N, and, lastly, T and NT. Consciousness increases, in Jungian terms, when the functions are differentiated, a trend throughout history. Newman mentions as well that there is an overwhelming bias in Western culture today toward NT, especially in science (and in his immediate concern, cognitive psychology). There is an assumption that the left side is superior, with the right side assisting or supplementing, a notion he refutes. Because of this bias, science knows more about what the left side does and where left functions are centered. It may be this bias that led, or misled, Princeton psychologist, Julian Jaynes, to place the ancient "voices" of the gods in the right posterior of the brain, communicating over the anterior commissure to the left posterior of the brain. An alternative idea would be the perfectly competent guidance of daily life by the right (SF) lobe, which when thrown into crisis heard voices from the language centers we know are located in the left posterior (N), in early times organized at a much more primitive and less regulated level than in modern times. Thus, the innovative Revelations of the Nabi and their eventual demise as the left functions became increasingly more differentiated and competent in the new balance that came into being in post-bicameral times. See Julian Jaynes, *The Origin of Consciousness in the Breakdown of the Bicameral Mind* (Boston: Houghton Mifflin, 1976). See also note 14 below.

5. Myers and McCaulley, *Manual*, pp. 33, 35. George R. Frisbie, "Cognitive Styles: An Alternative to Keirsey's Temperaments," *Journal of Psychological Type*, vol. 16, p. 18.

6. Northrop Frye, *Anatomy of Criticism: Four Essays* (Princeton, N.J.: Princeton University Press, 1957), pp. 158–239, and *Fables of Identity: Studies in Poetic Mythology* (New York: Harcourt, Brace & World, 1963), pp. 7–20.

7. James F. Hopewell, *Congregation* (Philadelphia: Fortress Press, 1987), pp. 67–85.

8. Hopewell includes a "World View Test" (pp. 203–211), which because of this "Empiric" designation for the north Ironic pole drastically skewed the results obtained among participants in the liberal Unitarian Universalist religion, to such an extent (most scored high on the Ironic pole) that an alternative questionaire, "What Is Your Opinion," was created by the Rev. Glenn Turner of Portland, Me., with more balanced results, true to the four original distinctions.

9. Mottoes for the four worldviews from Glenn Turner, worksheet, midwinter 1988.

10. Hopewell, *Congregation*, pp. 55–64.

11. Newman, *Cognitive Perspective on Jungian Typology*, p. 7.

12. Watson, trans., *Chuang tzu*, pp. 29–30.

13. The medicine wheel of Native American cultures has great potential for coordination with MBTI typology. An unusually incisive book presenting medicine wheel spirituality is that developed by the Four Worlds Development Project, *The Sacred Tree*, 1985. Mary E. Loomis, *Dancing the Wheel of Psychological Types* (Wilmette, IL: Chiron Publications, 1991), is an attempt to work with typology and the medicine wheel.

14. Laurens van der Post, *The Lost World of the Kalahari* (New York: Morrow, 1958), pp. 27–29; pp. 188–217. Post represents for me an unusual example of the ability of an NF author to appreciate his way (see primary deasil influences, above) into what appears to be a pure SF cultural milieu. The !Kung seem to have differentiated SF values to an exquisite degree but seem completely blind and uncomprehending when confronted with NT or ST perspectives. They will not survive the confrontation. See also van der Post's *Heart of the Hunter* (New York: Morrow, 1961).

CHAPTER NINE

1. The cosmic bodies coordinate well with the traditional four elements: fire (F, SF), air (T, NT), earth (S, ST), and water (N, NF).

2. This important theme for interfaith families is developed in a new curriculum now in the field-testing stage: Lucinda Duncan, *Oil and Water*, forthcoming from the Department of Education, Unitarian Universalist Association, Boston.

3. Diana L. Eck, *Encountering God* (Boston: Beacon Press, 1993) pp. 166–199.

4. Ibid. p. 168.

5. George Hunston Williams *The Radical Reformation* (Philadelphia: the Westminister Press, 1962) p. 719.

6. Charles B. Sanford, *The Religious Life of Thomas Jefferson.* (Charlottesville: University of Virginia, 1984). p. 32.

7. John Ackerman, *Spiritual Awakening* (Bethesda, MD: Alban Institute, 1994), p. 88; p. 100.

8. Dorothy Berkley Phillips, *The Choice Is Always Ours* (New York: Harper, 1960), p. 38.

9. Joseph Campbell, *The Hero with a Thousand Faces* (Cleveland: World, 1949), p. 36.; p. 16.

10. Campbell, *Power of Myth*, pp. 92, 117–18.

11. Robert K. Greenleaf, *Servant Leadership* (New York: Paulist Press, 1977). In a chapter called "Servant Leadership in Churches," p. 239, he writes:

   This is different from the traditional view in which the church and the school purveye knowledge and values for the use of individuals in their separate lives. Now we are saying that in a society dominated by a complex of institutions, the first such in the history of the world, the quality of life achieved within churches and schools may have more to do with their influence on society than what they teach or advocate.

Most charitable institutions, of which the church is one, have tended to view the problems of society as "out there," and it was assumed that service to the "out there" was the sole justification for their existence. Now the view is emerging that one begins "in here," inside the serving institution, and makes of it a model institution. This model, because it is a thing of beauty, in itself, becomes a powerful serving force.

12. Rebecca Parker, "A Different Call," sermon presented before the Unitarian Universalist Ministers' Convocation, Hot Springs, Arkansas, March 15, 1995.

RESOURCES

PSYCHOLOGICAL TYPE

Eleanor S. Corlett & Nancy B. Millner, *Navigating Midlife*. 1993.
Terence Duniho, *Wholeness Lies Within*. 1991.
W. Harold Grant, Magdala Thompson, Thomas E. Clarke, *From Image To Likeness*. 1983.
Sandra Hirsh, Jean Kummerow, *Life Types*. 1989.
David Keirsey, Marilyn Bates, *Please Understand Me*. 1978.
Otto Kroeger, Janet M. Thuesen, *Type Talk*. 1988.
Isabel Briggs Myers, *Gifts Differing*. 1980.
Isabel Briggs Myers, *Introduction to Type*, 5th ed. 1993.
Isabel Briggs Myers, Mary H. McCaulley, *Manual*. 1988.
James Newman, *A Cognitive Perspective on Jungian Typology*. 1990.
Roy M. Oswald, Otto Kroeger, *Personality Type and Religious Leadership*. 1988.
Loren E. Pedersen, *Sixteen Men*. 1993.
Naomi L. Quenk, *Beside Ourselves*. 1993.

SCRIPTURES

Analects of Confucius
Bible
Bhagavad Gita
Buddhist Scriptures
Chuang-tzu
Confucian Odes
Dhammapada
Emerson's *Essays*
Epic of Gilgamesh
Fuller's *Synergetics*
Gāthās
Granth
Hadith Qudsi
Hsün-tzu
Koran
Lao-tzu's *Tao Te Ching*
Little Flowers of St. Francis
Meng K'o
Nag Hammadi Library
Patanjali's *Yoga Sutras*
Shinto Scriptures
Tagore's *Gitanjali*
Upanishads
Vedas

RELIGIOUS TRADITIONS

Muhammad Asad, *The Road to Mecca*. 1954.
Swami Atmamanda, *The Four Yogas*. 1991.
Martin Buber, *On the Bible*. 1968.
Joseph Campbell, *The Power of Myth*. 1988.
Ananda Coomaraswamy, *Buddha and the Gospel of Buddhism*. 1964.
Herrlee G. Creel, *Confucius and the Chinese Way*. 1949.
Alain Danielou, *Yoga*. 1991.
Morton Scott Enslin, *The Prophet From Nazareth*. 1961.
Herbert Fingarette, *Confucius: The Secular As Sacred*. 1972.
R. Buckminster Fuller, *Critical Path*. 1981.
R. Buckminster Fuller, *No More Secondhand God*. 1963.
T. Glover, *The Conflict of Religions in the Early Roman Empire*. 1909.
M. Hiriyanna, *Outlines of Indian Philosophy*. 1964.
Rune E. A. Johansson, *The Psychology of Nirvana*. 1970.
Julian Jaynes, *The Origin of Consciousness in the Breakdown of the Bicameral Mind*. 1976.
Corliss Lamont, *The Philosophy of Humanism*. 1957.
Mai-mai Sze, *The Way of Chinese Painting*. 1956.
Rustom Masani, *Zoroastrianism*. 1962.
James McCartney, *Philosophy and Practice of Yoga*. 1978.
Kenneth L. Patton, *A Religion for One World*. 1964.
Joseph Politella, *Hinduism*. 1966.
Joseph Politella, *Taoism and Confucianism*. 1967.
Laurens van der Post, *The Heart of the Hunter*. 1961.
Laurens van der Post, *The Lost World of the Kalahari*. 1958.
Sarvepalli Radhakrishnan, *The Hindu View of Life*. 1979.
Bertrand Russell, *A History of Western Philosophy*. 1945.
D. S. Sarma, *Hinduism Through the Ages*. 1967.
Albert Schweitzer, *Indian Thought and its Development*. 1936.
K. M. Sen, *Hinduism*. 1961.
Huston Smith, *The Religions of Man*. 1986.
Rabindranath Tagore, *The Religion of Man*. 1930.
Rabindranath Tagore, *Personality*. 1917.
Rabindranath Tagore, *Sadhana*. 1913.
William Irwin Thompson, *The Time Falling Bodies Take to Light*. 1981.
Alan W. Watts, *The Way of Zen*. 1957.
Dudley Young, *Origins of the Sacred*. 1991.
Heinrich Zimmer, *Philosophies of India*. 1951.

CREDITS

INTRODUCTION

Page xiii. Copyright © P. Lal, 162/92 Lake Gardens, Calcutta, India. Reprinted by permission of P. Lal.

CHAPTER ONE

2. From *Gifts Differing* by Isabel Briggs Myers. Modified and reproduced by special permission of the publisher, Consulting Psychologists Press, Inc., Palo Alto, CA 94303. Copyright © 1980 by Consulting Psychologists Press, Inc. All rights reserved. Further reproduction is prohibited without the publisher's written consent.

CHAPTER THREE

Page 31. Excerpted with the permission of Simon & Schuster from *The Analects of Confucius*, by Arthur Waley, translator. Copyright © 1938 by Allen & Unwin Ltd.

CHAPTER FOUR

1. From *Out of my Life and Thought: An Autobiography by Albert Schweitzer.* Copyright © 1933, 1949 by Henry Holt and Co., Inc. Copyright © 1990 by Rhena Schweitzer Miller. Translation copyright © 1990 by Antje Bultmann Lemke. Reprinted by permission of Henry Holt and Co., Inc.

3. *The Stranger*, by Albert Camus. Copyright © 1946 by Alfred A. Knopf/Random House. Reprinted by permission of the publisher.

4. From *The Great Dialogues of Plato* by Plato, by W. H. D. Rouse, translator. Translation copyright © 1956 by J. C. G. Rouse. Used by permission of Dutton Signet, a division of Penguin Books USA Inc.

10. From *A Cry of Absence* by Martin E. Marty. Copyright © 1983 by HarperCollins Publishers. Reprinted by permission of the publisher.

22, 24–27. Excerpts from *The Seven Storey Mountain* by Thomas Merton. Copyright © 1948 by Harcourt Brace & Company and renewed 1976 by the Trustees of The Merton Legacy Trust. Reprinted by permission of the publisher.

29. From *Mysticism and Logic* by Betrand Russell. Reprinted by permission of Bantam Doubleday Dell Publishing Group, Inc.

35. Reprinted from *The Bhagavad Gita* by Winthrop Sargeant, translator. Reprinted by permission of the State University of New York Press.

44, 49. Copyright © P. Lal, 162/92 Lake Gardens, Calcutta, India. Reprinted by permission of P. Lal.

74. From *Zen Flesh, Zen Bones* by Paul Reps. Reprinted by permission of Charles E. Tuttle Co., Inc. of Tokyo, Japan.

81. From *The Edicts of Asoka*, by Nikam and McKeon, editors and translators Reprinted by permission.

CHAPTER FIVE

10. From *The Time Falling Bodies Take to Light* by William Irwin Thompson. Copyright © 1981 by William Irwin Thompson, St. Martin's Press, Inc. New York, NY. Reprinted by permission.

12, 15–16. From *The Gospel of Sri Ramakrishna* as translated into English by Swami Nikhilanada and published by the Ramakrishna-Vivekananda Center of New York. Copyright © 1942 by Swami Nikhilananda. Reprinted by permission.

26. From *The Book of Songs* by Arthur Waley. Copyright © 1960 HarperCollins Publishers Limited. Reprinted by permission of the publisher.

27. From *Mo Tzu* by Burton Watson, translator. Copyright © 1963 by Columbia University Press. Reprinted by permission of the publisher.

47. From *Bhagavad Gita in the Light of Sri Aurobindo* by Sri Aurobindo. Copyright © 1978 by Manoj das Gupta. Reprinted by permission.

63–64. From *The Sayings of Muhammad* by Allama Sir Abdullah Al-Mamun Al-Suhrawardy. Copyright © 1990 by Citadel Press/Carol Publishing. Reprinted by permission of the publisher.

CHAPTER SIX

Page 105. From *Hsun Tzu* translated by Burton Watson. Copyright © 1963 by Columbia University Press. Reprinted by permission of the publisher.

7. From *The Book of Songs* by Arthur Waley. Copyright © 1960 HarperCollins Publishers Limited. Reprinted by permission of the publisher.

15. Reprinted by permission of Penguin Books, India Pvt. Ltd.

25. From *Translations from the Chinese* by Arthur Waley, translator. Copyright © 1919 and renewed 1947 by Arthur Waley. Reprinted by permission of Alfred A. Knopf Inc.

26. From *The Sayings of Mencius* by James R. Ware. Translation copyright © 1960 by James R. Ware. Reprinted by permission of Dutton Signet, a division of Penguin Books, USA Inc.

30. From *Documents of the Christian Church* by Henry Bettenson, editor. Copyright © 1963 by Oxford University Press. Reprinted by permission of Oxford University Press.

34, 44. From *Hsun Tzu* by Burton Watson, translator. Copyright © 1963 by Columbia University Press. Reprinted by permission of the publisher.

51–52. From *The Sayings of Mencius* by James R. Ware. Translation copyright © 1960 by James R. Ware. Reprinted by permission of Dutton Signet, a division of Penguin Books, USA Inc.

53–54. From *Essential Works of Stoicism* by Moses Hadas, editor. Bantam Doubleday Dell. Reprinted by permission of the publisher.

76. Excerpt as submitted from *Religion in the Old Testament* by Robert H. Pfeiffer and edited by Charles Conrad Forman. Copyright © 1961 by Harper & Brothers. Copyright renewed 1988 by Louise A. Pfeiffer and Paul H. Pfeiffer. Reprinted by permission of HarperCollins Publishers, Inc.

78, 87. *On The Bible*, by Martin Buber. Copyright © 1968 by Alfred A. Knopf/Random House. Reprinted by permission of the publisher.

94. Excerpted with the permission of Simon & Schuster from *The Analects of Confucius*, by Arthur Waley, translator. Copyright © 1938 by Allen & Unwin Ltd. Reprinted by permission of the publisher.

100. Excerpt as submitted from *Confucius: The Secular as Sacred* by Herbert Fingarette. Copyright © 1972 by Herbert Fingarette. Reprinted by permission of HarperCollins Publishers, Inc.

101–103, 108, 110. Excerpted with the permission of Simon & Schuster from *The Analects of Confucius*, by Arthur Waley, translator. Copyright © 1938 by Allen & Unwin Ltd.

120. Excerpt as submitted from *Confucius: The Secular as Sacred* by Herbert Fingarette. Copyright © 1972 by Herbert Fingarette. Reprinted by permission of HarperCollins Publishers, Inc.

128. From *Hsun Tzu*, translated by Burton Watson. Copyright © 1963 by Columbia University Press. Reprinted by permission of the publisher.

CHAPTER SEVEN

10. *Letters To a Young Poet* by Stephen Mitchell, translator. Copyright © 1984 by Alfred A. Knopf/Random House. Reprinted by permission of the publisher.

12. Excerpt from "The Hidden Teacher" in *The Unexpected Universe*. Copyright © 1969 by Loren Eiseley. Reprinted by permission of Harcourt Brace & Company.

13–14. Reprinted by permission of Scribner, a Division of Simon & Schuster from *The Firmament of Time* by Loren Eiseley. Copyright © 1960 by Loren Eiseley. Copyright © 1960 by The Trustees of the University of Pennsylvania.

27. From *Chuang Tzu* by Burton Watson, translator. Copyright © 1964 by Columbia University Press. Reprinted by permission of the publisher.

29–30. From *The Works of Li Po* by Shigeyoshi Obata. Copyright © 1922, renewed 1950 by E. P. Dutton. Used by permission of Dutton Signet, a division of Penguin Books USA Inc.

32. From *Chuang Tzu* by Burton Watson, translator. Copyright © 1964 by Columbia University Press. Reprinted by permission of the publisher.

34. From *Dreaming the Dark* by Starhawk. Copyright © 1982, 1988 by Miriam Samos, Beacon Press, Boston. Reprinted by permission of the publisher.

42. Excerpt as submitted from *The Spiral Dance* by Starhawk. Copyright © 1979 by Miriam Simos. Reprinted by permission of HarperCollins Publishers, Inc.

44. From *The Revolt of the Masses* by Jose Ortega y Gasset. Copyright © 1932 by W. W. Norton & Company. Reprinted by permission of the publisher.

49. From *The Bhagavad Gita*, by Swami Nikhilananda, translator. Published by the Ramakrishna-Vivekananda Center of New York. Copyright © 1944 by Swami Nikhilananda. Reprinted by permission.

64–66, 73. Reprinted with the permission of Simon & Schuster from *Collected Poems and Plays of Rabindranath Tagore* (New York: Macmillan, 1937).

CHAPTER NINE

11. From *Servant Leadership* by Robert K. Greenleaf. Copyright © 1977 by Paulist Press. Reprinted by permission of the publisher.

INDEX